BBC
Speakout
3RD EDITION

B2

Student's Book and eBook

CONTENTS

LESSON	GRAMMAR/FUNCTION	VOCABULARY	PRONUNCIATION	READING
LEAD-IN p6				
1 identity BBC VLOGS | Who do you take after in your family?				
1A My ID p8	Present perfect simple and continuous	Personality adjectives; suffixes	Weak forms of *have* and *been*	
1B Memory p11	infinitive and *-ing* forms	Collocations about memory; idioms: memory	Connected speech: chunking: two-part collocations	Read an article about people who never forget
1C I'd much rather … p14	How to … express personal preferences	Emotions and feelings	Word stress: dependent prepositions	Read a travel guide to Lagos
1D Personality p16	*while*, *whereas* and *whilst*			
UNIT 1 REVIEW p18				
2 different worlds BBC VLOGS | What impact does social media have on your life?				
2A Real or virtual? p20	Future probability	Science and technology; word families	Connected speech: future probability	Read an article about the future of VR
2B Closer to nature p23	Quantifiers	Nature	Connected speech: quantifiers	
2C Amazing lives p26	How to … speculate	Lifestyle adjectives	Stress to show certainty	Read an article about people with amazing lives
2D The time traveller p28		Extreme adjectives		
UNIT 2 REVIEW p30				
3 showtime BBC VLOGS | What live events or performances do you enjoy and why?				
3A Festival p32	Relative clauses	Festivals; the environment	Pitch in non-defining relative clauses	Read three articles about eco festivals
3B Performers p35	Cleft sentences	Phrasal verbs: performing; phrasal verbs: communication	Emphatic stress	
3C Binge-watch p38	How to … use vague language	Film and TV	Linking and elision	Read an infographic about binge-watching
3D Music lover? p40	*do* and *did* for emphasis			
UNIT 3 REVIEW p42				
4 lifestyle BBC VLOGS | Name one change you could make to your life to improve your health.				
4A Making changes p44	Future continuous and future perfect	Health and lifestyle; illness and treatment	Connected speech: future perfect	Read an article about people making changes to their lifestyles
4B Sleep p47	Passives	Sleep	Sentence stress: content and function words	
4C Keep moving p50	How to … express agreement and disagreement	Exercise; sport: motivation and benefits	Stress in phrases for partial agreement	
4D Ancient traditions p52		Phrases related to time		
UNIT 4 REVIEW p54				

LISTENING/VIDEO	SPEAKING	WRITING
Listen to a podcast about identity	Use a diagram to explain your identity	Write a blog post describing yourself
	Describe a memory **FUTURE SKILLS** Communication	
	Agree on an itinerary for a day in a city **FUTURE SKILLS** Collaboration **MEDIATION SKILLS** create tourist recommendations for your town/area	
BBC Street Interviews about personality	Discuss personality traits	Write a letter of recommendation
	Make predictions **FUTURE SKILLS** Critical thinking	
BBC Radio *Why we should listen to trees*	Suggest ways to encourage people to spend time in nature **FUTURE SKILLS** Leadership	Write a for-and-against essay on the pros and cons of living in the countryside
Listen to a conversation about unusual lifestyles	Speculate about the lives of famous people	**MEDIATION SKILLS** summarise an informal interview
BBC Programme *Doctor Who*	Talk about an imaginary trip back in time	Write a competition entry
	Plan an eco-friendly festival **FUTURE SKILLS** Collaboration	Write a formal email proposing a new festival
Listen to a podcast about stage fright	Practise speaking in public **FUTURE SKILLS** Self-management	
Listen to a conversation about binge-worthy TV shows	Describe your favourite film or TV series	**MEDIATION SKILLS** describe a film
BBC Street Interviews about music	Ask and answer questions about the importance of music in your life	Write a forum comment
	Talk about how your life will be different in five years' time **FUTURE SKILLS** Communication	
BBC Radio *The science of sleep*	Discuss statements about sleep	Write an article about how to get a good night's sleep
Listen to a conversation about the benefits of exercise	Hold short debates on sports and exercise **MEDIATION SKILLS** decide how to contribute to an event	
BBC Programme *Earth from Space*	A discussion about traditional vs. modern lifestyles	Write a cause-and-effect essay

CONTENTS

LESSON	GRAMMAR/ FUNCTION	VOCABULARY	PRONUNCIATION	READING
5 work BBC VLOGS | Which professions do you admire and why?				
5A First day! p56	Past perfect simple and continuous	Time expressions	Connected speech: past perfect continuous	Read an article about first days at work
5B Change of plan p59	Past plans and intentions	Work and careers; areas of work	Connected speech: intrusive /w/ sounds	
5C You're on mute! p62	How to … describe problems and suggest solutions	Video conference calls **FUTURE SKILLS** Social responsibility	Intonation to show degrees of certainty	
5D Are you a team player? p64	Non-defining relative clauses for comments			
UNIT 5 REVIEW p66				
6 psychology BBC VLOGS | What things do you never find the time to get done?				
6A Pay attention! p68	Necessity, prohibition and permission	Prefixes	Word stress: prefixess	Read an article about avoiding distraction
6B Quiet p71	Reported orders, requests and advice	Reporting verbs	Consonant clusters	
6C Here's my advice p74	How to … ask for advice and give advice tactfully	Collocations with *get* and *take*	Pitch for sounding tactful	
6D Would I lie to you? p76		Fillers		
UNIT 6 REVIEW p78				
7 talent BBC VLOGS | Do you have any hidden talents?				
7A An unexpected passion p80	Past modals of deduction	Compound adjectives; chance	Connected speech: past modals of deduction	Read an article about an unexpected source of inspiration **FUTURE SKILLS** Communication
7B I wish! p83	*wish, if only, should have*	Idioms: regrets	Chunking in idioms	
7C Let me explain p86	How to … describe a process	Phrasal verbs: explaining	Stress in phrasal verbs	
7D Hard work or talent? p88	adverbials of concession			
UNIT 7 REVIEW p90				
8 community BBC VLOGS | What does 'community' mean to you?				
8A A new way of living p92	Participle clauses	Collocations with *go, have* and *make*; describing homes and living conditions	Pitch in participle clauses	Read an article about co-living
8B If the world … p95	Conditionals with conjunctions	World issues	Stress in conditional sentences	
8C Online communities p98	How to … develop an argument	Prepositional phrases	Sounding persuasive	
8D Second shot p100		Phrases with *get*		
UNIT 8 REVIEW p102				

WRITING BANK p104   **GRAMMAR BANK** p108   **VOCABULARY BANK** p136   **COMMUNICATION BANK** p142

LISTENING/VIDEO	SPEAKING	WRITING
	Tell an anecdote about the first time you did something **FUTURE SKILLS** Communication	
BBC Radio *Is one career in your life enough?*	Discuss a time when your life plans changed	Write a report about broadening young people's career aspirations
Listen to three problematic video conference calls **MEDIATION SKILLS** agree on a course of action	Practise describing problems and suggesting solutions	
BBC Street Interviews about working in a team	A discussion about working alone vs. in a team	A thank-you message
	Discuss your top three ways to avoid distraction **FUTURE SKILLS** Self-management	Edit notes to make them more concise
Listen to a conversation about introverts	Take a quiz about introverts and extroverts	
Listen to someone asking for advice	Practise giving advice tactfully	**MEDIATION SKILLS** add to posts in a thread, building on the advice of other people
BBC Programme *Would I Lie to You?*	A true or false story	An email giving news
	Speculate about a series of chance events	
Listen to people talking about missed opportunities	Discuss your regrets	Write a personal essay
Listen to someone explaining a recipe	Explain your way of doing something **FUTURE SKILLS** Communication **MEDIATION SKILLS** make a concept easier for someone else to understand	
BBC Street Interviews about talent and hard work	A discussion about talents	A social media post
	Discuss co-living spaces **FUTURE SKILLS** Collaboration	Write a job application letter/email
Listen to a talk about world issues	Discuss hypothetical situations **FUTURE SKILLS** Creative and critical thinking	
Listen to part of a debate about online communities	Hold a debate about online communities	**MEDIATION SKILLS** make a discursive argument on a topic
BBC Programme *Amazing Humans*	A presentation on a project	A mission statement

MEDIATION BANK p146　　**AUDIOSCRIPTS** p158　　**VIDEOSCRIPTS** p170　　**IRREGULAR VERBS TABLE** p175

LEAD-IN

GRAMMAR

1 A Read the text. Who is it? Look on page 142 to find out.

Who am I?

I'm one of the most famous British men who ever lived, but my family wasn't famous. My father made gloves! I got married at eighteen and became an actor. My career took off rapidly when I moved to London, but it wasn't acting. If the printing press hadn't been invented, you probably wouldn't have heard of me. People have been reading and watching my works for over four centuries, and some of my plays have been made into well-known films. In 2116, I will have been dead for 500 years.

B Read the text again and find examples of the following.
1. a relative clause
2. a conditional sentence
3. a verb in the present perfect continuous form
4. a verb in the future perfect form
5. a verb in the past perfect passive form
6. a phrasal verb
7. an adverb

COMMON ERRORS

2 A Correct the mistakes in the questions.
1. How long you have been studying English?
2. Do you enjoy listening music in English?
3. When was the last time you watch a film in English?
4. Do you like discussing about current affairs?
5. Are you looking forward to learn more English?
6. What would you do if you would have unlimited time and money?

B Which mistakes in Ex 2A feature:
1. a verb pattern?
2. a conditional form?
3. word order?
4. a verb tense?
5. a missing preposition?
6. an extra preposition?

C Work in pairs. Ask and answer the questions in Ex 2A.

PRONUNCIATION

3 A Match the sentence beginnings (1–10) with the endings (a–j) that rhyme.

1 I thought I could   a back on my farm.
2 I stayed although   b and I feel great.
3 She felt so calm   c while in the queue.
4 All that stuff   d the pot of gold.
5 I watch my weight   e they'd all find out.
6 We read the review   f escape this wood.
7 He had no doubt   g felt so rough.
8 When you cough   h I wanted to go.
9 The girl controlled   i that bit of earth.
10 It was worth   j it puts me off.

B Work in pairs. Think of other words in English that have the same rhymes as 1–10.

VOCABULARY

4 A Look at the nouns and noun phrases in the boxes. Which verb do they go with?

do or *make*?

> a choice   a fortune   a profit   business
> me a favour   notes   the laundry   your best

take or *have*?

> a chat   a course   a dream   a good time
> a relationship   an important step
> charge   your time

B Work in pairs. Say a noun or noun phrase from Ex 4A. Your partner says the correct verb, without looking at the book.

5 A Choose the correct prepositions to complete the sentences.
1. I get **on** / **in** / **up** well with my dad.
2. He gave **on** / **up** / **in** eating fast food.
3. This machine is out **of** / **in** / **to** order.
4. We'll always keep **in** / **on** / **to** touch.
5. We arrived **to** / **by** / **at** the stadium early.
6. We may be late. It depends **of** / **by** / **on** the traffic.
7. Ken is married **to** / **with** / **on** Jan.
8. Congratulations **on** / **for** / **of** your success!

B Complete the sentences with the correct form of the phrasal verbs in Ex 5A.
1. Who do you _____ well with in your family? Why?
2. Have you ever _____ anything _____? What and why?
3. How do you _____ with your friends and family?

C Work in pairs. Discuss the questions.

identity 1

VLOGS

Q: Who do you take after in your family?

1 ▶ Watch the video. Note down the family members that people mention and the characteristics they share.

2 Work in pairs. Discuss who you take after in your family. Give examples.

GSE LEARNING OBJECTIVES

1A LISTENING | Understand a podcast about identity: personality adjectives; suffixes

Talk about your identity: present perfect simple and continuous

Pronunciation: weak forms of *have* and *been*

Write a blog post about yourself

1B READING | Read an article about people who never forget: infinitive and *-ing* forms; collocations about memory; idioms: memory

Pronunciation: chunking: two-part collocations

Describe a memory

1C HOW TO … | express personal preferences; emotions and feelings

Pronunciation: word stress: dependent prepositions

1D BBC STREET INTERVIEWS | Understand street interviews about people's personalities

Talk about personality traits: *while*, *whereas* and *whilst*

Write a letter of recommendation

Unit 1 | Lesson A

1A My ID

GRAMMAR | present perfect simple and continuous
VOCABULARY | personality adjectives; suffixes
PRONUNCIATION | weak forms of *have* and *been*

VOCABULARY

personality adjectives

1 A Work in pairs and discuss the questions.
 1 How would you usually describe yourself to someone you have never met before?
 2 How do you think the factors in the box might influence someone's personality?

> the language you speak   where you live
> your family   your life experiences

B Read the article. Does it include any of your ideas?

C Work in pairs and discuss the questions.
 1 Which ideas in the article do you agree or disagree with? Which do you find surprising?
 2 Do you feel your personality changes when you speak a different language? In what way?
 3 What other things do you think can influence your personality?

2 A Complete the meanings with the adjectives in bold in the article.
 1 If someone doesn't follow the rules, you can say they are being ....
 2 When you are interested in learning about new things, you are ....
 3 When you have big plans to achieve a lot of things, you are ....
 4 If you like to go out with a lot of people and enjoy yourself, you are ....
 5 If you smile a lot and feel happy most of the time, you are ....
 6 People who often disagree with other people are ....
 7 If you're not afraid of going to new places and taking risks, you are ....
 8 If you refuse to change your mind about something, you are ....

B Work in pairs. Describe three people you know using words from Ex 2A. Explain why you chose each word.

C Learn and practise. Go to the Vocabulary Bank.

▶▶ page 136 **VOCABULARY BANK** suffixes

What shapes our personality?

Sarah Logan | Wed 6th Jan | 22.18 GMT

Our experiences have a huge impact on our personalities. The jobs we do, the people we meet, our achievements and disappointments all contribute to the kind of person we are. What other factors might also be important?

Family

A lot of people think that our personality is shaped by the size of our family and our position in it. Some argue that first-born children are more likely to be **ambitious** achievers. Younger children, on the other hand, might be more **rebellious** and willing to break rules. The youngest child of a family is often fun-loving and **adventurous** – always keen to try new things. We can inherit personality characteristics, too, like being **argumentative** or **stubborn**.

Language

Research suggests that the language we speak influences our personality and the way we think. In a recent survey of international students, Gosia, a Polish-born immigrant in the USA, says that when she speaks English, she feels 'more **curious** about the world'. Natasha, who speaks several languages, says that she feels more romantic when she's speaking in Portuguese, more **cheerful** and likely to smile when speaking Italian and more relaxed when speaking in Greek.

Geography

Other studies show that where we live or were born might also influence our lifestyle, our personality and the way that we interact with others socially. People living in warmer climates often see themselves as more sociable and **outgoing**, whilst people from mountainous areas seem to be more open to new experiences.

1A

LISTENING

3 A 🔊 **1.01** | Listen to a podcast on what makes us who we are. Who mentions the following topics? Matteo, Hana or both?
1. living in different countries
2. enjoying food from a particular country or area
3. having a mixed identity
4. identifying with a particular type of music
5. work experience
6. family influence

B 🔊 **1.01** | Listen again and answer the questions.
1. How was Matteo able to get an Italian passport?
2. How has Matteo's Italian background influenced his lifestyle?
3. Does Matteo feel British? Why/Why not?
4. How does Hana feel about the different countries she has lived in?
5. Which part of her personality does Hana think she gets from a parent?
6. Why does Hana think she is so ambitious and focused on her career?

C Work in pairs. Look at the quotes from the podcast. Are the comments true for you? Can you think of examples?
1. '… everything I grew up with – the food, the language, the people – all of that forms a big part of who I am.'
2. '… all of these different places [where I've lived] play a part in who I am, far beyond the idea of nationality or belonging to one single place.'
3. 'Everyone is an individual with different life experiences and different stories to tell.'

GRAMMAR

present perfect simple and continuous

4 A Work in pairs. Read each pair of sentences (a and b) and answer the questions (1–6).
a. We've been interviewing people out on the street.
b. We've had some really interesting replies.
1. Which tense focuses on the result of an activity?
2. Which tense focuses on the activity itself?

a. I've lived in lots of different places around the world.
b. I've been living in the UK for over five years now.
3. Which tense answers the question: How many?
4. Which tense answers the question: How long?

a. I've learnt that hard work always pays off.
b. I've been learning Dutch, but it's really hard!
5. Which tense describes a completed action?
6. Which tense describes an activity which is unfinished?

B Learn and practise. Go to the Grammar Bank.

▶▶ page 108 **GRAMMAR BANK**

PRONUNCIATION

5 A 🔊 **1.02** | weak forms of *have* and *been* | Listen and complete the questions.
1. How long _____ living here?
2. _____ lived in another country?
3. What _____ doing recently?
4. How long _____ studying English?

B 🔊 **1.02** | Listen again. Does the speaker use the strong forms of *have* and *been* (/hæv/ and /biːn/) or the weak forms (/həv/ and /bɪn/)?

C Work in pairs. Ask and answer the questions in Ex 5A.

SPEAKING

6 A Draw a pie chart like the one below to explain what makes you who you are. Make notes about why each part is important.

B Work in groups. Show your charts to each other and talk about the different parts of your personal identity. Whose ideas are similar to yours?

I think for a lot of people my age, how we present ourselves online forms a big part of our identity. Even more so for me as I've been posting YouTube videos about the places I go and the people I meet.

My family have been a huge influence on my identity. I'm very ambitious in terms of work and I get that from my mum.

Unit 1 | Lesson A

WRITING

a blog post

7 A Read the blog post. What do you learn about Sydney's family background, personality and attitude to work?

B Complete the blog post with Sydney's examples to support her ideas.

a Recently, I've taken up rock climbing and surfing.
b I love nothing more than getting together with a big group of friends!
c I love the Chinese New Year celebrations, and I'm crazy about Asian food!
d You will often find me working late at night to get the job done.

C Match the sentence beginnings (1–7) with the endings (a–g).

1 I would say that I
2 In my work, I'm very
3 You will often find me
4 In my personal life,
5 I would like to think
6 I love nothing more than
7 Recently I've taken up

a at my desk before anyone else arrives at work.
b I like to be sociable.
c that I'm cheerful and friendly.
d reliable. I will always complete a job I'm given.
e doing a job to the best of my abilities.
f work harder than most people I know.
g skateboarding and I'm really enjoying it.

D Write a *Who am I?* blog post describing yourself. Use the sentence beginnings in Ex 7C to help you, and include examples to support your ideas. Write about:

- your family background and identity.
- your personality and personal life.
- your attitude to work or studying.

Who am I?

My name is Sydney and I was born in Sacramento, in the USA. My parents are immigrants from China, so I've grown up speaking Mandarin at home but English at school and with my friends. We have family in China so we have always visited regularly. As well as my U.S. identity, I would say that I identify quite strongly with my Asian roots. [1] ....

In my personal life, I would like to think that I'm quite adventurous. I love trying out new experiences. [2] .... I'm not particularly good at either, but I'm quite stubborn, so I plan to keep going. I'm also outgoing and sociable. [3] ....

In my work, I'm very ambitious. I never settle for anything less than the best and always work hard. [4] .... In terms of my experience, I've been designing websites for over seven years. I co-founded WebDesignSY, an award-winning creative studio. I've designed websites for businesses, charities and individuals. I've also taught several courses in design at the California Institute of Arts and Technology. I love nothing more than thinking of interesting ways to represent you and your brand, so please get in touch.

1B Memory

GRAMMAR | infinitive and *-ing* forms
VOCABULARY | collocations about memory; idioms: memory
PRONUNCIATION | chunking: two-part collocations

GRAMMAR

infinitive and *-ing* forms

1 Work in pairs. Ask and answer the questions.

1 Can you remember …
- what you were doing on Sunday two weeks ago?
- the birthdays of all your family members?
- the last film you saw at the cinema?
- how you celebrated your birthday two years ago?
- what your first teacher looked like?

2 Do you generally have a good memory or are you forgetful?

3 Do you know any special techniques to improve your memory?

2A Work in pairs. Read about seven different ways to remember things. Which do you do already? Which would you like to try? Why?

B Match the phrases in bold in Ex 2A with the rules (1–4).

1 We can use an infinitive after the verb *be*.
to write

2 We can use an infinitive to express a purpose.

3 We use the *-ing* form after prepositions.

4 We can use some verbs followed by an infinitive or an *-ing* form, with a change in meaning (four phrases).

C Learn and practise. Go to the Grammar Bank.

▶▶ page 109 **GRAMMAR BANK**

1 When I have to **remember to do** things, I write notes to myself.

2 I like using visualisation – connecting facts to images. It works well for me. I **remember visualising** facts for a test last month and I passed!

3 Before a presentation, I **try to practise** in front of a mirror to make sure I don't forget what I'm going to say.

4 **To keep** a list in my head, I invent songs, which I sing to myself.

5 I heard sleep is good for your memory, so I **tried taking** naps after class.

6 I remember facts **by imagining** I'm in a building. Everything on the list is in a different room and I walk through the rooms.

7 My technique is **to write** a story that uses everything I need to remember.

Unit 1 | Lesson B

READING

3 A Work in pairs. Think about your family and friends. Who has the best memory? What kinds of things can they remember well?

B Read the article and answer the questions.
1 What kinds of things do Funes, Veiseh and Price remember?
2 What kinds of people are more likely to have HSAM?
3 What is the connection between emotions and memory?

C Scan the article again and find the information.
1 the author of the book *Funes the Memorius*
2 the significance of the date 15 December 2000
3 the age at which Jill Price first contacted Dr McGaugh
4 the date when Elvis Presley died
5 what the abbreviation HSAM stands for
6 the amount of time Dr McGaugh has spent researching memory

D Work in groups. Discuss the questions.
1 What do you think are the advantages and disadvantages of having abilities like Veiseh and Price?
2 Why do you think some people are better at remembering things than others?

VOCABULARY

collocations about memory

4 A Scan the article again. Complete the sentences with the correct form of the collocations in bold.
1 Your .... are things you can remember from when you were very young.
2 If you have a good .... , you can remember things for an extended period of time.
3 If you have .... , you can remember things exactly as they are, without making mistakes.
4 If something .... , it makes you think of something from the past.
5 If you are generally able to remember things well, you ....
6 When you .... , you learn them in such a way that you can repeat them from memory.
7 If you .... of something, you remember every small part and moment of it.
8 You have a good .... if you can remember things from a few moments ago.

B Work in pairs. Find the idiom *go in one ear and out the other* in paragraph five of the article. What do you think it means?

C Learn and practise. Go to the Vocabulary Bank.

▶ page 136 **VOCABULARY BANK**
idioms: memory

The people who never forget

What research is telling us about people with amazing memories

Ayodele Odetoyinbo
Mon 18th June

In Jorge Luis Borges's story *Funes the Memorius*, the title character falls off his horse, bangs his head, and suddenly remembers everything he's ever experienced. He remembers the changing shapes of clouds and the exact position of a dog at different times of day. He remembers every leaf on every tree he's ever seen and reconstructs his dreams at will.

Some people say that truth is stranger than fiction, and sure enough, there are real people with similar abilities to Funes. The designer, artist and entrepreneur Nima Veiseh can **remember every detail** of his late teenage years: the clothes he was wearing on any given day, what he ate at every meal, every painting on every wall of every art gallery he's ever visited. He can even remember the day he started to remember everything: 15th December, 2000.

But Veiseh wasn't the first. Before him was Jill Price. When Price was thirty-four, she contacted Dr James McGaugh, director of the Center for the Neurobiology of Learning and Memory at the University of California, Irvine. She explained that she had a problem: whenever she saw a date on TV, it **brought back memories** and she began reliving everything that had happened on that day. McGaugh invited her to the centre.

To test her memory, McGaugh used a book which contained summaries of the major news stories from every day of the twentieth century. He quizzed her. What happened on 16th August, 1977? Price told him Elvis Presley died that day and it was a Tuesday. When did the singer Bing Crosby die? 14th October, 1977. It was a Friday, and Price heard the news on the car radio on her way to football practice. Asked about the date of one major international event, she got the answer wrong. McGaugh corrected her, but she insisted. He checked another source and found that the book was wrong.

Jill Price was the first person to be diagnosed with HSAM (Highly Superior Autobiographical Memory), a condition which enables someone to remember the events of their life in great detail. Jill doesn't make the effort to **learn things by heart** – it just happens. However, her ability only functions with things she is interested in. When asked to recall a long series of numbers or other general information, she loses her **perfect recall**. Like the rest of us, things go in one ear and out the other. Her memory is connected to her individual identity and things that are important to her.

Dr McGaugh has spent half a century researching memory. He has led numerous experiments on **long-term memory** and **short-term memory**. One conclusion from the research is that people who have HSAM are more likely to enjoy daydreaming, creating fantasies and imagining different worlds. This may mean they have greater ability to create memorable pictures in their minds, which helps them remember things. Another conclusion is that **having a good memory** is aided by the ability to focus completely on what we are doing. Immersing ourselves deeply in a task means we are more likely to remember the details. A third finding is the importance of emotional connections. When we are engaged emotionally in something, we are less likely to forget it. That's why our **childhood memories** are often very powerful.

People in many walks of life – students, teachers, lawyers – need to remember information to be successful. Even if we can't recall details in the way Price, Veiseh and Borges's Funes can, maybe there *are* things we can learn from McGaugh's research. For example, we're more likely to remember information if we focus deeply on it, or if we can find an emotional connection with it. Understanding these things might benefit all of us.

1B

PRONUNCIATION

5 A 🔊 1.03 | chunking: two-part collocations | Listen to the sentences. Is there a pause between the words in bold, or are they said as one chunk?

1 I definitely don't have **perfect recall** when it comes to remembering appointments!
2 My **long-term memory** is pretty good.
3 There are lots of techniques for improving your **short-term memory**.
4 We love sharing our **childhood memories**.

B 🔊 1.03 | Listen to the sentences again. Then practise saying the collocations in bold as one chunk.

C Work in pairs and discuss the questions.

1 Which is better – your short-term memory or your long-term memory?
2 Are you good or bad at learning things by heart?
3 Do you enjoy talking about childhood memories with your family?
4 Are there any sounds or smells that bring back memories for you?

SPEAKING

6 A You are going to describe a memory. Think of something interesting or funny that happened to you recently or in your childhood. Use the prompts below to make notes.

- When did it happen?
- Where were you?
- Who was there?
- What happened?

B Read the Future Skills box and do the task.

> ### FUTURE SKILLS
> **Communication**
>
> When we tell a story, we need to maintain our listeners' interest. One way to do this is by describing details that are unusual, funny or interesting.
>
> Look at your notes in Ex 6A and add interesting details. Think about the place, the weather, the people, the sights, sounds and smells, etc.

C Work in groups. Tell your story. Remember to describe details to keep your listeners interested.

I'm going to tell you about a memory from when I was about ten. I remember meeting …

1C I'd much rather …

HOW TO … | express personal preferences
VOCABULARY | emotions and feelings
PRONUNCIATION | word stress: dependent prepositions

VOCABULARY

emotions and feelings

1 A Work in groups. Discuss the questions.
   1 What kind of things do you like doing when you visit a new city?
   2 When was the last time you visited a new place? Where was it and what did you do?

B Work in pairs. Read the travel guide entry about Lagos, Nigeria. Which of the activities would you like or not like to do? Why?

C Scan the guide again. Complete the sentences with the words in bold.
   1 If you're _passionate_ about something, you love it.
   2 If you're _____ of something, you like it.
   3 If you're _____ something, you feel worried about doing it.
   4 If you're _____ something, it frightens you a lot.
   5 If you're _____ the idea of something, you find it very exciting.
   6 If you're really _____ something, you like it a lot.
   7 If you're not _____ something, you don't like it much.
   8 If you are _____ something, you don't want to do it anymore.

PRONUNCIATION

2 A 🔊 1.04 | **word stress: dependent prepositions** | Listen to the sentences and look at the phrases in bold. Which word is stressed, the adjective or the preposition?
   1 I'm **terrified of** the traffic.
   2 I'm **passionate about** trying local food.
   3 I get **nervous about** taking taxis.
   4 I'm not **keen on** museums.
   5 I'm **fond of** the street markets.
   6 I was **thrilled by** the chance to explore.

B Work in pairs. Discuss the activities in the box using the phrases in Ex 1C.

> driving in foreign countries   getting lost in a new city
> going on boat rides   learning about new cultures
> trying unusual foods   visiting museums
> watching dance performances

A: I'm really into trying new or unusual foods.
B: Me too!

AFRICA > NIGERIA

Lagos

Welcome to Lagos

Are you **passionate about** fashion? **Thrilled by** the idea of discovering new and interesting art? Maybe you're **fond of** street markets? Or are you **really into** cities by the ocean? If you like any of these, Lagos might be the place for you.

The most populous city in Africa, Lagos is full of life: loud chatter, the smells of delicious street food, and non-stop music. Because it's so big, you may be **nervous about** getting lost or **terrified of** the crazy traffic. Never fear! Use tour buses or rent a private car with a driver. And plan ahead. It can take a while to get around.

For a perfect day in Lagos, start at Bogobiri House, a wonderful hotel with striking artworks on the walls. Next, go to Freedom Park to learn about Nigerian history and culture, and watch dancers and musicians performing. If you're **not keen on** culture but like shopping, go to Victoria Island, Lagos's equivalent of Manhattan, with stylish designer shops and great restaurants. By now, you may be **fed up of** the city centre, so head to Tarkwa Bay Beach and go for a relaxing boat ride. End the day with a meal of pepper soup followed by jollof rice and chicken. Perfection on a plate!

How to ...
express personal preferences

3 A 🔊 1.05 | Listen to two businesspeople discussing what to do on their day off in Lagos. What do they decide to do?

B 🔊 1.05 | Complete the sentences from the conversation. Then listen again and check.
1. The .... about it is the street life.
2. I'd be happy to go there ...., but maybe not more than a couple of hours.
3. I'm not a big .... shopping generally.
4. I'd .... to a park and just wander about for a bit.
5. I think I'd .... do that than to go wandering around the shops.
6. You know, ... really like doing is surfing.

C Complete the table with the phrases in the box. Use the sentences in Exercise 3B to help you.

> I'd be happy   I'd prefer
> I'd rather   I'm (not) a big fan of
> What I love about

expressing personal preferences

expressing likes and dislikes	I'm really into/I'm passionate about ... I'm (not) keen on 1 .... 2 .... /The thing I love/like about ... is ...
discussing options	3 .... (to do that) because ... 4 .... (do that) because ... I'd much rather ...
compromising	5 .... to ... , but ...

D Learn and practise. Go to the Grammar Bank.

⏩ page 110 **GRAMMAR BANK**

4 A Read the list of things to do in Prague. Which activities would you choose to do? Why?

Top 5 Things to do in Prague
1. Charles Bridge – walk across this famous, historical stone bridge with its thirty statues.
2. Farmers' Market, Náplavka – visit this great street market and try meat, fish, baked goods, etc.
3. Prague Castle – visit the historical castle, over 1,000 years old, with halls, towers, gates and gardens.
4. Gallery of Steel Figures – see amazing metal sculptures of superheroes, cars, bicycles, etc.
5. Westfield Chodov – spend time in this modern shopping centre with designer stores, restaurants and an eighteen-screen cinema.

B Work in pairs. Imagine you have a day to spend in Prague together. Take turns making suggestions and responding using the phrases in Ex 3C.

A: Why don't we go to the Farmers' Market? I'm really into trying new kinds of food.
B: Great idea! I'm passionate about food, too.

SPEAKING

5 A Work in groups. Brainstorm some cities you would like to visit, and choose one you are all interested in.

B Work alone. Imagine you are going to spend a day in the city you chose in Ex 5A. Make notes about:
- places to visit (e.g. famous sites, museums, green spaces, etc.).
- activities (e.g. shopping, concerts, city tours, etc.).
- how you'll get around.
- meals (e.g. what to eat, when, where, etc.).
- what to do in the evening.

C Read the Future Skills box and do the task.

FUTURE SKILLS
Collaboration

When we collaborate, we sometimes have to compromise, to find a solution that everyone can accept.

Look at your notes in Ex 5B. What ideas might you need to compromise on? Why? What other ideas would be acceptable to you, as a compromise?

D In your groups, try to agree on an itinerary for a day in the city. Use your notes in Ex 5B to help you. Then present your ideas to the class.

MEDIATION SKILLS
organising a group task
create tourist recommendations for your town/area

⏩ page 146 **MEDIATION BANK**

Speak anywhere   Go to the interactive speaking practice

Unit 1 | Lesson D

1D BBC Street Interviews
Personality

Collin

Anna

GRAMMAR | *while, whereas* and *whilst*
SPEAKING | discuss personality traits
WRITING | a letter of recommendation

PREVIEW

1 A Work in groups. Take turns describing the personality of someone in the group without saying their name. Try to guess who is being described.

B Match the sentence beginnings (1–8) with the endings (a–h).
1 Camille is really **bubbly** – she's always
2 Ali is very **committed** to
3 My sister loves trying new things. She's always **enthusiastic**
4 You should try to be more cheerful
5 I always seem to worry about things – I'd love to
6 My grandma is a very kind
7 I always try to stay
8 Everyone was very **welcoming** to

a when I suggest doing something different.
b and **loving** person.
c laughing and full of life.
d be more happy-go-lucky.
e **positive** when things go wrong.
f and less **grumpy**!
g the new club members.
h his job – he takes it very seriously.

C Work in pairs. Take turns using the adjectives in Ex 1B to describe your friends and family.

VIEW

2 A ▶ Work in pairs. Watch the interviews. Which of the speakers is similar to you? In what ways?

B ▶ Watch the first part of the interviews again. Note down at least one adjective each speaker uses to describe themselves. Which of the adjectives can describe you?

C ▶ Watch the second part of the interviews again. Choose the correct words to complete the sentences.
1 Elaine's personality changes when she is **in other countries** / **at work**.
2 Anna thinks she is more **serious** / **stressed** at work.
3 Valeria is more **direct** / **compassionate** at work.
4 Elijah talks more when he is with his **friends** / **mother**.
5 Gwen sometimes has the feeling she doesn't want to be at **work** / **a party**.
6 Roisin is less confident **with new people** / **at work**.
7 Collin says that his personality **changes a lot** / **never changes**.

D Choose the correct meanings (a or b).
1 Elaine: I try to make the best that I can out of life.
   a She tries to think positively even in bad situations.
   b She feels sad in many situations.
2 Anna: I'm a people person.
   a She thinks she is similar to many other people.
   b She likes people and gets on well with them.
3 Collin: I never give up.
   a He keeps trying even in difficult situations.
   b He is always generous to others.
4 Elaine: I'll need to be a little bit more professional.
   a She has to speak more.
   b She has to be more serious.
5 Gwen: It varies.
   a It always stays the same.
   b It changes, depending on the situation.

Q1: How would you describe your personality?
Q2: How does your personality change in different situations?

16

1D

BBC

Valeria

Roisin

Gwen

Elaine

Elijah

GRAMMAR

while, whereas and *whilst*

3 A Read the sentences from the interviews and choose the correct option to complete the rule.

1 At work, maybe I'm more serious, **whereas** when I go to, like, a café with my friends, er, I'm a lot more relaxed.
2 I'm probably less confident when I meet new people, **whilst** when I'm with my friends, I'm a bit more confident, a bit more chatty, a bit more comfortable.

We use *while*, *whereas* and *whilst* to introduce a second idea that is **similar to / different from** the first idea in the sentence.

B Learn and practise. Go to the Grammar Bank.

▶▶ page 111 **GRAMMAR BANK**

SPEAKING

discuss personality traits

4 A Make notes on the following questions.

1 How would you describe your personality?
2 How does your personality change in different situations (e.g. when you're hanging out with friends, with family, at work or when you meet new people, etc.)?
3 Has your personality changed as you've got older? If so, how?
4 In what ways is your personality similar to and different from other people in your family?
5 What personality traits are important in a friend?
6 What personality traits are important for the roles or jobs in the box? Why?

comedian   hairdresser   lawyer
manager   parent   police officer
sales representative   teacher

B Work in pairs. Discuss the questions in Ex 4A. Use your notes to help you.

C Work with a different partner. Describe your first partner's personality. What job do you think they would be good at? Why?

WRITING

a letter of recommendation

5 A Work in pairs. Discuss the questions.

1 Who would you ask to write a letter of recommendation for you? Why?
2 What do you think they might say about you?

B Write a letter of recommendation. Go to the Writing Bank.

▶▶ page 104 **WRITING BANK**

1 REVIEW

GRAMMAR

present perfect simple and continuous

1 A Use the prompts to write questions in the present perfect simple or continuous.

1. How long / you / learn / English?
2. How many teachers / you / have?
3. What / you / do / improve your English recently?
4. you / finish / today's homework?
5. you / study / a lot / recently?
6. you / watch / any films in English recently?

B Work in pairs. Ask and answer the questions.

infinitive and -ing forms

2 Complete the sentences (1–8) with the correct ending, a or b.

1. I stopped to call Omar because
2. I stopped calling Omar because
a. I needed his help.
b. he never wanted to talk to me.

3. Do you remember to send
4. Do you remember sending
a. those funny letters when we were children?
b. your mum a birthday message every year?

5. I forgot to take
6. I forgot taking
a. that photo. We were so young then!
b. a photo, so I can't show you where we went.

7. Sarita tried to take the medicine,
8. Sarita tried taking the medicine,
a. but it didn't help.
b. but she couldn't – it was too disgusting.

VOCABULARY

3 A Choose the correct words to complete the sentences.

1. I think this person is really **into** / **about** music.
2. I don't think they're very **keen** / **curious** on sport.
3. They're passionate **about** / **for** the environment.
4. This person seems to **have** / **keep** a good memory.
5. This person enjoys doing exciting things. They are very **adventurous** / **stubborn**.
6. They enjoy being with people – they're very **ambitious** / **outgoing**.
7. This person might be **nervous** / **terrified** about taking exams.
8. They are good at learning things by **memory** / **heart**.

B Work in pairs. Name someone in your class who you think matches each sentence in Ex 3A. Then talk to that student. Were you right?

A: Are you really into music?
B: No, not really. I listen to it at work, but that's about it. How about you?

4 A Choose the correct options (A–C) to complete the anecdote.

Stormy weather

Since I was very young, I ¹_____ the outdoors. As a ten-year-old, I read lots of books about explorers and I was extremely ²_____. I was happy wandering into the woods on my own, or exploring abandoned houses. ³_____ most children are ⁴_____ about the natural world, I was obsessed. I have one particular childhood ⁵_____ of a day with my grandfather. He was really ⁶_____ hiking and one day, when I was ten, he took me with him. The idea was ⁷_____ up a hill called Gomez Peak, and we needed to go at a good pace so ⁸_____ back by dinnertime. Unfortunately, we got caught in a storm. There was no escape. We tried ⁹_____ under a pine tree to stay dry, but it didn't work; we got soaked. As we stood there, he kept trying ¹⁰_____ me, saying, 'It's going to be OK.' He thought I'd be ¹¹_____ of all the noise and wind. But I wasn't scared – I loved it. I'll never forget ¹²_____ to the rain falling like drumbeats. To this day, I have never had so much fun in my life!

	A	B	C
1	have always been loving	always love	have always loved
2	adventurous	ambitious	nervous
3	While	Because	However
4	terrified	keen	curious
5	recall	memory	detail
6	keen	passionate	into
7	to go	going	by going
8	as we were	that we are	as to be
9	standing	stand	to stand
10	comfort	comforting	to comfort
11	fed up	terrified	not keen
12	listen	to listen	listening

B 🔊 **R1.01** | Listen and check your answers.

different worlds 2

VLOGS

Q: What impact does social media have on your life?

1 ▶ Watch the video. What impacts of social media do the people mention?

2 Work in pairs. Discuss the impact that social media has on your lives.

GSE LEARNING OBJECTIVES

2A READING | Read an article about virtual reality: science and technology; word families

Discuss possible future uses of virtual reality: future probability

Pronunciation: connected speech: future probability

2B LISTENING | Understand a radio programme about spending time in nature: nature; quantifiers

Talk about ways to encourage people to spend time in nature

Pronunciation: connected speech: quantifiers

Write a for-and-against essay on living in the countryside

2C HOW TO … | speculate: lifestyle adjectives

Pronunciation: stress to show certainty

2D BBC PROGRAMME | Understand a TV drama about time travel: extreme adjectives

Talk about an imaginary trip back in time

Write a competition entry

Unit 2 | Lesson A

2A Real or virtual?

GRAMMAR | future probability
VOCABULARY | science and technology; word families
PRONUNCIATION | connected speech: future probability

READING

1 A Work in pairs. Discuss the questions.

1 Have you ever used a virtual reality headset like the one in the photo? Would you like to?
2 What do you know about how VR is used now? How do you think it might be used in the future?

B Read the article. Which topics in the box do the people mention?

> education   gaming   health   shopping   sport
> training for work   travel

C Read the article again. Complete the table with the main points and supporting details it includes.

main point	supporting detail
People in the tech industry expect VR to be used more in the future.	¹ Microsoft and Google are spending a lot of money on it.
VR will be useful in schools.	²
³	Using VR can help reduce stress.
VR can help surgeons.	⁴
⁵	Firefighters need practice in real situations.
VR will never replace real travel.	⁶

D Work in pairs. Discuss the questions.

1 Which arguments in the article do you find the most convincing? Why?
2 Which uses of VR do you think will be the most useful? Why?
3 Which events in other countries would you most like to attend using VR? Why?

VOCABULARY

science and technology

2 A Scan the article again. Complete the sentences with the correct form of the words in bold.

1 I work as a **researcher**. I find out information by reading and speaking to people.
2 When you play a video game with ………………, you actually feel as if you are in the gaming world.
3 ……………… technology is controlled by computers and seems to make some decisions for itself.
4 After arranging scientific tests, we publish the ……………… so people can learn from them.
5 In 2020, two of the biggest brands in the ……………… were Facebook and Apple.
6 Many people now don't need to go into an office, but can work ………………, from anywhere in the world.
7 We ……………… information: we read it, test it, and explain the results.
8 Technology helps us to ……………… many things, like tomorrow's weather or the future of financial markets.

B Work in pairs. Discuss the questions.

1 Do you have to analyse anything in your work or studies? What do you do with the findings?
2 Name one thing you have to predict or research in your daily life.
3 When's the last time you did something remotely? How did it go?
4 What's your favourite smart device? Why?
5 Do you think the tech industry has too much influence? Why/Why not?

C Learn and practise. Go to the Vocabulary Bank.

▶ page 137 **VOCABULARY BANK** word families

Is virtual reality the future?

Many of us have experience of **virtual reality** in gaming, but does the technology have other, more serious uses? Many people in the **tech industry** certainly think so. Microsoft and Google have spent hundreds of millions of dollars developing VR projects, and when Facebook bought a company called Oculus VR for $2.3 billion, Facebook's CEO, Mark Zuckerberg, **predicted** that VR is going to become a part of daily life for billions of people. So, is VR really the future? We hear two different views.

YES — Yulia Ivanovich

VR has huge potential in education and training. Several studies have compared the performance of students taught traditionally to those taught using VR. The **findings** showed that students who used VR tended to perform better. It makes sense. Imagine you're learning about the Amazon rainforest. What's more effective: reading about it or going there? VR also helps in training for dangerous jobs like firefighting and mountain rescue, allowing people to practise dealing with difficult situations in a safe environment.

Another possible use for VR is in health. In one study that looked at using VR to relieve stress, participants spent time in a virtual forest. They reported feeling more positive afterwards, and the **researchers** concluded that spending time in a virtual forest can decrease stress as much as being in a real one. It could also help surgeons as they can practise their skills in a safe, virtual environment. This use is certain to become more common because it can save lives.

VR is also likely to be used more in the travel industry. People are becoming aware of the environmental costs of travel and tourism, so VR could provide a virtual alternative. Instead of flying halfway around the world to attend a festival or watch a sports event, people could experience it **remotely** without causing environmental damage.

NO — Noor El-Basany

When it comes to education and training, everyone says VR has potential, but it probably won't be used widely in schools. Why not? Firstly, it's too expensive, and secondly, when you **analyse** the research in detail, you realise there isn't much evidence that it works. Similarly, VR has some applications in training, but it will never replace real-life training. If you're a firefighter, fighting a fire in a virtual environment just isn't the same – you need real practice.

In health, VR may be useful in a few situations, but it's unlikely to be used as a serious treatment. Does anyone really believe that putting on a VR headset and visiting a virtual world is any kind of long-term solution to anything? It sounds more like escapism to me, rather than a serious solution to a problem.

Some people have said VR might replace some kinds of tourism, but it'll never work. The whole point of going to a festival or sporting event is to be part of the crowd. And travelling is about having experiences: seeing new sights, getting to know other cultures, and trying different food. No **smart** machine can ever replace that. Travel is also about showing off your photos and bragging to your friends about the amazing things you have seen. You can't do that if your trip consists of you sitting in your living room wearing a headset!

Unit 2 | Lesson A

GRAMMAR
future probability

3 A Read the sentences (1–8). Complete the uses (a–e) with the correct modal verbs and the phrases in bold.

1 VR **is going to** become a part of daily life for billions of people.
2 Surgeons who **are due to** operate on patients could practise their skills.
3 This use **is certain to** become more common because it can save lives.
4 VR **is likely to** be used in the travel industry.
5 People **could** experience it remotely.
6 It **will** never replace real-life training.
7 VR **is unlikely to** be used as a serious treatment.
8 VR **might** replace some kinds of tourism.

a We use will_____ and _____ to make general predictions.
b We use _____ to say we are sure something will happen.
c We use _____ to say we think something will probably happen. The opposite is _____.
d We use _____ and _____ to say we think something is possible.
e We use _____ to say something is scheduled to happen, e.g. a train to arrive.

B Learn and practise. Go to the Grammar Bank.

▶▶ page 112 **GRAMMAR BANK**

PRONUNCIATION

4 A 🔊 **2.01** | connected speech: future probability |
Listen and complete the sentences with the correct phrases.

1 VR _____ be used more in the future.
2 The new headsets _____ go on sale next week.
3 This game _____ be a big hit!
4 VR _____ replace our summer holidays.

B 🔊 **2.01** | Listen again. Notice how the phrases are pronounced in connected speech. Practise saying the full sentences.

C Work in pairs. Take turns completing the sentences with your own ideas.

1 Video games are certain to …
2 New technology is going to …
3 In the future, people are unlikely to …
4 The next football World Cup is due to …
5 In future, medical professionals could …
6 Teachers of the future might …
7 By 2030, tourists are likely to …
8 In the future, firefighters might …

SPEAKING

5 A Work alone. Read the predictions. Decide which ones you agree with, and which you disagree with.

By 2040 …
- offices will not exist. Former office workers will meet and socialise in virtual spaces.
- virtual university professors will give virtual lectures in the environments they are teaching about.
- most people will go to virtual concerts and sporting events instead of real ones.
- doctors will use VR to predict health issues. They will analyse findings based on VR simulations.

B Read the Future Skills box and do the task.

> **FUTURE SKILLS**
> **Critical thinking**
>
> Being accurate is an important part of critical thinking. For example, 'By 2040, nobody will eat meat.' is a big claim. It seems unlikely that every single person in the world will give up meat in the future. Something like, 'By 2040, the majority of people in the UK will have reduced the amount of meat in their diet.' is far more accurate and easier to evaluate.
>
> Think again about your responses to the predictions in Ex 5A. Think about how you can express your opinions accurately, to show how sure you feel about each one.

C Work in groups. Discuss the predictions in Ex 5A and answer the questions.

1 Which of the predictions:
- will happen?
- might happen?
- is unlikely to happen?
- definitely won't happen?
2 What do you think of the predictions? How would they affect our day-to-day lives?
3 What other uses do you think there will be for virtual reality in the future? What other predictions would you make about life in 2040?

2B Closer to nature

GRAMMAR | quantifiers
VOCABULARY | nature
PRONUNCIATION | connected speech: quantifiers

LISTENING

1 A Work in pairs. Read the information about the BBC Radio programme and discuss the questions.

Why we should listen to trees

Most of the world's population live in big, noisy cities, where we don't have many opportunities to get close to nature. For many of us, this means we miss out on some of the positive effects of spending time in nature. Alex Smalley explains.

1 Do you spend time out in nature? Why/Why not?
2 What kinds of natural places do you enjoy visiting?
3 Why do you think spending time in nature is good for us?

B 🔊 2.02 | Listen to the programme. Tick the ideas that are mentioned.

1 People have known for a long time that we benefit from spending time in nature.
2 In the past, doctors didn't recognise the benefits of spending time in nature.
3 In recent centuries, we seem to have forgotten the health benefits of being in nature.
4 The excitement of city life brings health benefits.
5 Spending time in or near nature helps restore balance.
6 Studies have indicated that listening to the sounds of nature can improve your well-being.

C Work in pairs and answer the questions.

1 According to the programme, how would most people describe their idea of paradise?
2 What did doctors in the 1700s recommend for their patients?
3 What has helped improve people's quality of life in the last 200 years?
4 What problems does living in 'big, busy and noisy cities' cause us?
5 How does spending time in a natural environment help us?
6 Why did some hospital patients in the 1980s recover faster than others?

D 🔊 2.02 | Listen again and check your answers.

GRAMMAR

quantifiers

2 A Work in pairs. Read the comments about the radio programme. Which do you agree with? Which do you disagree with? Why?

Rodrigo
07:56 | 13 June

Alex is right! **The majority of** the world's population now live in cities, and there is **a lack of** green public spaces where people can relax.

Fumi
08:20 | 13 June

I work in an office where most people spend **a good deal of** time stuck at a computer screen, and **very little** time outdoors. **Several** of us try to find time in the day to go out and enjoy nature, but we're definitely **in a minority**.

Alexis
10:47 | 13 June

I agree! There are ways to get closer to nature even if you live in a city, and have **no** time to spare. **Every** day, take **a few** moments to notice the nature around you. Sit outside with your morning coffee, grow **a handful of** plants on your desk, or take **a little** time to enjoy the view from your office window. **Each** time you do this, you'll feel more relaxed.

B Read the comments again. Match the quantifiers in bold with the meanings (1–4).

1 a large number or amount
2 a small number or amount
3 one individual person or thing
4 none

C Complete the rules with the type of noun: *singular, plural* or *uncountable*.

1 Use *several, few, a few, a handful of* + ... nouns.
2 Use *the majority of, a lack of, no* + ... nouns or .... nouns.
3 Use *each, every* + ... nouns.
4 Use *very little, a little, a good deal of* + ... nouns.

D Learn and practise. Go to the Grammar Bank.

▶▶ page 113 **GRAMMAR BANK**

Unit 2 | Lesson B

PRONUNCIATION

3 A 🔊 2.03 | connected speech: quantifiers | Listen to the sentence. Look at the quantifier in bold and draw (‿) between any words that link together.

The majority of the world's population now lives in cities.

B 🔊 2.04 | Draw (‿) to show connected speech in the quantifiers. Then listen and check.
1 **A good deal of** my time is spent commuting.
2 There's **a lack of** green public spaces.
3 **Several of us** walk along the beach in the morning.
4 People who live in the countryside are definitely **in a minority**.
5 I grow **a handful of** herbs on my balcony.

C Work in pairs. Take turns to complete the sentences with your own ideas.
1 A good deal of my time is spent …
2 There's a lack of …
3 Several of us …
4 People who … are definitely in a minority.

VOCABULARY

nature

4 A Complete the article with the words and phrases in the box.

| coastline | deserted | open space | river bank |
| scenery | sunlight | track | woodland |

Did you know?

New research has found that spending just two hours a week in nature is enough to improve your health and well-being.

For some people, this might mean sitting by the sea on a ¹_____ beach somewhere on a wild ²_____, looking up at a clear blue sky and listening to the sound of the waves crashing onto the sand. Or perhaps enjoying a wide ³_____ where the ⁴_____ is spectacular. For others, it might be walking through ⁵_____ near where they live and watching the morning ⁶_____ through the trees. Or maybe walking along a narrow ⁷_____ to a ⁸_____, to sit and watch the water flowing past.

B Read the article again. Which word or phrase:
1 means that there is no one else around?
2 refers to the land by the side of a river?
3 refers to a rough path or road?
4 is the opposite of a small, contained area?
5 refers to an area with a lot of trees?
6 is another word for landscape?
7 refers to the area of land near the sea?
8 refers to light from the sun?

C Work in pairs. Describe a natural place that you know or enjoy spending time in.

SPEAKING

5 A Work in groups. Imagine your school or college wants to encourage people to spend more time in nature to improve their well-being. Make notes about:
- green spaces nearby and how you could use them.
- changes you could make to the building (e.g. creating a rooftop garden).
- one-off events or activities you could do (e.g. a tree-planting event).
- changes you could make to ways of working or schedules.
- posters, leaflets, etc. you could create.

B Read the Future Skills box and answer the question.

> **FUTURE SKILLS**
> **Leadership**
>
> When you are working in a group, a discussion can sometimes get stuck on one topic for too long. When this happens, it is important to refocus the group by suggesting what you should discuss next.
>
> What expressions can you use to move the discussion on to a new topic?

C Work in your groups. Try to agree on five suggestions for your college or school. Remember to refocus the discussion if you get stuck on one topic for too long.

WRITING

a for-and-against essay

6 A Work in pairs. Write down five advantages of living in a city and five advantages of living in the countryside.

B Read the essay. Does it mention your ideas? Do you agree with the writer's point of view?

C Read the essay again. Then choose the correct words to complete the sentences.

1 The introductory paragraph **explains what the topic is and why we might be interested** / **gives the writer's opinion on the topic**.
2 Paragraph two gives points **for** / **for and against** the idea.
3 Paragraph three gives points **against** / **for and against** the idea.
4 The conclusion **asks the reader's** / **gives the writer's** opinion.

7 A Look at the sentences in bold in the essay. Find linkers which are used to show a contrasting idea. The first one has been done for you.

B Work in pairs and answer the questions.

1 What punctuation follows *However*?
2 Which verb form follows *despite*?
3 Which linker is used in the phrase '................... the fact that …'?
4 Which linker is used to start a sentence which contrasts with the previous ideas?

C Connect the ideas in two different ways using the linkers in brackets.

1 Some young people love living in the city / others don't like it at all. (although / however)

   Although some young people love living in the city, others don't like it at all.

   Some young people love living in the city. **However**, others don't like it at all.

2 Public transport can be very overcrowded / people still use it (despite the fact / while)
3 Life in the city is exciting / it can be stressful (while / however)
4 Pollution and crime are problems / many young people prefer living in the city (although / despite)

D Write notes for the four paragraphs of a for-and-against essay on living in the countryside. Then write the essay (180–200 words).

City living – pros and cons

Rural and urban living have always held a different appeal for different people. ¹**While some people love living in the countryside, others find it boring and can't wait to get back to the excitement of the city.** So, what are the pros and cons of living in the city?

For many people the city offers plenty of advantages. Firstly, cities are much more exciting. There are lots of things to do, from shopping and eating out to going to the theatre or the cinema. In a city, all of these things are easy to access on public transport, which makes life a lot easier. Secondly, there are a great number of professional opportunities available in the city which are not available if you live in the countryside. Many big businesses have their headquarters in the city. Therefore, there are more businesses to choose from and more jobs available. Also, you're likely to get a higher salary. Lastly, when you live in a city, you get the opportunity to meet a huge number of diverse people. ²**Although you can build a network of friends and professional contacts anywhere you live, being in a city makes this easier.**

³**However, there are some downsides to living in the city.** It's a lot noisier and more crowded than the countryside. The pace of life is very busy and this can feel stressful. ⁴**Despite having efficient public transport, life in the city means you often have to spend a lot of your time commuting to work.** Also, the cost of living is often higher in the city. In addition to this, you have to consider that pollution and levels of crime are likely to be worse than in the countryside.

On balance, I think the advantages of being in a city outweigh the disadvantages, especially for younger people. ⁵**Despite the fact that there are benefits to living a peaceful life in the countryside, it's no surprise that so many people choose to give this up in order to find more excitement and opportunities in the city.**

Unit 2 | Lesson C

2C Amazing lives

HOW TO ... | speculate
VOCABULARY | lifestyle adjectives
PRONUNCIATION | stress to show certainty

VOCABULARY

lifestyle adjectives

1 A Work in pairs. Look at the photos and answer the questions.
1 Where are the people?
2 What are they doing?
3 What is unusual about their lives?

B Read the article. What do you think is the hardest thing about each lifestyle?

2 A Scan the article. Complete the sentences (1–7) with the adjectives in bold.
1 My life is so busy and tiring – it's ....
2 My job is so .... – I do exactly the same thing every day, so I'm always bored.
3 My job gives me a lot of personal satisfaction, as well as a good income – it's very ....
4 My life is very .... , like everyone else's. There's nothing unusual about it.
5 I don't think anybody else lives like me. I have a(n) .... lifestyle.
6 My lifestyle is very .... I don't spend a lot of money on myself.
7 Life here is very .... , with very cold weather and a lot of snow in the winter.

B Work in pairs. Do any of the statements in Ex 2A apply to your life? Why/Why not?

Life at the extreme

This week, we continue our profiles of some of the world's most amazing people, by looking at three women with extreme lives.

Life at sea

Diana Botutihe's lifestyle is definitely **unique**. She has lived her entire life at sea. Born at sea, she has spent her whole life on boats that are typically 5 m long and 1.5 m wide. She visits land only to trade fish for other essentials such as rice and water. It's a simple, **modest** life. Her boat looks homely: filled with water cans, cooking pots, plastic utensils, a kerosene lamp and a couple of pot plants. Diana is one of the world's last marine nomads, a member of the Sama-Bajau ethnic group, a group of Malay people who have lived a traditional life at sea for centuries.

Life in space

Astronauts have been living on the International Space Station for more than a decade. Whilst floating in the air without gravity may sound like fun, there are plenty of challenges which make doing even **ordinary** things like washing your hair difficult. Karen Nyberg spent more than twenty years in a hugely fulfilling career working as an astronaut. While she was on the Space Station, Karen, who enjoys running and has run nine marathons, would typically spend at least two hours a day training on a running machine or an exercise bicycle. Life in space can be **tedious** at times, so as well as dealing with technical and practical problems on the Space Station, Karen also enjoyed creative pursuits like sewing and sketching.

Life around the world

Rosie Swale-Pope is the only person in history to have undertaken a solo, unsupported run around the world. Over nearly five years, she has travelled over 32,000 km, facing extreme danger, **harsh** Siberian winters, wolves and loneliness. Rosie runs pulling a trailer, which she then uses to camp inside. Life on the road can be **exhausting**, but also incredibly **rewarding**. She says she is happiest when sleeping alone in remote forests and meeting people as she runs by day, often starting before dawn to avoid the traffic.

How to ...
speculate

3 A 🔊 **2.05** | Listen to a conversation about a TV series. What factual information do you learn about Karen Nyberg and Rosie Swale-Pope?

B 🔊 **2.05** | Read the sentences from the conversation. Are they talking about Karen (K) or Rosie (R)? Then listen again to check.

1 **I'd guess** it must be so inspiring to see the world like that.
2 **I'd have thought** it would be exhausting to live like that all the time.
3 **I'd imagine** that was really hard.
4 **I reckon** it must be pretty lonely at times.
5 She's **clearly** the kind of person who just has to keep moving.
6 **I suppose** they had video chats.
7 **There's no way** I would ever consider doing that.
8 She's **bound to** feel scared sometimes.

C Work in pairs. Look at the words and phrases in bold in Ex 3B. Which can you use:

1 instead of saying 'I think ... '?
2 to talk about what you think as a result of the evidence you see?
3 to talk about something you think is not possible?

D Learn and practise. Go to the Grammar Bank.

▶▶ page 114 **GRAMMAR BANK**

PRONUNCIATION

4 A 🔊 **2.06** | **stress to show certainty** | Listen to the sentences and underline the words with the main stress.

1 There's no way I would ever consider doing that.
2 She's clearly the kind of person who just has to keep moving.
3 She's bound to feel scared sometimes.

B Write sentences about the lives of the people in the article in Ex 1B using the phrases in Ex 3B. Write about the topics in the box or your own ideas.

> entertainment   food   friends and family   sleep

C Work in pairs. Take turns to read your sentences. Do you agree with each other's ideas? Why/Why not?

SPEAKING

5 A Work in groups. You are going to talk about the lives of some famous people. Agree on four people you all know about from the categories below.

> actor   businessperson   fashion model
> influencer   singer   sports star

B Work alone. Think about the people you have chosen. Prepare to discuss the questions.

1 What do they enjoy about their life?
2 How do they feel about being famous?
3 Why might they feel unhappy sometimes?

C Discuss your opinions and assumptions about the people you chose in Ex 5A. Which person do you think has the best life? Why?

MEDIATION SKILLS
note taking and summarising
summarise an informal interview

▶▶ page 147 **MEDIATION BANK**

Speak **anywhere** Go to the interactive speaking practice

27

Unit 2 | Lesson D

2D BBC Entertainment
The time traveller

VOCABULARY | extreme adjectives
SPEAKING | an imaginary trip back in time
WRITING | a competition entry

PREVIEW

1 A Work in groups. Discuss the questions.

1 Which famous artists can you name? What do you know about their lives?
2 What do you know about Vincent van Gogh?

B Read the programme information. What did you learn about Vincent van Gogh?

Doctor Who

Doctor Who is a BBC science-fiction series about a character called the Doctor who can travel backwards or forwards in time. In this episode he and his companion, Amy, go to France to visit the artist Vincent van Gogh. Van Gogh was a 19th-century painter from the Netherlands. During his lifetime, he was unsuccessful and had a difficult life. He was often unhappy because no one recognised his talent. After he died, his work became popular and he is now one of the most famous artists in history.

VIEW

2 A ▶ Watch the video. What does van Gogh learn about his paintings by the end of the episode?

B ▶ Number the events in order. Then watch the video again and check.

a Van Gogh talks about the wonders of the universe.
b Van Gogh hears a tour guide speaking about his work.
c Van Gogh takes the Doctor and Amy to his cluttered home.
d The Doctor and Amy go back in time and meet van Gogh in a café.
e A guide in a museum tells visitors about van Gogh. 1
f The Doctor has an idea.
g Van Gogh tries to give the Doctor a gift.
h The group go to a museum called the Musée d'Orsay.

C Work in groups. Discuss the questions.

1 Why do you think the Doctor took van Gogh to the Musée d'Orsay?
2 How do you think van Gogh feels by the end of the episode? How has his life changed?

2D

VOCABULARY

extreme adjectives

3 A Read the sentences from the programme. Choose the correct meanings for the adjectives in bold.
1. Those final months of his life were probably the most **astonishing** artistic outpouring in history.
   a sad and dark
   b very surprising or amazing
2. That's **incredible**, don't you think, Amy?
   a extremely good or great
   b not believable
3. You know, you should be careful with these [paintings]. They're **precious**.
   a valuable and important
   b very large
4. This is the **mighty** Musée d'Orsay, home to many of the greatest paintings in history.
   a very large and important
   b extremely old
5. Van Gogh is the **finest** painter of them all.
   a most famous
   b best
6. His command of colour, the most **magnificent**.
   a extremely good
   b very bright or shiny

B Which of the adjectives in Ex 3A can you use with *very*? Which are extreme adjectives?

C Work in groups. Try to name the following:
- a magnificent work of art.
- an astonishing scientific achievement.
- a very fine film or piece of music.
- something precious in your country.
- a mighty person.
- an incredible time to be alive in history.

D Compare your ideas with other groups.

SPEAKING

an imaginary trip back in time

4 A 🔊 2.07 | Listen to someone explaining where they would go if they could travel back in time. Where do they choose and why?

B 🔊 2.07 | Listen again. Tick the phrases that you hear.

> **KEY PHRASES**
>
> To start with, …
> So, what would I do?
> With that in mind, I'd …
> What else?
> Another possibility would be to …
> And last but not least, I'd …

C Read the Key phrases again and answer the questions.
1. Which two phrases introduce a new topic?
2. Which phrase refers to something just mentioned earlier?
3. Which two phrases can we use to show a sequence of events?

5 A Imagine you could travel back in time. Make notes about:
- where you would go (e.g., which area, city, country, etc.).
- which time you would go back to.
- who you would like to meet.
- what you would do.

B Work in groups. Take turns to explain which time periods you would visit and why. Whose trip sounds the most exciting?

WRITING

a competition entry

6 A Work in pairs. Discuss the questions.
1. Have you ever won a competition? What was the prize?
2. Have you ever entered a creative competition (e.g., with a piece of writing, art, music, etc.)? Did you win?

B Write a competition entry. Go to the Writing Bank.

⏩ page 104 **WRITING BANK**

2 REVIEW

GRAMMAR
future probability

1 A Write as many predictions as you can using the topics in Box A and structures in Box B.

A

> future holidays   the weather   your future career
> your plans for the weekend

B

> be going to   certain to   could   due to   likely to
> may   may not   might   might not   unlikely to
> will + certainly/definitely/possibly/probably   won't

I might go the cinema at the weekend. I'll definitely speak to my parents.

B Work in pairs. Take turns reading your predictions. Are any of them similar?

quantifiers

2 A Read the results of a survey about a group of language learners. Then choose the correct words to complete the sentences.

LANGUAGE LEARNING SURVEY
Participants: 20 students, aged 18–52, average age 26

use a book to learn the language	18
use online resources	20
use some kind of dictionary	13
use a pronunciation app	5
don't have enough time to study	16
review the lesson for ten minutes or more afterwards	10
read in the target language for more than four hours a week	2
prefer to learn with others	16

1 **Few / Several / The majority** use a book to learn the language.
2 **Every student / Several / A handful** use(s) the internet to get input.
3 **A minority of / Few / Plenty of** students use a dictionary.
4 **The majority / A handful / Plenty** of students use a pronunciation app.
5 Most students mention having **a lack of / a bit of / plenty of** time to study.
6 Half say they do **all / a little / a good deal of** revision outside class.
7 **Very few / No / The majority of** students read a lot in the target language.
8 **A large number of / A lack of / Few** students prefer learning with others.

B Work in pairs. Guess which of the sentences are true for your class.

VOCABULARY

3 Complete the sentences with the words in the box. There are two words you don't need.

> coastline   deserted   findings   predict   scenery
> smart   sunlight   track   virtual reality

1 It's impossible to .... the future.
2 Researchers should publish their ....
3 .... is almost as realistic as real life.
4 You should go up into the mountains because the .... is amazing!
5 After midnight the town is ....
6 The .... is very wild and dramatic.
7 Open the curtains! We need some ....!

4 A Choose the correct options (A–C) to complete the text.

Another world: Finding solitude

Anyone looking for solitude [1].......... find it in a 21st-century city, but there are still [2].......... of places one can be alone. In the 19th century, the American writer Henry Thoreau did an experiment in solitary living. He went to live on a patch of [3].......... owned by his friend Ralph Waldo Emerson. Thoreau built a hut on the [4].......... of Walden Pond. He spent over two years there and wrote a book, *Walden*, about his experiences.

More recently, the Italian writer Paolo Cognetti left Milan and rented a shepherd's hut near the mountains of Valle d'Aosta. There he lived for [5].......... months, surrounded by [6].......... scenery and [7].......... noise besides the wind. While there, he took time to [8].......... his life and think about what he [9].......... do next. Like Thoreau, he wrote a book: *The Wild Boy*.

[10].......... people are able to escape like Thoreau and Cognetti. [11].......... of us are lucky if we get a few days on a [12].......... beach. But there will always be quiet places for those with the desire and resources to find them.

	A	B	C
1	is due to	will definitely	is unlikely to
2	plenty	good deal	a lack
3	track	woodland	scenery
4	coastline	open space	banks
5	a good deal of	few	several
6	incredible	precious	mighty
7	the majority of	each	very little
8	research	analyse	predict
9	might	is going to	was due to
10	Few	Little	Enough
11	Several	The minority	The majority
12	coastline	deserted	woodland

B 🔊 R2.01 | Listen and check your answers.

showtime 3

VLOGS

Q: What live events or performances do you enjoy and why?

1 ▶ Watch the video. Which events are mentioned and why?

2 Work in pairs. Which live events or performances you do enjoy? Why?

GSE LEARNING OBJECTIVES

3A READING | Read an article about a sustainable music festival: festivals; the environment; relative clauses
Plan an eco-friendly festival
Pronunciation: pitch in non-defining relative clauses
Write a formal email about an event

3B LISTENING | Understand a podcast about stage fright: phrasal verbs: performing; phrasal verbs: communication; cleft sentences
Speak in public
Pronunciation: emphatic stress

3C HOW TO ... | use vague language: film and TV
Pronunciation: linking and elision

3D BBC STREET INTERVIEWS | Understand people talking about music
Talk about a music questionnaire: *do* and *did* for emphasis
Write a forum comment about music

Unit 3 | Lesson A

3A Festival

GRAMMAR | relative clauses
VOCABULARY | festivals; the environment
PRONUNCIATION | pitch in non-defining relative clauses

VOCABULARY

festivals

1 A Work in pairs. Which music festivals have you been to? Which would you like to go to? Why?

B Read *Festivals: The good, the bad and the ugly*. What problems associated with festivals does the writer mention?

C Scan the article again. Complete the sentences with the words in bold.
1 People who attend a festival can be called ....
2 Another word for places where events take place is ....
3 The people who plan an event are the ....
4 An actor, musician or performer who entertains people on stage is a(n) ....
5 Instead of 'go to' an event we can say people .... an event.
6 The list of performers for an event is the ....
7 If you make people want to come to an event, you .... them.
8 When we talk about the feeling that a place or event gives you, we call it the ....

2 A Work in groups. Discuss the questions.
1 What kinds of things create a good festival atmosphere and attract large crowds?
2 How important is it for event organisers to think about their impact on the environment?
3 How can festival-goers reduce their impact on the environment when they attend events?

B Find words in the text related to the environment.

C Learn and practise. Go to the Vocabulary Bank.

▶▶ page 137 **VOCABULARY BANK** the environment

Festivals: The good, the bad and the ugly

Everybody loves a good music festival, right? Sleeping in a tent for days to catch a glimpse of your favourite **act** on stage, and being outside with old friends and people you've only just met. Festivals are one of the highlights of summer, which is why they **attract** millions of people each year. Often set in **venues** in some of the most stunning locations, with a fantastic **line-up** of performers, they're a great place for people to get together and enjoy a few days of arts and live music in a truly relaxed **atmosphere**.

However, festival **organisers** are becoming increasingly aware that events like these can have a hugely negative impact on the environment. They generate a lot of waste and carbon emissions. It's estimated that in the UK alone, over 100 million plastic cups are used at festivals and live events. And then there's the rubbish that gets left behind by **festival-goers** – each of the major festivals in the USA generates 100 tonnes of waste per day, and after Glastonbury Festival in the UK, more than 5,000 tents and 6,500 sleeping bags are often left behind.

Luckily, if you want to **attend** a festival but also want to keep a clear conscience, there are plenty of great sustainable festivals happening all over the world.

READING

3 A Work in groups of three. You are each going to read about a festival, before telling your classmates about it. Read about your festival. Student A: Read the text below. Student B: Read the text on page 142. Student C: Read the text on page 144. Makes notes.
- Name of the festival • Venue • Dates
- Activities, events and features of the festival
- Eco-friendly ideas

B Summarise the information about your festival to your group. Use your notes from Ex 3A to help you.

C Discuss and comment on all three festivals. Use the questions below to help you.
1 Which of the festivals would you choose to go to? Why?
2 Which one do you think has the best eco-friendly ideas? Why?

Burning Man

Where: USA   When: August/September

Burning Man is unique. Held every summer in Nevada's Black Rock Desert, this famous festival attracts travellers from all over the globe. It's officially an art festival and as you wander around the desert you will find all types of amazing art installations. But there is much more to the festival than just art. The desert location becomes a temporary city, filled with people wearing costumes and enjoying complete freedom and creative expression. Nobody uses money – people give each other gifts of food and drink. The week-long event (they don't like the word 'festival') is dedicated to art and community. There's no fixed line-up as such – things just 'happen'. At the end of the festival everyone gets together to watch the burning of a huge statue of a man.

Despite the name, the iconic Burning Man event operates with the aim of 'leaving no trace'. Throughout the festival, people are encouraged to pick up any rubbish they find and put it in their pocket to dispose of later. Festival-goers are also encouraged not to buy things which will later be thrown away. The organisers aim to be carbon negative and to sustainably manage their waste by 2030. They are keen to use the city as an example of how a sustainable city of the future could work. They use solar power for electricity and electric cars to get around the desert. Every year, they create Black Rock City in the middle of the Nevada desert, and every year they take it down, pack up and leave the area without a trace.

GRAMMAR

relative clauses

4 A Complete the sentences about the festivals with *who*, *which* or *where*.
1 Burning Man festival, _____ takes place at the end of August, attracts huge crowds.
2 Fuji Rock Paper reuses wood _____ would otherwise go to waste.
3 People _____ attend the festival are encouraged to arrive by bus.
4 The festival appointed Damon Gameau, _____ is a world-renowned filmmaker, as their Eco Ambassador.
5 Fuji Rock offers hot springs _____ festival-goers can relax.
6 These are the eco-initiatives _____ the festival encourages.

B Work in pairs. Answer the questions.
1 Which sentences contain defining relative clauses? Which sentences contain non-defining relative clauses?
2 In which sentences can you replace the pronoun with *that*?
3 In which sentence can you omit the relative pronoun?
4 Are commas used with defining or non-defining relative clauses?

C Learn and practise. Go to the Grammar Bank.

▶ page 115 **GRAMMAR BANK**

PRONUNCIATION

5 A 🔊 3.01 | **pitch in non-defining relative clauses** | Listen to sentences 1 and 4 from Ex 4A. Does the speaker use a high or low pitch in the non-defining relative clause? Why?

B Add commas to the text where there are non-defining relative clauses. Then practise reading it.

The Green Man festival which is held annually in Wales is an independent arts and music festival. Being environmentally friendly is fundamental to Green Man whose organisers encourage festival-goers to bring their own water bottles and take home all their waste. They also send any tents which have been left unwanted at the site to refugee charities. Green Man which started with just a few hundred people in 2003 is now one of the UK's best-loved festivals.

C 🔊 3.02 | Listen and compare your pronunciation with the recording.

SPEAKING

6 A You are going to work in a group to plan a new eco-friendly festival. Think of your own ideas first and make notes.

B Work in pairs. Read the Future Skills box and do the task.

> **FUTURE SKILLS**
> **Collaboration**
>
> When you discuss a plan with others, use language to suggest ideas, ask for people's opinions and check that everyone agrees. For example:
> 'One idea we could consider is …
> What do you reckon? Don't you think it would be better to … ? Is everyone agreed that … ?'
>
> Make a list of other useful phrases to help you encourage discussion, invite others to join in and say what they think, etc.

C Work in groups and plan your festival. Use the questions to help you.

1 When will the festival be held? What will it be called? What is the venue for your festival?
2 How will you attract festival-goers and ensure a good atmosphere? What acts are in the line-up? How much will it cost? Will there be any special food or events?
3 How will you make the festival sustainable and protect the local environment?

D Present your festival to the class. Which do you think is the best? Why?

WRITING

a formal email

7 A Work in pairs. Read the email and answer the questions.
1 What is the purpose of the email?
2 What are the main features of the proposed festival?
3 How will the festival be sustainable?
4 What do you think of the ideas suggested?
5 Is the email formal or informal? How do you know?

To M.Drapers@council.org
From T.Stubbings@ecofest.net
Subject Ecofest – Festival Proposal

Dear Ms Draper,

¹We are writing to you with a proposal for a new family- and eco-friendly music festival, which we would like you to consider. Ecofest would be held annually in Riverside Park on the last weekend in June.

²The festival would feature local artists and musicians as well as a line-up of popular acts. Music to suit all tastes would be provided, and there would also be plenty of entertainment for children on offer, such as drumming workshops and arts and crafts activities.

³The festival would have a strong eco-theme which encourages families to move towards a more sustainable way of living through recycling and reducing our dependence on natural resources. Ecofest itself aims to keep a low carbon footprint by using solar power to run the festival and banning single-use plastic on site. We would like to assure you that there would be no mess left in the park. A team of volunteers will organise a clean-up at the end of the festival and dispose of any waste that is left by festival-goers.

⁴I hope you will consider our proposal. If you require any further information about Ecofest, please feel free to contact us. We look forward to hearing your response.

Kind regards,
Toni Stubbings
Manager of Ecofest

B Read the email again. Match the paragraphs (1–4) with their functions (a–d).

Paragraph 1   **a** eco-friendly initiatives
Paragraph 2   **b** why you are writing and the name of the festival
Paragraph 3   **c** closing sentences and future steps
Paragraph 4   **d** the main features/activities of the festival

C Find formal phrases in the email which match the informal phrases below.

1 We can't wait to hear your answer
2 Please get in touch
3 With best wishes
4 Hi!
5 If you need to know anything else …
6 Please think about our ideas.
7 You can be sure that …

D Read the situation and write a formal email with your proposal.

Your local authority intends to allow only one festival this summer because it is worried about the environmental impact on the local area. Write an email explaining why they should choose your festival and what you will do to make it sustainable.

3B Performers

GRAMMAR | cleft sentences
VOCABULARY | phrasal verbs: performing; phrasal verbs: communication
PRONUNCIATION | emphatic stress

VOCABULARY

phrasal verbs: performing

1 Work in pairs. Rank the following from 1 (the most frightening) to 4 (the least frightening).
- giving a presentation in English
- making a speech in public
- performing in front of an audience
- competing in a live sporting event

2 **A** Read the social media thread. Have any of these things ever happened to you?

B Read the thread again and match the phrasal verbs in bold with the definitions below.
1 to use a method or plan after other options have failed **fall back on**
2 to continue doing something
3 to think of an idea, plan, or solution
4 to make a mistake or do something badly
5 to be as good as people expect or hope
6 to accept a bad situation without complaining
7 to make it difficult for someone to focus
8 to finally do something

C Choose four topics below and write your answers.
- one thing I never mess up
- an event that lived up to my expectations
- a good idea I came up with recently
- something I ended up doing by accident
- a hobby I started as a child and carried on doing
- something I have to put up with every day

D Work in pairs. Take turns to read your answers and guess which topic they match.
B: Is it a hobby you started as a child and carried on doing?
A: Yes.
B: When did you start?

E Learn and practise. Go to the Vocabulary Bank.

▶▶ page 138 **VOCABULARY BANK** phrasal verbs: communication

Jaxfunnyguy_123
1 hour ago
Like | Comment | Share

Advice needed!
Does anyone have any advice for performing in public? I just did my first stand-up comedy act and, let's just say, it didn't quite **live up to** my expectations. Actually, it was a complete disaster. The worst thing is, I thought I was well prepared. I **came up with** loads of jokes beforehand and learnt them all, and I thought they were pretty funny. I was determined not to **mess up**. So I went up on stage and the lights were in my eyes and it was really hot. I started telling a joke and then someone in the crowd shouted something. It completely **put me off** and I forgot everything. I **ended up** running off stage and hiding for the rest for the evening.

Strawby_King2
55 minutes ago
Like | Comment | Share

Urgh! I'm sorry you had to **put up with** a heckler. As an actor, what puts me off is when people in the audience start coughing or looking at their phones! My advice is to ignore them. You just have to **carry on** and hope they stop!

SamiraPRS
47 minutes ago
Like | Comment | Share

Try again. I remember being told I had to give a huge presentation at work once. I was so nervous I felt sick. But once you've done it a few times, it gets easier because you have more experience to **fall back on**. So when things go wrong, you know how to cope.

Unit 3 | Lesson B

LISTENING

3 A Work in pairs. What do you think are the best ways to prepare for a public performance?

B Read the information about a podcast. Who do you think it is mainly aimed at?

Up in lights
Entertainment
★★★★

Up in lights is a weekly radio podcast in which Pauline Hazany talks to performers about everything from getting your foot in the door and auditioning, to writing your own material and finding an agent.

29 Jan
Stage fright >

In this episode, Pauline discusses stage fright with a musician, an actor and a motivational speaker.

4 A  **3.03** | Listen to an extract from the episode on stage fright. What do all three performers discuss in their interview?

1 They talk about their experiences and give advice.
2 They explain why stage fright means they no longer enjoy performing.
3 They discuss the differences between performing in a studio and performing in public.

B **3.03** | Answer the questions. Then listen again and check.

Which speaker, Katherine (K), Rufus (R) or Mahmoud (M) …

1 received advice from someone with the same job?
2 imagines performing in front of familiar people?
3 imagines the consequences if things go wrong?
4 prepares less than in the past?
5 imagines they are a different person?
6 tries to remember why the audience is there?

C Work in groups. Discuss the questions.

1 Which pieces of advice from the recording do you think are the most useful? Why?
2 What is 'visualisation'? In what situations do you think it might be effective?

5 A Read the extract from the recording. Does the example of hyperbole in bold make the sentence sound more or less dramatic?

You've practised **a thousand times**.

B Read the sentences and underline the examples of hyperbole.

1 My time on stage seemed to go on forever!
2 Every time I had to go on stage, I could hardly stand up, I was shaking so much.
3 You feel as if you're going to die of fright.
4 I used to get incredibly nervous before giving my talks. I mean like a total disaster.
5 Every day I had to go on stage, it was like the worst day of my life!

GRAMMAR

cleft sentences

6 A Read sentences a–d from the podcast. Then complete the rules (1 and 2).

a What I needed to do was prepare both physically and mentally.
b It's the character that's important, not me.
c It was the build-up beforehand that scared me.
d What worked for me was approaching the presentation differently.

We can use a cleft sentence to add emphasis or focus attention on one part of the sentence.

1 We start the cleft sentence with *it* or ....
2 We use the correct form of the verb ....

B Learn and practise. Go to the Grammar Bank.

➤ page 116 **GRAMMAR BANK**

PRONUNCIATION

7 A | **emphatic stress** | Work in pairs. Read the sentences (1–4). Which words do you think are stressed? Why?

1 What helped me was breathing deeply.
2 What works for me is to prepare well.
3 It was a friend who made this suggestion.
4 It's the music that's important.

B **3.04** | Listen and check. Which words are stressed? Choose a or b.

a the verb *be*.
b the words or phrase that are/is the main focus of the cleft structure.

C Work in pairs. Take turns to complete the sentences with your own ideas. Focus on putting the stress in the correct place.

- When I needed advice, it was … who (taught/told me) …
- When I'm nervous, what helps me …
- When I want to have fun, it's … who I call.
- When I need to relax, what I do is …
- When I have a lot of work to do, what works for me is …
- It's … who/that always cheers me up when I'm feeling sad.

SPEAKING

8A You are going to practise speaking in public. Follow the instructions below.
- You have to get from A to B across the grid.
- You can move straight across or diagonally, one square at a time.
- When you move to a square, you have to talk about the topic for thirty seconds.
- First, look at the topics and plan your way from A to B.
- Then take turns to speak.
- Time each other to make sure you speak for thirty seconds.

Talk about:

A ──► B

a type of food you've never eaten	the first time you did something	a number or date that's important to you	two favourite books	something funny
which animal makes the best pet	something in the news	a photo	something you always carry with you	sport
a place you want to visit	a musician or singer	an app	coffee	a great actor
something you hear every morning	two pieces of technology	two favourite items of clothing	one thing that would make your life easier	smells you love
video games	someone who should be (more) famous	your favourite moment of the week	the last thing you watched on TV	something you did yesterday

B How did you perform in the speaking activity in Ex 8? Read the Future Skills box and discuss the questions.
1. What did you find difficult about the task?
2. Which topics did you find it easy and difficult to talk about?
3. What techniques do you think might help you cope better in the future?
4. What advice would you give to someone who is preparing for a speaking exam in English?

FUTURE SKILLS
Self-management
Many people feel nervous or experience some difficulties when they have to speak in front of other people. After you have spoken in public, it is a good idea to reflect on what you did well and what you can improve next time.

Unit 3 | Lesson C

3C Binge-watch

HOW TO... | use vague language
VOCABULARY | film and TV
PRONUNCIATION | linking and elision

VOCABULARY

film and TV

1 Work in pairs. Look at the infographic and discuss the questions.
   1 Which facts surprise you most?
   2 Do you ever binge-watch? How many hours have you binge-watched in one go? Which programmes?
   3 Which of these things have you done in order to continue watching your favourite show?

   > called in sick at work   cancelled social plans
   > stayed at home all day   stayed up all night

2 A Work in pairs. Match the sentence beginnings (1–9) with the endings (a–i). Then discuss the meaning of the words in bold.
   1 I had to watch the whole series so that
   2 I love that film, especially the **scene**
   3 Ela's dress was beautiful! In fact,
   4 That's the film with brilliant actors. It's got
   5 I enjoy watching films in other languages
   6 The film is **based** on
   7 Have you watched the last episode? It's got
   8 I loved the music so much that
   9 It's a detective drama which is **set** in

   a the true story of a famous scientist.
   b and learning a few words by reading the **subtitles**.
   c all the **costumes** were amazing.
   d Sweden.
   e I've downloaded the **soundtrack**.
   f I could see the **ending** and find out what happened.
   g a brilliant **twist** at the end.
   h where she finally tells him she loves him.
   i a fantastic **cast**.

   B Work in groups. Discuss the questions.
   1 What films have you seen that were based on true stories?
   2 How do you feel about watching films with subtitles?
   3 What's your favourite film soundtrack?
   4 What films or series have you watched recently with a good cast?

BINGE! The stats behind our viewing obsession

The average American watches 2.8 hours of TV per day or nearly 20 hours each week. Much of that time is spent binge-watching. 38% of people surveyed said they binge-watched weekly for an average of 4.2 hours per session.

In the UK, 18–34-year-olds watch an average of **1 hour of Netflix per day.**

37% of Netflix users binge-watch at work.

24% of Americans have cancelled social plans in order to watch a show.

94 hours The world record for the longest binge watch — set by New York resident, Alejandro 'AJ' Fragoso.

76% of 18–29-year-olds in the USA have stayed up all night to watch a TV show.

7.1% of men worldwide reported spending between five and seven hours watching an online series in one sitting, and just under 2% said that they did so for more than ten hours at a time.

One in five British workers admits to calling in sick at work so they can stay at home and binge-watch TV shows.

How to ...
use vague language

3 A Work in pairs. What kinds of TV programme do you enjoy most? Why?

B 🔊 **3.05** | Listen to three friends talking about two shows they have binge-watched. What did they enjoy about them? Tick the points they mention.

- the acting
- the cast
- where it's set
- who/what the story is based on
- the soundtrack
- plot twists
- interesting characters
- costumes
- the ending

C 🔊 **3.05** | Work in pairs. What did the speakers say about each topic? Listen again and check.

4 A 🔊 **3.06** | Complete the extracts from the conversation with the words and phrases in the box. Then listen and check.

| and that kind of thing | around the 1950s |

Alice: So, it's about a woman, Beth Harmon, who is a chess prodigy. It's set in the USA ¹.................... and it shows her rise to becoming, like, a world-class chess player, you know, beating all the grand masters ² ....

| and stuff | bit |

Alice: Yes, I loved that ³ .... at the end when ... well, I won't spoil it for you, but it's really good. And it's beautiful to watch, too, you know, the costumes ⁴ .... It's done really well.

| or something | young-ish | what's her name |

Alice: It's like a murder mystery ⁵ ....
Sam: That's right. Oh, it's brilliant. It's based on a book by um, ⁶ .... ? You know, that Australian author ... Liane Moriarty. It tells the story of five ⁷ .... women ...

| sort of | that kind of thing |

Sam: Every episode is ⁸ .... incredibly tense and gripping to watch. You get really caught up in the drama and ⁹ ...., all the plot twists.

| about | something like that |

Alice: The show I'm watching at the moment has got ¹⁰ .... ten seasons, or ¹¹ ....

B Work in pairs. Read the examples of vague language (a–f) and answer the questions.

- **a** It's sort of like *Groundhog Day*, but set in the future.
- **b** It's a book by what's his name? You know, that ...
- **c** I watched for a couple of hours or so.
- **d** It's a kind of detective drama.
- **e** He's tall-ish and very good looking.
- **f** I watch a lot of action films, crime drama and that kind of thing.

1 Which sentence refers to people without saying their name?
2 Which refer to approximate numbers?
3 How can we change adjectives to make them more vague?
4 How do you say something is similar, but not exactly the same?
5 How can we avoid giving a long list at the end of a sentence?

C Find more examples of the different types of vague language in Ex 4A.

D Learn and practise. Go to the Grammar Bank.

⏩ **page 117 GRAMMAR BANK**

PRONUNCIATION

5 A 🔊 **3.07** | linking and elision | Listen to the sentences and look at the parts joined by a ⌣. Which show:
- **a** linking between words which end in a consonant sound and words which begin with a vowel sound?
- **b** elision (when a consonant sound disappears before another consonant sound)?

1 It's based ⌣ on ⌣ a book by what's her name?
2 Every episode is sort ⌣ of incredibly tense.
3 You get ⌣ caught ⌣ up in the drama and that ⌣ kind ⌣ of thing.
4 It's got ⌣ about ten seasons ⌣ or something like ⌣ that.

B Practise saying the sentences.

SPEAKING

6 Work in groups. Take turns telling each other about a film or TV programme you would recommend. Ask questions to find out if you would enjoy it.

- A: You really should watch *Stranger Things*. It's a really gripping story!
- B: What's it about?
- C: Is it scary?

MEDIATION SKILLS
giving general and personal views
describe a film

⏩ **page 148 MEDIATION BANK**

3D BBC Street Interviews

Music lover?

GRAMMAR | *do* and *did* for emphasis
SPEAKING | a music questionnaire
WRITING | a forum comment

Oby
Leanne
Roisin

PREVIEW

1 Work in groups. Discuss the questions.
   1 Which types of music in the box do you like and why?

   > classical   contemporary R&B
   > film scores   folk   hip hop   jazz
   > opera   rap   rock   soul

   2 Who are your favourite artists in these genres?
   3 What other types of music do you like?
   4 Do you ever go to gigs or concerts? If so, who was the last act you saw? If not, which bands or singers would you most like to see live?
   5 How important is music in your life?

Q1: What kind of music do you like and why?

Q2: How important is music in your life?

VIEW

2 A ▶ Watch the video. Which genres does each speaker like? How many speakers say that music is really or very important to them?

B ▶ Watch the first part of the video again. Match the speakers (1–8) with what they say about music (a–h).
   1 Kaelan   a I enjoy music from films.
   2 Roisin   b I enjoy singing along while I'm listening.
   3 Ryan   c I listen to songs that are quite relaxed.
   4 Aslan   d I like music that is good to dance to.
   5 Oby   e I like the lyrics and the beat behind the music.
   6 Leanne   f I can express myself freely and improvise when I play.
   7 Sophia   g I listen to rap while I'm doing exercise.
   8 Lucy   h I like music with guitars and drums in it.

C ▶ Watch the second part of the video again. Are the statements True (T) or False (F)?
   1 Kaelan is a professional musician.
   2 Roisin likes going to live music performances.
   3 Ryan only listens to music at home.
   4 Aslan always listens to music while he's working.
   5 Oby played an instrument in the past.
   6 Leanne listens to music to help her relax.
   7 Sophia listens to music for most of the day.
   8 Lucy often goes to festivals.

D Work in pairs. Discuss the questions.
   1 What do you think Ryan means when he says that music is the soundtrack to his life?
   2 Leanne likes to put music on in the background when she's doing things. Do you do this? If so, what do you listen to?

3D

Kaelan

Ryan

Aslan

Sophia

Lucy

GRAMMAR

do and *did* for emphasis

3 A Work in pairs. Read the extracts from the interviews. Why do the speakers use *do* and *don't*?

1. I **do** listen to music on Spotify, like, public platforms, but I **don't** play any instruments.
2. There's certain bits of work where I **do** listen to music while I'm working and there's certain bits of work where I **don't**, where I can't, if it's very technical, or if I'm trying to be very creative, then I can and **do** listen to music.
3. I have to say I **don't** like orchestra music so much, but I **do** like background music, listening to relaxing things.
4. Although I **don't** go to festivals, I **do** listen to it a lot at home and I play the piano as an instrument.

B Learn and practise. Go to the Grammar Bank.

▶▶ page 118 **GRAMMAR BANK**

SPEAKING

a music questionnaire

4 A Read the questionnaire and make notes on your answers.

How important is music in your life?

1. Have your music tastes changed since you were younger? How?
2. Can you play an instrument? If so, how long have you been playing it? If not, which instrument would you most like to learn?
3. Are you a good singer? Have you ever sung karaoke? If so, what did you think of the experience?
4. Do you listen to music to motivate yourself and/or to help you concentrate? If so, what type of music?
5. What is your favourite band or song?
6. Do you listen to a lot of music in English?
7. Who is the most famous musician from your country? What do you think of them?
8. What is the first song you ever remember?

B Work in groups. Ask and answer the questions in the questionnaire. Use your notes and the Key phrases to help you.

KEY PHRASES

I absolutely love …
I'm really into …
I'm a big fan of …
I couldn't live without …
I'm not very keen on …
I don't like … , but I do like …
I can't stand …

WRITING

a forum comment

5 A Work in pairs. Discuss the questions

1. Which online discussion forums have you used in the past?
2. Do you prefer to read online discussions or take part in them?
3. What are the main advantages and disadvantages of forums?

B Write a forum comment. Go to the Writing Bank.

▶▶ page 105 **WRITING BANK**

3 REVIEW

GRAMMAR

relative clauses

1 A Complete the relative clauses in the sentences. Add commas where necessary.

1 I met a woman yesterday. She was Aki's mother.
   The woman .... Aki's mother.
2 He wrote his books with this pen.
   This is the pen ....
3 That girl's father predicted the disaster.
   She's the girl .... disaster.
4 The event first took place in 1923.
   1923 is the year .... place.
5 Jan is a circus performer. He's Lia's boyfriend.
   Jan .... a circus performer.
6 He's famous for this book.
   This is the book ....

B Which relative clause in Ex 1A is non-defining? In which sentences can the relative pronoun be omitted?

C Work in pairs. Take turns defining the things in the box using relative clauses. Guess who or what your partner is describing.

> a city   a famous person   an object in your bag
> a person you both know   a TV series or film
> something you use every day

She's the politician who …

cleft sentences

2 A Put the words into the correct order to make cleft sentences.

1 What / about / we / scenery / the / New Zealand / is / like
2 The / is / thing / that / about / I'm / my / nervous / exam
3 It / arrive / on / was / that / she / Monday / was / to / due
4 What / learning / difficult / heart / is / I / things / find / by
5 The / was / grandmother / who / me / person / my / taught
6 The / about / passionate / is / thing / location / she's / the

B Work in pairs. Take turns completing the sentences with your own ideas.

- It was … who taught me …
- It was in the year … that I …
- What I'd like to do next weekend …
- What I've always liked about …

VOCABULARY

3 A Choose the correct words to complete the sentences.

1 When someone corrects me while I'm speaking English, it puts me **on / off**.
2 I love the lively **atmosphere / venue** you get when you're in a big festival crowd!
3 I know which bands and singers would be in my perfect festival **act / line-up**!
4 When I speak in public, I think I come **across / back** as too formal.
5 I love films that are **based on / set in** true stories.
6 I don't study at home because I can't put **up to / up with** the noise.
7 I don't enjoy watching films where I have to read the **soundtrack / subtitles**.
8 I sometimes find it hard to get my message **across / up** in English.

B Work in pairs. Which sentences in Ex 3A are true for you?

4 A Choose the correct options (A–C) to complete the story.

The show goes on

I once took on the challenge of trying to put on a show with people who had never performed on stage before. At first it seemed impossible. People kept ¹................ their lines. After a few weeks, I really didn't want to continue, but everyone was so enthusiastic that in the end, I ²................ agree to carry on. But then I realised that we were trying to rehearse in the evenings, ³................ everyone was tired. So I ⁴................ the idea of rehearsing early in the mornings instead, ⁵................ was much more successful because everyone was fresh. ⁶................ I liked about working with people new to acting was that they were completely free – they had no expectations to ⁷................ .

As the day of the performance approached, I must admit I became more nervous. We had put up posters to ⁸................ an audience, but I wasn't sure how many would ⁹................ . Thankfully, the theatre was full. My amateur cast ¹⁰................ giving an incredible performance, and the audience loved it!

1 A ending up	B messing up	C speaking up
2 A did	B have	C do
3 A which	B what	C when
4 A put up with	B came up with	C got on with
5 A where	B who	C which
6 A What	B Which	C This
7 A live with	B live for	C live up to
8 A attract	B act	C come
9 A set	B attend	C attract
10 A came up	B put up	C ended up

B 🔊 R3.01 | Listen and check your answers.

42

lifestyle 4

VLOGS

Q: Name one change you could make to your life to improve your health.

1. ▶ Watch the video. What changes do they mention?

2. Work in pairs. Discuss one change you could make to your health.

GSE LEARNING OBJECTIVES

4A READING | Read an article about healthy lifestyle choices: health and lifestyle; illness and treatment

Discuss your future lifestyle: future continuous and future perfect

Pronunciation: connected speech: future perfect

4B LISTENING | Understand a radio programme about sleep: sleep

Discuss sleep: passives

Pronunciation: sentence stress: content and function words

Write an article about sleep

4C HOW TO … | express agreement and disagreement: exercise; sport: motivation and benefits

Pronunciation: stress in phrases for partial agreement

4D BBC PROGRAMME | Understand a documentary about beekeeping: phrases related to time

Talk about traditional vs. modern lifestyles

Write a cause-and-effect essay

Unit 4 | Lesson A

4A Making changes

GRAMMAR | future continuous and future perfect
VOCABULARY | health and lifestyle; illness and treatment
PRONUNCIATION | connected speech: future perfect

READING

1 A Work in groups. Which of the following are important for a healthy lifestyle? In what ways?

> exercise   food   money   sleep
> stress   where you live

B Read *How to live well: the thinker, the bather and the eater.* Answer the questions.
  1 What change did each person make?
  2 Why did they make the change?
  3 What are their goals for the future?

C Choose the correct option (a or b) for each question (1–3).
  1 How does Felipe feel about the other students on his course?
    a astonished that they are so young
    b pleased that they have accepted him
  2 How does Fiona feel about swimming in the Okavango Delta?
    a excited that it might happen
    b concerned that it might be dangerous
  3 How does Derek feel when he thinks about his diet in the past?
    a ashamed at how unhealthy it was
    b surprised that he didn't realise it was harming him

D Work in groups. Discuss the questions.
  1 What do you think of the changes the people in the text are making?
  2 What other positive changes could they make?
  3 Do you know anyone who has made similar lifestyle changes?

VOCABULARY

health and lifestyle

2 A Complete the sentences with the correct form of the phrases in the box. Use the phrases in bold in the article to help you.

> cut down on   ~~do a regular workout~~   do a sedentary job
> expand your horizons   keep mentally active
> keep up my progress   stay in shape   transform my lifestyle
> vary my diet   work long hours

  1 I <u>do a regular workout</u> in the gym once or twice a week.
  2 I'd hate to .... where I have to sit in an office all day.
  3 I try to .... and eat lots of different foods, to get a balance of all the things my body needs.
  4 I think travelling is a great way to .... and help you understand other people's lives.
  5 I exercise because I enjoy it, not because I want to ....
  6 I'd like to .... my screen time; I spend too long in front of a computer.
  7 I don't need to .... I'm already very healthy and happy.
  8 In my job I have to .... , sometimes up to ten hours a day!
  9 I like doing puzzles as a way to ....
  10 Starting an exercise programme is easy. I'm fine for a few weeks, but I find it hard to ....

B Work in pairs. Are the sentences in Ex 2A true for you? Why/Why not?

C Learn and practise. Go to the Vocabulary Bank.
  ▶▶ page 138 **VOCABULARY BANK** illness and treatment

How to live well

4A

Life is full of turning points, when either we decide to make a change ourselves, or change is forced upon us. This month, we speak to three people who recently reached a turning point in their lives and decided it was time to **transform their lifestyle**. We ask them: Why did you make a change and where do you see yourself in two years' time?

the thinker

'I worked until the age of seventy in a job that was both interesting and intellectually stimulating. When I retired two years ago, I decided I needed to **keep mentally active**, so I signed up for a university degree in sociology. I'm the oldest student by a long way, but luckily the others on my course don't see that as a problem. I also started going to French classes because I'd always wanted to learn another language. I'm really enjoying both things, and I've made loads of new friends. Doing this degree has really helped me to **expand my horizons** and think about society and my place in it.

Personally, I think it's really important to **stay in shape** both mentally and physically. I hope it will help me fight off illnesses like Alzheimer's, and it also motivates me and gives me something to aim for. Where do I see myself in two years? Well, I'll have graduated, so I'll have a degree, and hopefully my French will have improved, too. There are lots of volunteer roles related to social issues, so maybe I'll be working as a volunteer two or three days a week. I guess it's also possible I'll be travelling around France and using my new language skills.'

Felipe Ortega

the bather

'For years I **did a sedentary job** and **worked long hours** in a corporate office. It was well paid, but high stress, and it was definitely having a damaging effect on my health. I didn't sleep well and had no time to exercise. I reached a point where I knew that I needed to change, so I started going to the gym and **doing regular workouts**. Then I saw a TV programme about wild swimming and I decided to give it a go. I loved it from the start, and now I swim 365 days a year in rivers, oceans and the occasional waterfall. It doesn't matter what time of year it is, or how cold the water is – I'll be there. I feel much happier and healthier now. There's a huge wild-swimming community worldwide, so I'm starting to plan a few trips abroad to places like the fjords in Iceland, where the water is beautiful, but apparently extremely cold. What will I be doing in two years' time? Well, I definitely want to **keep up my progress** and if I'm lucky, I'll be swimming in the Okavango Delta in Botswana – one of my dreams! I hope there won't be any crocodiles, but I doubt it will stop me even if there are! I've also started posting blogs about my experiences, and I'm getting quite a few followers, so who knows, maybe I'll have given up my job and I'll be earning a living as a wild-swimming influencer.'

Fiona Karlsson

the eater

'I was never particularly interested in healthy eating when I was younger – I would always choose a burger and chips over a salad! Then a few years ago, I started noticing that I didn't have much energy, and I was having a few health issues. I came across an article online about the effects of junk food on the body, and I suddenly realised how unhealthy my diet was – full of sugar and salt. So, I made the decision to **vary my diet** more and **cut down on** processed foods. And it worked. I started to feel better almost immediately, so I've since made more changes to the way I eat. I've started buying a lot of my food directly from local producers – butter and cheese from farmers and seafood from local fishermen. I've also started growing a few vegetables in my garden. When I look back, it seems really strange that it took me so long to work out what my diet was doing to me. The difference in my energy levels now is incredible. So, in two years' time? I'll have given up meat completely, and I'll have transformed my whole garden into a mini farm! Hopefully, I'll be growing most of my own fruit and vegetables, and I'll be eating fresh, seasonal produce all year round.'

Derek Mankham

45

Unit 4 | Lesson A

GRAMMAR

future continuous and future perfect

3 A Read the sentences (a–d) and answer the questions (1–2).
  a In two years I'll have graduated.
  b I'll have transformed my whole garden into a mini farm.
  c If I'm lucky, I'll be swimming in the Okavango Delta in Botswana.
  d I'll be growing most of my own fruit and vegetables.
  1 Which sentences are about things that will be completed before a specific time in the future?
  2 Which sentences are about things that will be in progress at a specific time in the future?

B Learn and practise. Go to the Grammar Bank.
  ⏩ page 119 **GRAMMAR BANK**

PRONUNCIATION

4 A 🔊 **4.01 | connected speech: future perfect** | Listen and complete the sentences. Which words link together? Do we use the strong or weak form of *have*?
  1 This time next year, ... graduated from university.
  2 I hope .... cut down on junk food by then.
  3 When you next see me, ... started working out.
  4 I hope .... found a new job by the summer.

B Complete the sentences with your own ideas, using the future perfect. Then read your sentences to a partner. Make sure you link the words and pronounce *have* correctly.
  • By the end of today, I'll have …
  • By next weekend, I'll have …
  • By next summer, I'll have …

SPEAKING

5 A Think about your lifestyle in five years' time. Do you have any goals? How might your life be different? Choose two topics from the box and make notes on your goals and predictions.

> achievements   activities/experiences
> English   health and lifestyle   home
> studies and/or work   travel

B Read the Future Skills box and do the task.

> **FUTURE SKILLS**
> **Communication**
>
> When you talk about your goals and predictions, it is a good idea to add examples and reasons, to make your answers more interesting.
>
> 'I want to vary my diet more. **For example**, I hope I'll be cooking dishes from different countries.'
>
> 'I hope I'll have transformed my lifestyle **because** I'm too stressed at the moment.'
>
> Look at your notes in Ex 5A. What examples and reasons can you add?

C Work in pairs. Discuss what you will be doing in five years' time, and how your life will have changed. Ask your partner questions to learn more details.
  A: In five years' time, I'll have graduated from university and hopefully have found a good job!
  B: What kind of job would you like to do?

4B Sleep

GRAMMAR | passives
VOCABULARY | sleep
PRONUNCIATION | sentence stress: content and function words

VOCABULARY

sleep

1 A Work in pairs. How many hours' sleep did you get last night? Was it a normal amount for you?

B Read the quiz. Then complete the sentences (1–10) with the words and phrases in bold.
1. You can say that you _____ to mean that you fall asleep.
2. A short sleep during the day is called a _____ .
3. Someone who often or always has trouble sleeping is a(n) _____ .
4. When you are very tired, you are _____ .
5. If you do not wake up easily, even when it's noisy, then you're a _____ , and you usually go into a very _____ .
6. If you make a rough breathing noise when you sleep, then you _____ .
7. A dream where something bad happens is a _____ .
8. If you deliberately stay in bed later than normal, you _____ .
9. If you stop other people from sleeping, you _____ them _____ .
10. If you don't wake up when you are supposed to, then you _____ .

C Work in pairs. Ask and answer the questions in the quiz. How similar are your sleep habits?

How well do you sleep?

1 Do you ever **oversleep**?
  a) No, I'm a very light sleeper, so my alarm always wakes me up.
  b) Yes, I'm a **heavy sleeper**, so I often sleep through the alarm.
  c) Yes, but I don't mind. Sometimes it's good to **have a lie-in**.

2 How long does it usually take you to fall asleep?
  a) Not long at all. I **drop off** as soon as my head hits the pillow.
  b) Quite a long time. I usually read for an hour. It helps me to switch off.
  c) It depends. I sometimes lie awake in bed thinking about work or family problems.

3 Do you do anything to help you get to sleep?
  a) Yes, I sometimes do relaxation exercises.
  b) If I can't sleep, I count or do maths problems in my head.
  c) I listen to podcasts or check my phone until I feel tired.

4 How often do you have trouble going to sleep?
  a) Never.
  b) Occasionally. It's usually because I'm worried about something.
  c) All the time. I'm an **insomniac**, so I often have a **nap** in the afternoon to try and catch up on sleep.

5 Do you usually remember your dreams?
  a) I sometimes remember my dreams, especially if I've been in a **deep sleep**.
  b) I never remember my dreams.
  c) I don't usually remember dreams except when I wake up after having a **nightmare**.

6 Do you ever **snore**?
  a) Sometimes when I'm really **exhausted**.
  b) Only if I have a cold.
  c) Yes, I'm very noisy. I sleep in a room on my own so that I don't **keep** my partner **awake**.

LISTENING

2 A Work in groups. Read the information about the BBC Radio programme and answer the questions.

> **The science of sleep** BBC
>
> We spend around a third of our lives asleep, but the reason we sleep is still a mystery. Could it be the biggest mistake the evolutionary process has ever made? What does sleep actually do for us? David Edmonds meets Matthew Walker, one of the world's leading sleep scientists, to find out.

1 On average, how many hours a night do you think people in the developed world sleep?
2 Why do you think humans sleep? Is it just a waste of time?

B 4.02 | Listen to the programme. Number the topics in the order they are mentioned.

a sleep and the brain
b the number of hours people sleep on average
c why sleep seems an odd thing for humans to do
d the effects of changing the clocks twice a year

C 4.02 | Work in pairs. Answer the questions. Then listen again and check.

1 Why does the presenter say that sleep seems 'a monumental waste of time'?
2 What do you learn about sleep in the 1940s, compared to now?
3 What happens to people's health when the clocks change in the spring and the autumn?
4 Why is sleep important for making decisions?

D Work in groups. Discuss the questions.

1 What happens to you if you don't get enough sleep?
2 Do you have an expression in your language meaning 'to sleep on a problem'?

GRAMMAR

passives

3 A 4.03 | Listen and complete the extract from the programme.

.... if sleep doesn't serve an absolutely vital function, then it's the biggest mistake the evolutionary process has ever made.

B Read the sentences (1–3) about sleep and look at the verbs in bold. Then choose the correct words to complete the rule.

1 **It is believed that** most people need eight hours' sleep.
2 In ancient cultures, **it was thought that** dreams could predict the future.
3 **It is expected that** if we sleep less, we can be more productive.

We can use passive structures with *it* to talk about **general ideas or beliefs / our own ideas or beliefs**.

C Learn and practise. Go to the Grammar Bank.

▶▶ page 120 **GRAMMAR BANK**

PRONUNCIATION

4 A 4.04 | **sentence stress: content and function words** | Listen to the sentence and underline the stressed words.

It's believed that most people need eight hours' sleep.

B Look at the sentence in Ex 4A again. Do we stress the content words (verbs, nouns, adjectives, etc.) or the function words (pronouns, articles, auxiliaries, etc.)? Why?

C 4.05 | Work in pairs. Read the sentences and predict which words will be stressed. Then listen and check.

1 It's expected that as we get older, we need less sleep.
2 It has been suggested that our use of technology affects our sleep.
3 It was thought a hot drink would help you to sleep better.
4 It's believed that if we sleep less, we can be more productive.

5 Work in pairs. You are going to guess whether some statements about sleep are true or false. Student A: Go to page 142. Student B: Go to page 144.

SPEAKING

6A Work in groups. Discuss the statements about sleep (1–9). Do you think they are true, or are they myths? Can you give examples from your own experience?

Reality or myth?

1. It is believed that some adults only need five or fewer hours of sleep a night.
2. It's been suggested that, in health terms, it doesn't matter whether you sleep during the day or at night.
3. It is known that some people walk around in their sleep and can carry out complex activities, such as driving and cooking.
4. It's thought that boredom can make you sleepy.
5. It's been suggested that adults need less sleep as they get older.
6. It's been suggested that it is fine to sleep very little during the week, then catch up at the weekend.
7. It's thought that watching TV in bed is a good way to relax before going to sleep.
8. It's been suggested that doing exercise before going to bed will stop you from going to sleep.
9. It's believed that scrolling on your phone before you go to sleep or during the night makes it more difficult for you to wake up the next day.

A: I think it's a myth that some adults only need five hours of sleep.
B: I agree. I know that if I get less than seven hours, I feel terrible!

B Go to page 142 and find out which of the statements are true.

WRITING

an article

7A Work in pairs. Read the article. Then discuss the questions.
1. What is the main argument being made by the writer? Do you agree with it? Why/Why not?
2. What reasons does the writer give for people sleeping less?

Why we're just not getting enough sleep
Kirsty Whitall | Wednesday 26 May

It is thought that the average adult requires seven to nine hours of sleep per night. However, we know that many people in the developed world are **not only** sleeping much less than this, **but also** suffering health problems as a result. In the USA, it has been suggested that people are sleeping at least one hour less than they did thirty years ago. There are many reasons why people might be sleeping less.

To start with, there is a problem with modern expectations of work since consumers expect information, entertainment **and** food to be available 24 hours a day. **Furthermore**, this 24/7 culture means that **as well as** consumers staying awake for longer than they used to, workers who provide us with these goods and services are expected to work longer hours or night shifts in order for companies to meet the demand.

In addition to this, in a fast-paced and competitive world of business, employees are often expected to work long hours, with more work to do and less time to do it. As a result, many employees are willing to sleep less in order to progress their careers. **Moreover**, with increased pressure at work, many employees find it difficult to find time to take holidays, with stress and burnout as likely consequences.

B Look at the linking words and phrases in bold in the article. Can you think of any more words and phrases we use to present additional ideas?

C Rewrite the sentences. Use the prompts in brackets to connect the ideas.
1. It's been suggested that people don't sleep well because they consume more caffeine than in the past. Another reason is that they spend a lot of time on screens. (not only … , but also …)
2. Many people sleep fewer than six hours a night and always feel tired. They are more likely to develop health problems. (Furthermore)
3. One problem is that people are required to travel long distances to get to work. Another problem is that people are working longer hours than before. (In addition to this, …)
4. Lack of sleep increases your risk of heart attacks. It also means that you are more likely to be in an accident. (As well as …)

D Write an article with the title *How to get a good night's sleep*. Use some of the ideas you discussed in Ex 7A. Use linking words to present additional ideas.

Unit 4 | Lesson C

4C Keep moving

HOW TO ... | express agreement and disagreement
VOCABULARY | exercise; sport: motivation and benefits
PRONUNCIATION | stress in phrases for partial agreement

VOCABULARY

exercise

1 A Work in groups. Discuss the questions.
1. How much exercise do you do in a typical week?
2. What kinds of exercise do you do?
3. How easy or difficult do you find it to make yourself do exercise?

B Read the article. How much exercise is recommended per week? Do the majority of people manage this amount?

C Work in pairs. Look at the words and phrases in bold in the article and answer the questions.
1. Which involves more effort: moderate exercise or vigorous exercise?
2. Which quality allows you to lift heavy objects?
3. Which quality allows you to continue to run or cycle for a long time without getting tired?
4. Is skipping with a rope high-impact or low-impact exercise?
5. Is yoga an aerobic exercise?
6. Which quality allows you to bend and move your body easily?

D Complete the statements with the correct words and phrases from the article.
1. My .... is quite good. I can touch my toes easily.
2. I try to avoid ....-impact exercises such as running.
3. I think I need to do some training with weights to improve my ....
4. I can run a short distance, but I don't have much ...., so I can't go more than a few kilometres.
5. I don't like getting too out of breath, so I prefer .... exercise.

2 A Work in pairs. Discuss which statements in Ex 1D are true for you.

B Learn and practise. Go to the Vocabulary Bank.

▶▶ page 139 **VOCABULARY BANK** sport: motivation and benefits

Getting and staying fit

Salim Rashid | Wednesday 27 May | 17.01 GMT

The world's strongest men pull twenty-tonne trucks on a rope. Ultra-marathon runners run 100-kilometre races, sometimes through the desert in forty-degree heat. Top surfers routinely surf six-metre waves. That's the crazy end of exercise. What about normal people? We all know it's important to exercise, but how much exercise should we do? And how can we stick at it even when we're tired or bored and it's raining outside?

According to one study from the UK, adults should be doing 150 minutes of **moderate exercise** or seventy-five minutes of **vigorous exercise** each week. This includes **strength** exercises such as lifting weights and **aerobic** exercises that make your heart beat faster, like jogging and cycling, which improve **stamina**. Experts recommend a mixture of **low-impact** exercise (where you keep at least one foot on the ground at all times) and **high-impact** activities such as running and jumping. Another recommendation is exercises that improve **flexibility**, for example yoga.

While such recommendations have been well known for a number of years, one report reveals that less than half the world's population does enough exercise. The key is motivation. People need to find an exercise type that they enjoy and then make it part of their daily routine, like having their morning cup of coffee.

4C

How to ...
express agreement and disagreement

3 A 🔊 4.06 | Listen to two people discussing exercise. Who does more exercise – Martin or Leah?

B 🔊 4.06 | Read the statements. Do Martin and Leah agree, disagree, or partially agree about each one? Listen again and check.
1 Everyone should do 150 minutes of moderate exercise each week.
2 Everyone should do an hour of exercise every day.
3 Martin doesn't need to do any exercise because he has a physical job.
4 Yoga is the best way to relax.
5 Martin should do some kind of exercise occasionally.

4 A Work in pairs. Complete the table with the words and phrases in the box. Then check your answers in the audioscript on page 162.

> agree more   although   fair point   see your point
> the other hand   up to a point

expressing agreement and disagreement

agreeing/ disagreeing	I couldn't ¹ ....
	That's a good/² .... , although it could also be argued that …
	I completely disagree.
	I take/³ ....
	But on ⁴ .... …
partially agreeing	I know what you mean, but …
	I agree ⁵ .... , but …
	That's a fair point, ⁶ .... it could also be argued that …

B Learn and practise. Go to the Grammar Bank.

⏩ page 121 **GRAMMAR BANK**

PRONUNCIATION

5 A 🔊 4.07 | **stress in phrases for partial agreement** | Listen to the sentences. Which word in the phrases in bold do we stress?
1 **I agree with you up to a point**, but not everyone has time to exercise every day.
2 **That's a fair point, although** strength training doesn't suit everyone.
3 **I take your point, but** it's important to make an effort to keep fit.
4 **I see your point, but** you can't expect everyone to enjoy going to the gym.

B 🔊 4.07 | Listen again and repeat the sentences.

6 A Choose the correct words to complete the conversations.
1 A: As far as I'm concerned, all sport is a waste of time and shouldn't be on TV.
   B: I **couldn't / can't** agree more. It's just a distraction from serious issues.
2 A: If you ask me, football is the best sport because anyone can play it.
   B: I **am / completely** disagree with you. I find football totally boring.
3 A: Personally, I believe sport is good for your character.
   B: I agree with you **for / up to** a point, but not if it teaches you to cheat.
4 A: In my view, countries spend too much money on the Olympic Games.
   B: True, but on **the other / another** hand, don't you think it's fun to watch?

B Work in pairs. Which of the ideas in Ex 6A do you agree with? Why?

SPEAKING

7 A Read the statements. Do you agree, partially agree or disagree? Why? Think of as many reasons as you can and make notes.
- 'All children should do sport at school at least once a day.'
- 'Some sports such as rugby and boxing are too dangerous and should be banned.'
- 'It's the government's duty to provide free gyms and sports equipment for everyone.'

B Work in groups. Discuss the statements in Ex 7A. Explain why you agree or disagree.

> **MEDIATION SKILLS**
> making group decisions
> decide how to contribute to an event
>
> ⏩ page 150 **MEDIATION BANK**

Speak anywhere   Go to the interactive speaking practice

Unit 4 | Lesson D

4D BBC Documentary
Ancient traditions

VOCABULARY | phrases related to time
SPEAKING | a discussion about traditional vs. modern lifestyles
WRITING | a cause-and-effect essay

PREVIEW

1 A Work in pairs. Look at the photos and answer the questions.
  1 What ancient tradition is shown in the photos?
  2 What do you know about this tradition?

B Read about the programme. What do you think you might learn about the beekeepers' lives? What problems might they face?

Earth from Space

Earth from Space is a BBC series that uses cameras in space to tell stories about life on our planet from a different perspective. In this episode, we watch a group of nomadic beekeepers who travel across China to harvest honey. But they've run into a problem and time is not on their side.

VIEW

2 A ▶ Watch the video. Check your answers to Ex 1B.

B ▶ Watch the video again. Complete the sentences with one word or a number.
  1 Nearly .... percent of the world's rapeseed oil comes from this part of China.
  2 The thick cloud makes it too .... for the bees to fly.
  3 The fields will be sprayed with pesticides in .... weeks' time.
  4 Mr Dai waits .... days for the weather to change.
  5 The bees need to visit two .... flowers to make a single jar of honey.
  6 Bees play an essential part in .... production.
  7 The total number of .... is falling each year.
  8 Mr Dai has .... of honey and is happy to move on.

VOCABULARY

phrases related to time

3 A Work in pairs. Read the sentences from the video. What do you think the phrases in bold mean?

1 They've travelled across China **just in time** for the bloom.
2 These bees aren't going anywhere and **time is running out**.
3 Pesticides are contributing to a worldwide decline in the number of honeybees and their **future is under threat**.
4 Mr Dai's **window of opportunity** is short.
5 Mr Dai has plenty of honey. And **not a moment too soon**.
6 The fields will be sprayed in two days. **It's time to** move on.

B Work in groups. Take turns to complete the sentences with your own ideas.

1 The future of the planet is under threat from …
2 Time is running out for …
3 We have a small window of opportunity to …
4 If we manage to … , it will be not a moment too soon.
5 It's time to …

SPEAKING

a discussion about traditional vs. modern lifestyles

4 A 🔊 4.08 | Listen to someone talking about how lifestyles have changed in her community. Make notes about the differences she mentions between traditional and modern lifestyles.

B 🔊 4.08 | Listen again. Tick the phrases you hear.

> **KEY PHRASES**
>
> I would say that (my modern lifestyle) is different from …
> Nowadays, … , whereas in the past …
> Traditionally/In the old days, …
> He/She/They used to/would … (get up early)
> We still have … , but it's … (smaller/more difficult)
> These days, it seems like …/it appears that …
> Our modern-day lifestyle is much more … than in the past.

C Make notes about traditions in your community. Use the questions to help you.

1 What traditions do your family or community preserve?
2 How do you think lifestyles have changed between the generations?
3 Which older traditions are under threat? Why?
4 Which older traditions do you think the next generation may be interested in?

D Work in groups. Discuss how traditions have changed in your communities. Whose community is the most traditional? Whose is the most modern?

WRITING

a cause-and-effect essay

5 A Work in pairs. How might the following affect people's lifestyles?

- larger populations in cities
- increased pollution
- better access to technology

B Write a cause-and-effect essay. Go to the Writing Bank.

▶▶ page 105 **WRITING BANK**

4 REVIEW

GRAMMAR

future continuous and future perfect

1 A Complete the sentences with the correct future continuous or future perfect form of the verbs in brackets.

1 Two years from now, I _____ in the same place. (not live)
2 By the time I'm old, I hope I _____ at least fifty countries. (visit)
3 A year from now, I expect I _____ with all the friends I have now. (still communicate)
4 In five years' time, I _____ (working) in the tech industry.
5 In five years, I _____ my degree. (complete)

B Work in pairs. Are any of the sentences true for you? Change some of the sentences so that they are true.

passives

2 A Complete the second sentence using an appropriate passive verb and *it*.

1 The media has reported that drinking coffee stops you from growing.
   _____ in the media that drinking coffee stops you from growing.
2 People expect that in the future more people will choose a vegetarian diet.
   _____ in the future, more people will choose a vegetarian diet.
3 In the past, people suggested that walking 10,000 steps a day would keep you fit.
   In the past, _____ walking 10,000 steps a day would keep you fit.
4 People believe that natural sugar is better for you than processed sugar.
   _____ natural sugar is better for you than processed sugar.

B Work in pairs. Are the statements in Ex 2A true or myths? Check your answers on page 142.

VOCABULARY

3 Complete the sentences with the words in the box.

asthma	cut down	keep up	long hours
medication	run-down	sedentary	shape
transform	vary	workout	

1 I try to do a regular _____, but recently I've been feeling a bit _____ and I haven't been able to.
2 I work _____ so I don't have much time for cooking. I should _____ my diet more, and I should also _____ on the amount of fast food I eat.
3 I have been thinking of ways I could _____ my lifestyle.
4 I do a _____ job which sometimes makes it hard for me to stay in _____.
5 I've started running in the morning, and now I'm up to 7 km. I hope I can _____ my progress.
6 I suffer from _____, so I take regular _____.

4 Choose the correct words to complete the sentences.

1 I don't sleep very well at night because my husband **snores / naps** so loudly!
2 I get so tired during the week that at the weekend I like to **have a lie-in / keep me awake**.
3 My son is a very **heavy / exhausted** sleeper – nothing wakes him up.
4 I have some very noisy neighbours and they **keep me awake / drop off** some nights.
5 I **snored / overslept** and very nearly missed my connecting flight.
6 Jack is a(n) **insomniac / heavy sleeper** so he's always tired!

5 A Choose the correct options (A–C) to complete the text.

Health is the new wealth

Tara Williams | Monday 25 Feb | 13.00 GMT

In recent years, health and fitness has grown into a multi-billion-dollar industry as many of us strive to eat healthily and [1]_____ in shape. With modern technology, the average lifestyle has become increasingly [2]_____. We are also busier and in general work [3]_____ hours than in the past. So, to make up for it, we follow healthy-eating gurus on Instagram and try to [4]_____ our diet by drinking fresh vegetable juice and eating superfood salads. We join gyms, buy fitness technology, take online yoga classes and [5]_____ regular workouts. It is [6]_____ that Americans spend more than $40 billion trying to improve their health and fitness every year.

And future trends look even more extreme. Some are predicting that within the next ten years, a lot of fitness training [7]_____ moved outside. The [8]_____ of training outdoors include exposure to the sun and fresh air, and running where the ground isn't flat. In addition, it's likely that more of us [10]_____ personal tracking devices, which will offer us computer-generated personal training programmes based on our individual health metrics.

	A	B	C
1	stay	go	make
2	exhausted	sedentary	vigorous
3	higher	bigger	longer
4	vary	cut down	maintain
5	make	do	keep
6	thought	thinking	think
7	has	will have	won't be
8	motivations	incentives	benefits
9	will have worn	will be wearing	wear

B 🔊 R4.01 | Listen and check your answers.

work 5

VLOGS

Q: Which professions do you admire and why?

1 ▶ Watch the video. What jobs do the people mention? Why?

2 Work in pairs. Discuss which professions you admire and why.

GSE LEARNING OBJECTIVES

5A READING | Read an article about first days at work: time expressions; past perfect simple and continuous

Tell a story about the first time you did something

Pronunciation: connected speech: past perfect continuous

5B LISTENING | Understand a BBC radio programme about portfolio careers: work and careers; areas of work

Talk about a change of plan: past plans and intentions

Pronunciation: connected speech: intrusive /w/ sounds

Write a report about the future of work

5C HOW TO ... | describe problems and suggest solutions: video conference calls

Pronunciation: intonation to show degrees of certainty

5D BBC STREET INTERVIEWS | Understand street interviews about people's work: non-defining relative clauses for comments

Talk about working alone vs. in a team

Write a thank-you message

Unit 5 | Lesson A

5A First day!

GRAMMAR | past perfect simple and continuous
VOCABULARY | time expressions
PRONUNCIATION | connected speech: past perfect continuous

READING

1 A Work in groups. Discuss the questions.
1. What kind of things do people worry about or feel excited about when they start a new job?
2. Have you ever had a funny or embarrassing experience in a new job or study environment?

B Work in pairs. Read the title and headings in the article *Oops! When things go wrong on your first day at work*. What do you think happened to each person?

C Read the article and check your ideas.

D Read the article again. Are the sentences True (T) or False (F)?
1. Lee was an experienced driver.
2. Lee's colleagues told him about their own similar experiences.
3. Emma asked permission to explore the building.
4. Emma's story was embarrassing for her.
5. Soumaya and the other new employees were expected to socialise.
6. Soumaya was embarrassed because she didn't recognise a well-known member of the company.

2 A Work in pairs. Scan the article again for the following phrases. What do you think they mean?
1. I wanted the earth to swallow me up. (story 1)
2. I had some time to kill. (story 2)
3. I let curiosity get the better of me. (story 2)
4. I decided to take a peek. (story 2)
5. You have to 'work the room'. (story 3)
6. I'd been making small talk. (story 3)
7. He laughed it off. (story 3)

B Work in pairs. Discuss the questions.
1. Which story do you think is the most embarrassing?
2. What do you think the writers should have done differently? Why?
3. What would you have done in these situations?

GRAMMAR

past perfect simple and continuous

3 A Work in pairs. Read sentences 1–6. Which verbs are in the past simple? What tense are the other verbs: past perfect simple or past perfect continuous?
1. I'd been trying to get a place for ages so I was really excited.
2. Someone found out what I'd been doing …
3. I'd been making small talk for hours and was exhausted.
4. I'd only passed my test the year before.
5. I then had to stay with that colleague whose car I had destroyed …
6. By the time I noticed this friendly looking man, I'd already met at least thirty people.

B Look at the verbs in Ex 3A again. Match each description (1–3) with the correct tense: past simple, past perfect simple or past perfect continuous.
1. the main events in a story
2. finished actions that happened before the main events
3. actions that continued for a period of time before the main events

C Learn and practise. Go to the Grammar Bank.

▶▶ page 122 **GRAMMAR BANK**

PRONUNCIATION

4 A 🔊 **5.01** | connected speech: past perfect continuous | Listen and complete the sentences.
1. I .... been trying to get a job for ages.
2. We'd .... waiting to meet our new boss.
3. .... been listening to a presentation.
4. She .... sleeping all afternoon.

B 🔊 **5.01** | How do we say *had been* in connected speech? Listen again and check.

C Work in pairs. Take turns completing the sentences.
1. Before I started … , I'd been …
2. Before I went … , I'd been …
3. Before I got … , I'd been …

OOPS!

When things go wrong on your first day at work

Amal Khatri | Friday 29 October | 17.01 GMT

Your first day in a new job is always a bit worrying, but what do you do when something truly terrible happens?

The crash

I'd been looking forward to starting my new job in sales. On my first day I was handed the keys to a company car and sent to one of the regional offices. I felt a bit nervous because I hadn't driven for a while. In fact, I'd only passed my test the year before.

I got into the car, but then my foot slipped as I was reversing, and I drove straight into the car behind me. I'll never forget the crunching sound it made. I just sat there in total shock. I wanted the earth to swallow me up.

It turned out the car belonged to one of my colleagues. As if that wasn't bad enough, I then had to stay with that colleague, whose car I had destroyed just moments earlier, while we talked to the insurance people on the phone. I remember apologising a lot, but everyone was really lovely about it. They kept checking that I was OK and reassuring me that these things happen. I ended up staying with the company for two decades.

Lee

Locked out

I was finally accepted onto a graduate scheme at a bank. I'd been trying to get a place for ages so I was really excited.

I arrived early and checked in with reception. I had some time to kill before the training session, so I wandered around. Then I let curiosity get the better of me and I got into a lift with a couple of other people. One of them got out at the 22nd floor and I followed him. I noticed some empty management suites and directors' offices, and I decided to take a peek, even though I knew it probably wasn't allowed. After all, I figured I might end up there one day, and up to that point I'd never been in a director's office.

I had a little look around, then suddenly realised my training session was about to start. So I quickly walked back to the lift, but it wouldn't open. It turned out I needed a key card, and I hadn't been given one. I tried the door to the stairwell. Locked. I was trapped on the 22nd floor. After ten minutes of panic, I called reception. They sent security to rescue me and I was marched into the training room in disgrace. Everyone was looking at me – it was awful! There followed a week of jokes about me being an intruder. Then someone found out what I'd been doing and they nicknamed me 'Boss Woman'.

Emma

An unfamiliar face

There was a meet-and-greet reception for all of us new employees. It was in one of the big, stylish meeting rooms, and there must have been about seventy people there. At these things, you have to 'work the room' and ask everyone's name and position. In no time, I'd met about twenty colleagues. However, I'd been making small talk for hours and I was exhausted.

By the time I noticed this friendly looking man, I'd already met at least thirty people. I went up to him and said, 'So what do you do here?' He paused and then explained that he was the founder and CEO of the company. I then realised that I'd seen him on the cover of various magazines. He was a billionaire who had won lots of industry awards. He was also the person who had indirectly hired me. I'd never been so embarrassed in my life. Fortunately, he was very nice and he laughed it off.

Soumaya

Unit 5 | Lesson A

VOCABULARY

time expressions

5 A Read the sentences from the article. Match the time expressions in bold (1–6) with their meanings (a–f).

1. I felt a bit nervous because I hadn't driven **for a while**.
2. **In no time**, I'd met about twenty colleagues.
3. I had to stay with that colleague, whose car I had destroyed **just moments earlier**.
4. I'd been trying to get a place **for ages**.
5. **Up to that point** I'd never been in a director's office.
6. **By the time** I noticed this friendly looking man, I'd already met at least thirty people.

a until or before a specific moment
b after a very short period of time
c at the point when something happened
d for a very long time
e for a period of time
f a few seconds before

B Choose the correct time expressions to complete the sentences.

1. I met the CEO in June. **Just moments earlier / Up to that point**, I hadn't met any of the management team.
2. I was sad when my friend May left the company. I'd worked with her **by the time / for ages**.
3. **By the time / For a while** I started the job, I'd already worked in the industry for thirty years.
4. On realising her abilities, they promoted her, and **in no time / for ages** she became CEO.
5. I got lost because I hadn't been there **for a while / just moments earlier**.
6. I sent off the final design, then found out they had cancelled the project **by the time / just hours earlier**.

SPEAKING

6 A You are going to talk about the first time you did something. Choose one of the ideas below and make notes.

First …
- day at work/school/university
- time you met someone important to you
- trip abroad
- time you played a game/did an activity
- time you performed or gave a talk in public

B Read the Future Skills box and do the task.

FUTURE SKILLS
Communication

When we tell a story, we can make it more interesting by describing how we felt, and how we (and other people) reacted.

Look at your notes from Ex 6A. What details can you add about feelings and reactions to make it more interesting?

C Work in groups. Take turns telling your stories.
- Describe what happened and when it happened.
- Describe people's feelings and reactions.
- Ask questions about your classmates' stories.

A: I'll always remember the first time I rode a bike. I went to the park with my mum and we just stayed there for hours with her running alongside me.
B: How old were you?

5B Change of plan

GRAMMAR | past plans and intentions
VOCABULARY | work and careers; areas of work
PRONUNCIATION | connected speech: intrusive /w/ sounds

LISTENING

1 A Work in pairs. Discuss the questions.
  1 What did you want to be when you were growing up?
  2 What, if anything, changed your mind?

B What do you think a 'portfolio career' is? Read the information about a BBC Radio programme to check.

Is one career in your life enough? BBC

It's the question that everyone asks a small child: 'What do you want to be when you grow up?' But in a rapidly changing world of work, the idea that you leave school, get a job in a company, and spend the rest of your working life there, is often no longer a reality. Sarfraz Manzoor finds out how and why increasing numbers of us are preparing to branch out, gain new skills and either switch career or develop a variety of different occupations, known as a 'portfolio career'.

2 A 🔊 5.02 | Listen to the programme. What advantages of a portfolio career do the people mention?

B 🔊 5.02 | Work in pairs. Are the statements True (T) or False (F)? Listen again and check.
  1 Emily Wapnick says that portfolio careers allow people to do multiple things they enjoy.
  2 Emily Wapnick believes that portfolio careers are only possible for younger people.
  3 Charles Handy says that most people who work for large companies are unhappy with their jobs.
  4 Charles Handy thinks that people enjoy working for themselves, even if they don't earn much money.
  5 Heather McGregor suggests it is important for people to focus on just one job to advance their career.

C Work in groups. Discuss the questions.
  1 Do you think it is a good idea to develop skills in many different areas or to focus on developing skills in one area only? Why?
  2 Do you think we ever get too old to learn new skills?
  3 How easy or difficult would it be for you to switch career plans? Why?

VOCABULARY

work and careers

3 A Complete the sentences from the programme with the correct form of the words and phrases in the box.

> advance entrepreneur part-time reinvent
> retrain set up start out switch

  1 You'll have people who have five different _____ jobs, each of which they love for a different reason.
  2 They've got, you know, three different businesses that are just thriving or they're a serial _____ or they've got a career in two different areas.
  3 Is there an age limit to when one can _____ oneself or, you know, open a new door in their career or in their enthusiasms?
  4 Professor Heather McGregor, … of the *Financial Times*, _____ in PR and communications, _____ as an investment banker, _____ a highly successful business and is now an academic.
  5 If one career isn't enough, is it best to establish yourself and then _____ to another in mid-life?
  6 You know, everybody should have other things that they do in their career, apart from their main job. Otherwise, they will never _____ their career.

B 🔊 5.03 | Listen and check your answers.

C Complete the questions with the correct form of the words and phrases in Ex 3A.
  1 Have you ever considered _____ your own company? Why/Why not?
  2 If you could choose to _____ in a new profession, which would you choose?
  3 What do you think are the best ways to _____ your career?
  4 What should people consider before they decide to _____ careers?
  5 What are the pros and cons of being an _____ ?
  6 Have you ever had more than one _____ job?

D Work in pairs. Discuss the questions in Ex 3C.

E Learn and practise. Go to the Vocabulary Bank.

▶▶ page 140 **VOCABULARY BANK** areas of work

Unit 5 | Lesson B

GRAMMAR

past plans and intentions

4 A Read the comments about the radio programme and answer the questions (1–4).

1 Who ended up doing the job they didn't want to do originally?
2 Who changed the subject they were studying because they didn't like the course?
3 Who decided to study something different because their grades were not high enough for their first choice?
4 Who found their job by developing a new skill in their spare time?

Guillermo
12.07 | 3 June

I was supposed to become a lawyer, but halfway through my training I changed my mind because I wasn't enjoying the course. I ended up setting up my own business instead.

Rachael
12.24 | 3 June

I wasn't meant to become a teacher. Both my parents were university lecturers and I was determined to do something different. By chance I got a summer job as a teaching assistant while I was at university, and I quickly realised that I love being in the classroom.

Amit
12.27 | 3 June

I was thinking of being a musician, but I quickly realised that I wasn't good enough and I would never make ends meet, so I retrained as an accountant. I didn't really enjoy the job, but it paid the bills. In my spare time, I started writing articles about the economy. Now I'm a full-time writer.

Maite
12.36 | 3 June

I was planning on studying medicine at university, but my exam results weren't good enough so I had to find another option. Now, I'm studying Spanish and Portuguese and I'm really enjoying it.

B Look at the comments in Ex 4A again and answer the questions.

1 Do we use *I was meant to*, *I was supposed to*, *I was thinking of* and *I was planning on* when we talk about plans that did happen or didn't happen?
2 Which phrases are followed by the infinitive? Which phrases are followed by the *-ing* form?

C Learn and practise. Go to the Grammar Bank.

▶▶ page 123 **GRAMMAR BANK**

PRONUNCIATION

5 A 🔊 5.04 | **connected speech: intrusive /w/ sounds** | Listen to the sentences. Notice the /w/ sound that appears between the marked sounds.

1 I was going to apply to university.
2 I was supposed to open a new account.
3 I was meant to interview her last year.

B Work in pairs. Look at the sentences again. Are the sounds before and after the /w/ sound consonants or vowels?

C Work in pairs. Complete the sentences with your own ideas. Then practise saying them.

- I was supposed to apply to …
- I wasn't meant to open …
- I was going to ask if …

SPEAKING

6 A Make notes about a time you had to change your plans, e.g. a childhood ambition, your work, holiday plans, etc. Use the questions to help you.

1 What was the original plan? Why did you think it was a good idea?
2 What happened? What made you change your mind?
3 How did things turn out? What were the consequences of your change of plan?

B Work in groups. Take turns telling your stories. Ask questions to learn more about your classmates' experiences.

WRITING

a report

7 A Work in pairs. Read the report and answer the questions.

1. What is the purpose of the report?
2. What problems does it describe?
3. What is the recommendation?
4. Is the language formal or informal? Give examples.

Report on how young people's career ambitions are lagging behind the new world of work

1 ....

The aim of this report is to outline the difference between young people's career aspirations and the reality of the modern workplace and to suggest ways in which young people can be encouraged to have more up-to-date and realistic career expectations.

2 ....

Many young people appear to be choosing their dream job from among traditional occupations. They want to be writers, actors, lawyers, teachers, health professionals, police officers and firefighters. **It appears that** young people often base their ideas for their future careers on the jobs of their parents, friends and neighbours, and on TV.

3 ....

However, the world of work is rapidly changing, with new jobs and careers appearing all the time, and many traditional roles disappearing due to the increased use of technology. **It seems that** industries which are likely to see the most growth are renewable energies, healthcare, information technology, cybersecurity and data analysis. Despite this, **studies have shown that** the career expectations of young people have not changed a huge amount over recent years. Young people seem to ignore or know little about jobs in these growth industries. **There has been a slight increase in** the number of young people (eleven percent) who want to pursue modern career paths in social media and emerging technologies.

4 ....

To conclude, young people should be encouraged to explore different career options. **It is recommended that** closer connections are made between new industries and schools, for example by giving work placements to students and training teachers how to help young people make smarter career choices.

B Complete the report with the following headings.

A Background situation
B Introduction
C Conclusion/recommendations
D Main issues

C Read the report again. Complete the table with the phrases in bold.

introduction	1 .... The purpose/intention of this report is to … This report looks at … This is a report concerning/regarding … This report contains/outlines/examines/assesses …
background situation and main issues	2 .... It has been suggested that … 3 .... 4 .... /a decrease in … However, … 5 ....
conclusion and recommendations	6 .... /To sum up,/In conclusion,/On the whole, … 7 .... /I conclude/recommend/would suggest that …

8 A Work in pairs. Read the task and make notes about the key issues and possible solutions.

> The director of your college wants to encourage more female students to pursue careers in STEM (Science, Technology, Engineering and Maths) or Management. She has asked you to attend a conference on the future of work and write a report with recommendations for the college.

B Work in pairs. The following ideas were discussed at the conference. Compare the list to your own ideas. Decide which ideas you would like to include in your report.

Problems

- Female students often choose not to pursue careers in STEM or management.
- Female students tend to choose roles that are seen as 'female', e.g. teacher, nurse. Problem of stereotypes. Not enough young women are choosing newer career options like computer coding and data analytics.

Possible solutions

- Ensure that female students have access to role models for their possible future careers. 'You can't be what you can't see.'
- Frequently invite visitors to the school to share their expertise with the students, particularly women who are successful scientists, engineers, entrepreneurs, etc.
- Organise specialist science and business events to be attended by all students.
- Organise careers events for young people where they have a chance to find out about a range of different career options.
- College literature and social media should aim to represent a wide range of jobs being done by both men and women to counter stereotypes.

C Write your report. Use some of the ideas above and your own ideas.

5C You're on mute!

Unit 5 | Lesson C

HOW TO ... | describe problems and suggest solutions
VOCABULARY | video conference calls
PRONUNCIATION | intonation to show degrees of certainty

VOCABULARY

video conference calls

1 A Work in groups. Discuss the questions.

1. How often do you have video calls? What for?
2. Do you prefer face-to-face meetings or video conferencing? Why? What are the advantages and disadvantages of each?
3. Is there any behaviour during video conferencing that annoys you?

B Read the article. Which rules do you think are the most important? Why? What other rules can you think of?

C Work in pairs. Answer the questions about the words in bold in the article.

Which ...

1. two phrases mean 'silent' and 'change so you're not silent'?
2. two words mean there is something wrong with the sound? How are their meanings different?
3. phrase refers to something you need so you can get online?
4. phrase refers to a place where you can post messages?
5. word refers to something you receive when someone asks you to go to the meeting?
6. phrase means your picture on screen has stopped moving?
7. word refers to something that takes you to a page on the internet?
8. phrasal verb means you can access a virtual meeting?
9. word refers to the person who invited everyone and usually controls the meeting?
10. word means the level of sound?

D Work in pairs. Read the Future Skills box and discuss the questions.

FUTURE SKILLS
Social responsibility

When we're in a video conference, we need to manage our behaviour so we are good participants. Read 1, 5, 7 and 9 in the text again. Do you always follow these rules? How could you improve your participation in video conferences?

Turn your video on!

10 golden rules of video conferencing

You've probably heard some funny video conferencing stories: the professor whose small children came into the room during a live BBC interview, the executive who accidentally shared a beach holiday photo instead of a work document, and the lawyer whose child had changed the settings so he appeared as a cartoon cat during a trial. You can't predict everything that might go wrong, but there are some basic rules you should follow.

1 Respond to the **invite** and be on time, as you would be for a face-to-face meeting.

2 Check the technology is working. Check your settings and your **internet connection**.

3 Make sure your face is lit from the front and not behind, so you aren't in shadow. Check the webcam is at eye level.

4 Make sure your background is suitable. A white wall or a bookshelf is fine. Piles of dirty dishes or a busy office are not.

5 Keep your camera turned on and look into it when speaking. This gives the impression of eye contact with others.

6 Put yourself **on mute** if you aren't speaking, so no one has to hear your dog barking or your toddler screaming. Remember to **unmute** yourself when talking.

7 Focus on the meeting. Switch off notifications and messaging services, and don't start answering emails. People will notice if you're not focused.

8 If you're the **host**, know your responsibilities. Check the **chat box** regularly, make sure everyone can **get in** at the beginning, and check no one **is frozen**. Stay until the end, as if hosting a meeting in person.

9 If you need to post a **link** or show a document, have the right file ready. The other participants won't want to wait while you try to locate it.

10 Check the sound. Make sure there isn't an **echo** or a **delay**, and that your **volume** is up so you can hear everyone.

5C

How to ...
describe problems and suggest solutions

2 A 🔊 **5.05** | Listen to parts of three video conferences. Which of the rules in the article do the speakers not follow?

B 🔊 **5.06** | Work in pairs. Complete the extracts from the conversations. Then listen and check.

Conversation 1
1 Why don't you try .... down the volume on your speakers?
2 It's .... a try because sometimes the echo's from the mic.

Conversation 2
3 There .... to be a problem with my internet connection.
4 Perhaps you could .... logging off and on again?
5 That .... work because sometimes the computer just seems to fix itself.

Conversation 3
6 Hang on. I can't .... the screen share working.
7 David, maybe you .... post the document as a link in the chat box.

C Complete the table with the phrases in the box.

| It might be worth + -ing form ... isn't working |
| It sometimes helps if you + infinitive (without to) because ... |

describing problems	I can't get the ... working. There seems to be a problem with ... There's something wrong with my ... 1 ....
suggesting a solution	Perhaps you could try ... Maybe you could ...? Why don't you try ...? 2 ....
explaining why a solution would work	That might work because ... It's worth a try because ... 3 ....

D Learn and practise. Go to the Grammar Bank.

▶▶ page 124 **GRAMMAR BANK**

PRONUNCIATION

3 A 🔊 **5.07** | **intonation to show degrees of certainty** | Listen to the same suggestion said in two different ways. Which speaker sounds more confident, a or b?

B 🔊 **5.08** | Listen to more suggestions and choose the speakers that sound more confident, a or b.
1 Maybe you could send a link.   a / b
2 You could try clicking on the invite. a / b
3 It might be worth checking the chat box. a / b
4 Perhaps you could log off and on again. a / b

C 🔊 **5.08** | Listen again. Repeat the sentences and copy the intonation.

D Work in pairs. Take turns to read the problems and offer solutions. Use intonation to show how confident you are.
1 My computer keeps crashing.
2 My car won't start.
3 My phone keeps running out of battery.

SPEAKING

4 A Work in pairs. Imagine you are taking part in a video conference. Student A: Choose one problem and have the conversation with Student B.

Student A
Explain a problem (frozen screen/ microphone not working/can't open a document).

Student B
Suggest a solution and say why it might work.

Say the suggestion doesn't work. Ask for other ideas.

Make another suggestion.

Say it works!

B Now swap roles. Explain a different problem and offer solutions.

MEDIATION SKILLS
encouraging people to expand on their ideas
agree on a course of action

▶▶ page 151 **MEDIATION BANK**

Speak anywhere Go to the interactive speaking practice

63

5D BBC Street Interviews

Are you a team player?

GRAMMAR | non-defining relative clauses for comments
SPEAKING | a discussion about working alone vs. in a team
WRITING | a thank-you message

Aslan

PREVIEW

1 Work in groups. Discuss the questions.
1 Which of the activities in the box do you prefer doing alone?

> driving long distances   exercising
> going to the cinema   having dinner
> studying   working on projects

2 Which do you prefer doing with other people? Why?
3 What are the advantages and disadvantages of working in a team or working alone?

Q1: Do you prefer working alone or as part of a team?

Q2: Tell us about a good or bad experience of working in a team.

VIEW

2 A ▶ Watch the video and answer the questions.
1 Do more of the speakers prefer working alone or in a team?
2 How many talk about a bad experience?

B ▶ Watch the first part of the video again. Look at the photos at the top of the page and match the speakers with the things they say.
1 I like to share things, **share accomplishments**. ....
2 [In a team, you can] **support each other**. ....
3 I'm self-employed, so it **suits me** to work alone. ....
4 I'm **a bit of a perfectionist**. ....
5 [In a team you can] **bounce ideas off of other people**. ....

C Work in pairs. Look at the sentences in Ex 2B again.
1 What do you think the words and phrases in bold mean?
2 Which of the sentences are true for you?

D ▶ Watch the second part of the video again. Are the statements True (T) or False (F)?
1 Kathiane preferred working with her old team more than she does with her new team.
2 Aslan can't think of any bad experiences he has had when working in a team.
3 Olivia didn't like working online with other students because of language difficulties.
4 Onika mentions a fun activity her company did once a week.
5 Hannah talks about a time when her team stopped a dangerous situation.

GRAMMAR

non-defining relative clauses for comments

3 A Read the extracts from the interviews and underline the relative clauses.

   a Erm, my old team never wanted to do the work until the last minute and would rather play around, which was incredibly frustrating because …
   b We had to do the whole project online, which was really difficult because …
   c We had a group lunch, which was really fun.
   d I was in a dangerous situation, which was very scary.

B Work in pairs. Ask and answer the questions.

   1 Do the extracts in Ex 3A contain defining or non-defining relative clauses?
   2 Do these relative clauses add more factual information or give an opinion?

C Learn and practise. Go to the Grammar Bank.

⏩ page 125 **GRAMMAR BANK**

SPEAKING

a discussion about working alone vs. in a team

4 A Think about a time when you worked well alone and another time when when you enjoyed working in a team. Make notes about:
- what you were doing and why.
- what issues or problems you had.
- why you were so successful.

B Work in groups. Talk about your experiences and discuss the questions.

   1 Do you think that working as part of a team usually achieves better results? Why?
   2 Does your group prefer working alone or in a team?

WRITING

a thank-you message

5 A Work in groups. Discuss the questions.

   1 Do you think it's important to thank your team when they do something well? Why/Why not?
   2 What's the best way to do it (e.g., as a group, individually, via email, in person, etc.)? Why?

B Write a thank-you letter. Go to the Writing Bank.

⏩ page 106 **WRITING BANK**

5 REVIEW

GRAMMAR

past perfect simple and continuous

1 Complete the second sentence using the past perfect simple or continuous form of the verbs in brackets.

1. I waited for over an hour, then the bus arrived.
   When the bus arrived, I .... for over an hour! (wait)
2. I got to the restaurant, then I realised my purse was still at home!
   When I got to the restaurant, I realised that I .... my purse at home. (leave)
3. The show was nearly over when we got to the theatre.
   The show .... by the time we got to the theatre. (nearly / finish)
4. I went for a two-hour run on Saturday morning, then I was tired in the afternoon!
   I was tired on Saturday afternoon because I .... for two hours in the morning. (run)

past plans and intentions

2A Complete the sentences with the correct form of the words in brackets.

1. I .... physics at university, but I didn't get the grades. (mean / study)
2. I .... camping last weekend, but the forecast was so awful that I stayed at home. (think / go)
3. I .... this course so much. (not expect / enjoy)
4. I .... to the USA last year, but I couldn't take the time off. (hope / travel)
5. I wasn't enjoying my job and I .... careers, but I couldn't decide what to do! (consider / switch)
6. I .... trying the new restaurant, but then I realised I didn't have any money. (go / suggest)

B Change three of the sentences in Ex 2A so they are true for you. Then compare with a partner.

VOCABULARY

3A Complete the conversations with the correct form of the words in the box.

| advance   construction   consultancy   part-time |
| reinvent   retrain   set   start   switch |

1. A: I'm thinking of ¹............ careers and ²............ to work in journalism.
   B: Have you ever done any journalism before?
   A: Yes, I actually had a ³............ job with a publishing company just after I finished university.
2. A: I'd always been interested in buildings, so I ⁴............ out working in ⁵............ . But I found it hard to ⁶............ my career. So recently I've ⁷............ up my own business in financial ⁸............ .
   B: You've completely ⁹............ yourself!

B Work in pairs. Do you know anyone who has retrained, set up their own business, switched careers or reinvented themselves? Tell your partner about them.

4 Choose the correct words to complete the sentences.

1. I was quite nervous when I started work as I hadn't done anything like that **for / since** a while.
2. There it is – I've been looking for that jumper **in / for** ages!
3. I couldn't answer the last question in the exam, but it went OK up to **that / the** point.
4. I remember when I first met you, because I'd left my job just moments **soon / earlier**.
5. Anton, we can't hear you – I think you're **in / on** mute.
6. Can everyone type their answers into the **chat / talk** box?
7. I think you need to make me the **host / guest** before I can share my screen.
8. Sorry, can you say that again? Your voice keeps repeating because of the **mute / echo**.

5A Choose the correct words to complete the article.

It's never too late ...
In Young Kim | 30 November

It probably feels like there's never a good time to ¹**switch / advance** careers, giving up a successful job for one that's a lot more uncertain. However, some people do manage to successfully ²**reinvent / mute** themselves.

Michelle Obama ³**was supposed to / had been** working in an office doing legal work when she decided that she wanted to leave her job and do something more satisfying. For her, that meant working in public service, ⁴**which / that** was a big career change. The rest, as they say, is history!

Giorgio Armani, one of the world's top fashion designers, didn't ⁵**start out / set up** in the world of fashion. He was ⁶**thinking / planning** to become a doctor, and ⁷**had been studying / studied** medicine for three years when he decided to leave university and join the armed forces. He worked in a military hospital in Verona before moving into fashion. First, he worked in a shop in Milan and then he started designing his own clothes before ⁸**setting up / advancing** his own company in 1975.

Harrison Ford, who starred in *Star Wars* and *Raiders of the Lost Ark,* started acting when he was a young man. However, a few years later, he wasn't satisfied with the opportunities that he had been offered ⁹**just moments earlier / up to that point**, so he decided to ¹⁰**retrain / reinvent** as a carpenter. He continued in this profession for fifteen years in order to support his wife and children before he was offered the role in *Star Wars*.

B 🔊 R5.01 | Listen and check your answers.

psychology 6

VLOGS

Q: What things do you never find the time to get done?

1 ▶ Watch the video. What things do the people mention?

2 Work in pairs. Give examples of things that you never find the time to do.

GSE LEARNING OBJECTIVES

6A READING | Read an article about staying focused: prefixes

Talk about how you stay focused: necessity, prohibition and permission

Pronunciation: word stress: prefixes

Edit notes to make them more concise

6B LISTENING | Understand a conversation about introversion: reporting verbs; reported orders, requests and advice

Discuss whether you are an introvert or an extrovert

Pronunciation: consonant clusters

6C HOW TO … | ask for advice and give advice tactfully: collocations with *get* and *take*

Pronunciation: pitch for sounding tactful

6D BBC PROGRAMME | Understand a TV comedy programme in which contestants guess if a story is true or false

Talk about a true or false story: fillers

Write an email giving news

Unit 6 | Lesson A

6A Pay attention!

GRAMMAR | necessity, prohibition and permission
VOCABULARY | prefixes
PRONUNCIATION | word stress: prefixes

VOCABULARY

prefixes

1 A Work in groups. Read the three opinions. Which do you agree with and why?

B Read the statements in Ex 1A again. Match the prefixes in bold with the meanings in the box.

again   below/under   incorrectly/badly
not (x2)   opposite action

C Learn and practise. Go to the Vocabulary Bank.

⏩ page 140 **VOCABULARY BANK** prefixes

When doing a task, we should avoid **un**necessary distractions. This might mean **dis**connecting our devices or closing the door.

When we're distracted, we often **mis**understand instructions or produce **sub**standard work.

Multitasking is a bad idea. It's **im**practical to concentrate while doing several things at once, and it often means we have to **re**do the tasks which we messed up!

PRONUNCIATION

2 A 🔊 6.01 | **word stress: prefixes** | Underline the stressed syllables in the words in bold. Then listen and check.

1 I got distracted while I was writing my essay, so I had to **rewrite** the whole thing!
2 The idea of avoiding distractions completely is **impractical**.
3 Sorry, I **misunderstood** what you were saying.
4 I can always tell when she isn't concentrating, because her work is **substandard**.
5 It is **unknown** exactly how much time is lost at work due to distractions.

B Read the sentences in Ex 2A again. Choose the correct word(s) to complete the rule.

When words are formed with prefixes, the stress is usually on the **prefix / part of the root word**.

C Work in pairs. Take turns giving examples of the following:

- a time you had to rewrite something.
- a plan that was imperfect or unrealistic.
- something you misread, misunderstood or misheard.
- an impractical/unrealistic ambition you used to have.
- advice that was unhelpful.

READING

3 A Read the article and choose the best summary (1–3).

1 Why some people are better at multitasking.
2 How to concentrate and avoid getting distracted.
3 Why you should switch off your phone more often.

B Read the article again and answer the questions.

1 If you do things 'simultaneously' (paragraph 1), how do you do them?
2 What do you think 'odd jobs' are? (paragraph 3)
3 What's the difference between external and internal triggers? (paragraph 4)
4 What are 'moments of transition' (paragraph 6)? Why are they a problem?
5 What two-word phrase (paragraph 7) means 'able to influence what happens'?

C Work in groups. Discuss the questions.

1 Do you agree with Eyal that internal triggers are a bigger problem than external triggers?
2 Would any of the ideas in *A Short history of staying focused* work for you? Why/Why not?

The art of doing

[1] There's a good chance if you asked a North American sixteen-year-old exactly what they're doing right now, they'd be unable to tell you. That's because they're not doing just one thing at any one time – they are simultaneously doing their homework on a laptop, checking their Twitter feed, watching a programme on Netflix, making a snack and messaging their best friend! Actually, it's not only North Americans or teenagers. Much of the world's population is busy multitasking and living in the 'nearly now'. Distraction is a way of life.

[2] It's tempting to blame the internet for our distractedness. There are apps for everything, and it's very easy to spend hours staring at a phone screen. There are even apps (oh, the irony!) to help us stay offline by locking us out of social media. But according to behavioural psychologist and author, Nir Eyal, tech isn't the problem.

[3] A few years ago, Eyal found himself getting distracted. So, he bought an old flip phone with no apps on it and started using a 1990s word processor with no internet connection. But he soon discovered that the tools didn't matter. Instead of working, he'd tidy his desk or take out the rubbish. These odd jobs didn't need doing; they were just distractions.

[4] His mistake? He'd believed that the problem was external triggers – things outside himself like phones and social media. But instead, he realised the problem was internal triggers – emotional states we want to escape. For example, when we're feeling lonely, we might check Facebook. When we're uncertain, we turn to Google. When we're bored, we find things to read or watch online.

[5] While researching his book, *Indistractable: How to Control Your Attention and Choose Your Life*, he found some solutions to help us stay focused. One of these is to plan your day, not with a to-do list, but by giving an idea of how long you think you'll spend on each task. Another idea occurred to him when he noticed that people have their devices on all day and check them constantly. He suggests checking social media and email only at certain times of the day, for fixed amounts of time, for example only checking your emails from 9.00–9.30 a.m.

[6] One of Eyal's ideas is that we should be careful about moments of transition, when we're moving from one task to the next. Often, we're tempted to do something 'quick', like catching up with messaging friends, which turns out not to be so quick. We find ourselves spending far more time on it than we'd planned, and the result is distraction.

[7] Eyal also reminds us of a psychological truth: we're not powerless. If we believe we're in control of our internal triggers, we're more likely to overcome them.

A short history of staying focused

Could Eyal's ideas work for you? If not, maybe you should take inspiration from what people did in the days before smartphones and texting.

366 BCE
Look terrible

Demosthenes built an underground study, where he practised public speaking and shaved half his hair off. He was so ashamed of his appearance he had to stay inside.

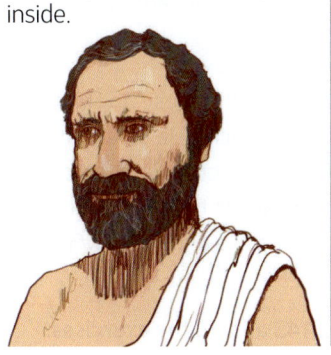

1876
Be so ill you can't have fun

Charles Darwin was sick constantly. But he saw it as a gift. It allowed him to concentrate on science free from 'the distractions of society and amusement'.

1912
Work at night

The novelist Franz Kafka suffered from insomnia and lived in a noisy Prague apartment, so his books needed to be written at night. He started at around 10.30 p.m. and ended at 3.00 a.m.

1984
Get locked in

When Douglas Adams' novel *So Long, and Thanks for All the Fish* needed finishing, his publisher booked him into a hotel. Adams wasn't allowed to leave the hotel until he'd finished the book.

Unit 6 | Lesson A

GRAMMAR

necessity, prohibition and permission

4 A Read the sentences from the article. Underline the words and phrases that describe necessity, prohibition or permission.
1. Douglas Adams's novel *So Long, and Thanks for All the Fish* needed finishing.
2. It allowed him to concentrate on science.
3. Adams wasn't allowed to leave the hotel.
4. Kafka's books needed to be written at night.

B Work in pairs. Answer the questions about the verb forms you underlined in Ex 4A.
1. Which phrase describes permission using verb + object + infinitive?
2. Which phrase is followed by a passive structure?
3. Which phrase describes prohibition?
4. Which word describing necessity can be followed by an *-ing* form?

C Learn and practise. Go to the Grammar Bank.

▶▶ page 126 **GRAMMAR BANK**

SPEAKING

5 A Read the tips for avoiding distractions. Can you think of any others?

10 top tips for avoiding distraction
1. switch off your phone
2. take breaks every twenty minutes
3. keep a strict routine
4. work at night
5. work somewhere boring
6. stay in the moment
7. work in a room with others who are working
8. lock the door
9. eat before you start working
10. listen to music

B Which three tips are the most useful? Why? Make notes.

C Work in groups. Tell other students which three you chose. Ask questions to see if they agree or not.

D Work in pairs. Read the Future Skills Box and discuss the question.

> **FUTURE SKILLS**
> **Self-management**
> Staying focused is essential for learning a language. Which of the new ideas for staying focused that you've read in this lesson do you think would help you in your studies?

WRITING

editing notes

6 A Read two versions of notes that summarise Nir Eyal's ideas in the article. Which version is clearer (1 or 2)? Why?

1

‹ Notes · · ·

Eyal describes external triggers as the things outside you such as phones and social media.

He goes on to say that internal triggers are the emotional states from which we want to escape. One of Eyal's ideas is to plan your day focusing on how long you'll spend on each task.

Another solution is the idea of checking social media and email only at certain times of the day, for fixed amounts of time.

Eyal thinks we should be careful about moments of transition, when we are moving from one task to the next. These 'quick' transitions often aren't quick.

Eyal also thinks we should remember we're not powerless.

2

‹ Notes · · ·

Eyal's ideas:

external triggers = phones, social media, etc.

internal triggers = emotional states

plan your day – how long to spend on each task?

check social media/email at set times, e.g. 9–9.30

be careful with transitions – can take more time than expected

'we're not powerless'

B Work in pairs. Read the ideas for making notes more concise (shorter). Which are the most useful ideas? Why?
1. choose only the most important points/key words
2. use headings and subheadings to organise the notes
3. write full sentences
4. use imperative sentences ('do this')
5. use reported speech ('He said that … ')
6. write definitions of complicated ideas
7. use your own words to summarise
8. cut small words like *a*, *the* and *of* if the meaning is clear without them

C Turn to page 143 and do the exercises.

6B Quiet

GRAMMAR | reported orders, requests and advice
VOCABULARY | reporting verbs
PRONUNCIATION | consonant clusters

LISTENING

1 A Work in pairs. Complete the definitions with *introvert* or *extrovert*.

> ¹........... **noun** (C)
>
> someone who is quiet and shy, and prefers spending time alone to being with other people

> ²........... **noun** (C)
>
> someone who is active and confident and prefers spending time with other people to being alone

B Work in groups. Discuss the questions.
1. What is the typical image of an introvert and an extrovert?
2. In what ways do you think the typical ideas about extroverts and introverts might be wrong?

C 🔊 **6.02** | Listen to a conversation between two friends, Miriam and Nishma. Answer the questions.
1. What are Miriam and Nishma talking about?
2. What happened when Nishma found herself working in a busy office?
3. Do you think Miriam and Nishma are introverts or extroverts? Why?

D 🔊 **6.02** | Choose the correct words to complete the summary. Then listen again and check.

> In her book *Quiet: The Power of Introverts in a World That Can't Stop Talking,* Susan Cain explores the idea that we live in a world which favours ¹**introverts / extroverts**, where the people who do all the talking tend to be ²**more / less** successful. She suggests that society doesn't reward or acknowledge the important contribution of introverts. She also questions some of the assumptions around introverts, like introverts are always ³**shy / quiet** and they're not very good at ⁴**focusing on a task / public speaking**. She argues that introverts often have to ⁵**train themselves to be more like extroverts / choose different jobs** in order to succeed in the things they are required to do for school or work.

2 A 🔊 **6.02** | Listen again. Write down one fact and one opinion that the speakers give about each topic.
1. the book that they discuss
2. team-building exercises
3. Barack Obama
4. an office that Nishma worked at
5. Nishma's manager

B Work in pairs. Which of the speakers' opinions in Ex 2A do you agree with? Why?

C Work in groups. Discuss the questions.
1. Do you think the terms 'introvert' and 'extrovert' are useful? Why/Why not?
2. Do you think most people are either introverts or extroverts, or a mixture or both?

GRAMMAR

reported orders, requests and advice

3 A Choose the correct words to complete the reported sentences from the conversation.
1. I asked my manager **letting / to let** me work somewhere a bit quieter.
2. She told me **to get / getting** back to my desk.
3. He advised me **to talk / talking** to my manager about working from home.

B Match the sentences (1–3) in Ex 3A with the type of information they report (a–c).
a advice   **b** a request   **c** an order

C Rewrite the sentences in Ex 3A using the exact words the person might have said.
1 'Do you think you could let me work somewhere a bit quieter?'

4 A Work in pairs. Choose the correct option to complete the rule.

To report requests, orders and advice, we use a reporting verb + subject + **infinitive with *to* / *-ing*** form.

B Learn and practise. Go to the Grammar Bank.

⏭ page 127 **GRAMMAR BANK**

Unit 6 | Lesson B

VOCABULARY

reporting verbs

5 A Work in pairs. Do you prefer working with introverts or extroverts? Why?

B Read the forum posts. Whose opinions are similar to yours?

C Choose the correct direct speech equivalents of the reported sentences from the forum posts. Use the reporting verbs in bold to help you.

1 I **suggested** having just one meeting a week.
   a 'I think it would be a good idea if we had just one meeting a week.'
   b 'We're only having one meeting a week from now on.'

2 At first people **refused** to take the idea seriously.
   a 'We're not sure that's a very good idea.'
   b 'You must be joking – that's a crazy idea!'

3 I **emphasised** how much time we could save.
   a 'We might be able to save a bit of time if we had fewer meetings.'
   b 'I'm sure we could save about ten hours a week if we had fewer meetings.'

4 I **threatened** to stop coming to meetings.
   a 'Would it be OK if I didn't come to all the meetings?'
   b 'I'll stop coming to meetings if we don't reduce the number.'

5 He **boasted** about his achievements.
   a 'I think what I've managed to do is amazing!'
   b 'I can assure you I never did that.'

6 He **claimed** to have worked as the manager of a well-known restaurant.
   a 'I've worked as the manager of Chez Luis, so I know what I'm talking about.'
   b 'I'm thinking of applying for a job as manager of Chez Luis.'

7 I **questioned** him about the details.
   a 'Have you heard about the manager's job at Chez Luis?'
   b 'What year did you work there?'

8 He **admitted** that it wasn't true.
   a 'Actually, I haven't been entirely honest about that.'
   b 'I can't believe you would accuse me of lying!'

D Learn and practise. Go to the Vocabulary Bank.

▶▶ page 140 **VOCABULARY BANK**
reporting verbs

Nish468
1 day ago
7 Comments | Share | Reply

Do you prefer working with introverts or extroverts?
So, random question I know, but my friend and I were talking about it today and I wanted to know what everyone else had to say!

noname
23 hours ago
7 Comments | Share | Reply

I prefer working with introverts. The extroverts at work are always talking about ideas and organising meetings instead of actually doing anything! So, recently I suggested having just one meeting a week, so we could get more work done. At first people refused to take the idea seriously, but I emphasised how much time we could save and threatened to stop coming to meetings at all. In the end I persuaded people to at least reduce the number of meetings they organised!

brassicpark
22 hours ago
7 Comments | Share | Reply

I agree with @noname. I worked in a bistro once where the manager was really extroverted. He spent loads of time talking about himself and he boasted about his achievements in the industry. He claimed to have worked as the manager of a well-known restaurant, but when I questioned him about the details, he admitted that it wasn't true.

PRONUNCIATION

6 A 🔊 6.03 | **consonant clusters** | Listen and complete the sentences with the correct reporting verbs.

1 She .... to stop speaking to me if I didn't go with her.
2 They .... us to go on holiday with them.
3 He .... the most important points.
4 She .... leaving the office early.
5 They .... practising the presentation beforehand.
6 She .... she had a lot of management experience.

B Look at the sentences in Ex 6A again. Underline the consonant groups in the reporting verbs.

C 🔊 6.03 | Listen again. Practise saying the sentences, making sure you pronounce the consonant clusters accurately.

D Work in pairs. Can you think of any situations where the following things have happened? Explain what happened.

1 Someone asked you to do something you didn't want to do.
2 Someone claimed that something was true, when it wasn't.
3 Someone suggested doing something that turned out to be a bad idea.
4 You admitted to making a mistake.
5 You threatened to do something but didn't really mean it.
6 You boasted about doing something in order to impress someone.

SPEAKING

7 A Work in groups. Discuss the quiz questions.

Are you an introvert or an extrovert?

Do the quiz to find out if you are an introvert, an extrovert, or somewhere in-between.

1 In a big group of friends, would you spend more time talking or listening? Why?
2 What would you do if someone asked you to give a presentation to a large group of people?
3 It's the weekend and you want to see your friends. What sort of thing would you organise?
4 You are in the middle of something important and your phone rings. How do you usually react? Why?
5 Imagine you go to a big networking event. How many people will you try to talk to? Why?
6 Imagine you're working on a big project. Would you choose to work for long, uninterrupted periods, or in smaller chunks of time? Why?
7 You're having dinner with friends and the conversation turns to something you know nothing about. What do you do?
8 Imagine you have a completely free morning. What do you do? Why?
9 Do people sometimes describe you as calm, serious or mysterious? Why?
10 When it's a special occasion (e.g. your birthday), how do you like to celebrate? Why?

B Who in your group is generally more extroverted? Who is more introverted? Why? Give examples of the answers they gave.

I would say Marta is more of an extrovert. Her senior manager asked her to give a presentation to a large group of people, and she agreed immediately!

Unit 6 | Lesson C

6C Here's my advice

HOW TO ... | ask for advice and give advice tactfully
VOCABULARY | collocations with *get* and *take*
PRONUNCIATION | pitch for sounding tactful

VOCABULARY

collocations with *get* and *take*

1 A Work in pairs. Discuss the questions.
1. Who do you speak to when you need advice?
2. When was the last time you gave someone advice? What was it about?
3. Have you ever had to give someone honest advice that they didn't want to hear?

B Read the blog post about giving advice. Which of the statements are true, according to the post?
1. Most people enjoy giving advice.
2. Advice from friends is usually very helpful.
3. People who want to talk about their problems don't usually want advice.
4. It is sometimes difficult to give people honest advice.
5. People usually listen to the advice that others give them.

C Scan the post again. Complete the definitions with the correct form of the collocations in bold.
1. If you ...., you try to help in a situation.
2. If you .... someone, you manage to help them understand something.
3. If you .... off your ...., you talk about something that is worrying or upsetting you.
4. If you .... someone's .... a problem, you help them forget about it for a while.
5. If you .... something ...., you make a mistake with it.
6. If you say something to someone and they ...., they get upset and think that you are criticising them.
7. If you ...., you accept it and act on it.
8. If someone ...., they understand what you are saying to them.

Want my advice?

Emily Atkins | Friday 12 July | 11.22 GMT

Advice is a funny thing, isn't it? Many of us love to **get involved** and give advice to someone with a problem. It's so satisfying to play the part of the wise friend! But actually, when people want to talk about their problems, they very rarely want advice. All they want is to **get something off their chest**. They want someone to listen to them in a sympathetic way, and help them **take their mind off** their problems for a while. They're very unlikely to **take advice** from anyone, because they actually need to work out the solutions for themselves.

On the other hand, we've all been in situations where someone desperately needs some honest advice. Maybe they're putting all their efforts into trying to make it as an actor, and they can't understand why they aren't a famous film star yet. The truth is, they can't act, but not even their closest friends are able to **get through to** them. Whatever their friends say, they don't seem to **get the message**.

Also, a lot of us find it hard to give truly honest advice, even if our friends desperately need it. We don't want to **get it wrong** and suggest something that ruins their life. And we don't want them to **take it personally** and be upset.

But it's important to help people when they need it. So, if you want my advice: stick to sympathy when someone comes to you with a problem, and give honest suggestions when you can.

D Work in pairs. Take turns talking about the situations below.
1. a piece of advice you took
2. one thing people shouldn't take personally (but always do)
3. a time you helped take someone's mind off their problems
4. a time when you tried to give someone advice, but they didn't get the message
5. a time when you decided not to get involved in a situation

A friend advised me to study English and I took the advice because ...

How to ...
ask for advice and give advice tactfully

2 A 🔊 **6.04** | Listen to two conversations and answer the questions.
1. What is the problem in each situation?
2. What advice does the speaker give in each conversation?
3. Is it easy for the speakers to give the advice? Why/Why not?
4. Do you think the people will take the advice?

B 🔊 **6.04** | Complete the expressions from the conversations by adding one word in each gap. Listen again and check.

Conversation 1
1. Ryan, I hope you don't take this the .... way, but I'm not sure it's a good idea to stop studying.
2. Look, I'm telling you this as a .... , Ryan.
3. Well, have you .... about getting some lessons?
4. To be .... , it might be useful to focus a bit more on your technique.
5. So, what .... you do?
6. But if I .... you, I definitely wouldn't leave university!

Conversation 2
7. Don't take this .... , but you do go out a lot, don't you?
8. Yes, but perhaps you .... to see friends just at the weekends?
9. What do you .... ?
10. Well, it .... be an idea to buy fewer clothes.
11. I don't want you to get the wrong .... , but I just think generally you could be a bit more careful with money.
12. My .... would be to set a budget each month.

3 A Choose the correct words to complete the conversations.
1. A: I hope you don't **take** / **get** this the wrong way, but I think you take your parents for granted. They're always paying for you.
   B: So, what do you think I **should** / **might** do?
2. A: I'm just telling you this **for** / **as** a friend. Your new haircut really doesn't suit you.
   B: Thanks. I don't mind. It'll grow soon enough.
3. A: Can you give me **an** / **some** advice? I'd really like to become a professional actor.
   B: Don't **hear** / **take** this personally, but my advice **should be** / **would be** to give up acting.
4. A: What **would** / **might** you do?
   B: It **might** / **should** be a good idea to talk to her one-to-one.
5. A: If you want **this** / **my** advice, you should study harder.
   B: I don't want you to get the **bad** / **wrong** idea, but I thought the same about you.

B Learn and practise. Go to the Grammar Bank.

▶▶ page 128 **GRAMMAR BANK**

PRONUNCIATION

4 A 🔊 **6.05** | **pitch for sounding tactful** | Listen to the advice. Do the speakers start with a high pitch or a low pitch? Do they get higher or lower?
1. Perhaps you should try to cut back on your spending a bit.
2. It might be a good idea to get there on time in future.
3. Have you thought about maybe going to bed a bit earlier?
4. My advice would be to maybe go to a more experienced hairdresser.

B Work in pairs. Take turns reading the situations and giving each other advice. Focus on the pitch of your voice.
1. A flatmate cooks a meal for you. The food is terrible.
2. A friend wants to sing a solo at your wedding. She's the world's worst singer.
3. A neighbour wants to show you his holiday photos. He took over 600!

SPEAKING

5 Work in pairs. Student A: Read the information below and take turns to ask for and give advice. Student B: Look at page 144.
1. Listen to your partner's problem. You know that they always come to work late and in the wrong clothes. They don't understand why they never get promoted. Give tactful advice.
2. Start a conversation. The neighbours in your block of flats always seem angry with you. They barely say hello anymore. Ask your partner for advice.
3. Listen to your partner's problem. You know that they always copy their classmates' homework and never help anyone else. Now their classmates won't work with them out of class.
4. Start a conversation. You used to give lifts to your friend on your motorbike. You never asked for money for petrol. Now your friend doesn't want to ride with you anymore. Ask your partner how you can restart the friendship.

MEDIATION SKILLS
building on other people's ideas
add to posts in a thread, building on the advice of other people

▶▶ page 152 **MEDIATION BANK**

Unit 6 | Lesson D

6D BBC Entertainment

Would I lie to you?

VOCABULARY | fillers
SPEAKING | a true or false story
WRITING | an email giving news

PREVIEW

1 A Work in groups. Look at the photo of Pelé. What do you know or can you guess about his life and achievements?

B Read about the programme. What is the connection between Pelé and the programme you are going to watch?

Would I Lie to You?

Would I Lie to You? is a BBC comedy panel show in which celebrities tell stories about themselves that may or may not be true. The other celebrities in the studio ask questions to help them guess whether or not the story is true. In this episode, BBC TV presenter Dan Walker describes an experience he had with Pelé, one of the most famous footballers in history.

VIEW

2 A ▶ Watch the video. Choose the sentence which best summarises the story.
   1 Pelé didn't want to sign Dan's bag because he'd already signed his shirt.
   2 Dan told Pelé not to sign his bag because he really liked it.

B ▶ Work in pairs. Answer the questions. Then watch again and check.
   1 What kind of bag did Dan have?
   2 How was Pelé connected to the New York Cosmos?
   3 In which year did Dan meet Pelé?
   4 What was in the bag when Dan got it?
   5 What two letters did Pelé write on the bag?

C Work in groups. Discuss the questions.
   1 While you were watching, did you think the story was true?
   2 Do you think Dan was rude to stop Pelé? Why/Why not?
   3 Have you ever met anyone famous? What happened?

6D

BBC

SPEAKING

a true or false story

4 A 🔊 **6.06** | Listen to Olga playing the game in the BBC programme. Discuss the questions.

1 Do you think the other players believe her story?
2 Do you think her story is true? Why/Why not?

B 🔊 **6.07** | Listen and check your ideas from Ex 4A.

C 🔊 **6.06** | Listen to Olga's story again. Tick the phrases you hear.

> **KEY PHRASES**
>
> Let me think.
> That's a good point.
> That's a good question.
> That's a difficult question for me to answer.
> I'll have to think about this.
> That's an interesting question.
> I'm just trying to remember.

D Look at the phrases again. Why are they used?

a to avoid answering a question completely
b to gain time while they are thinking about what to say

5 A You are going to play the game in the BBC programme. Choose a story to tell (true or false) and make notes. Use the questions to help you.

- Where were you?
- What happened?
- What was unusual about the situation or events?

B Work in groups. Follow the instructions to play the game.

1 Take turns telling your story.
2 Listen and ask questions.
3 Decide as a group if you think the story is true.
4 Reveal the answer.

VOCABULARY

fillers

3 A Work in pairs. Read the sentences (a–d) and answer the questions about the words in bold.

a **Well**, that's very interesting. Is that a Brazil bag?
b **So**, you already had that bag?
c **OK**, that's … that's interesting.
d **Right**, so I'd taken a Brazil shirt with me.

1 Why do people use these words in informal speech?
2 What other words or phrases can you use in a similar way?

B Work in pairs. Take turns answering the questions. Answer some truthfully and lie about others. Use the fillers in Ex 3A to give yourself time to think. Guess which answers are true and which are lies.

1 What's your favourite film?
2 Where did you grow up?
3 What's the most amazing thing you've ever done?
4 Who's the most famous person you've ever met?

WRITING

an email giving news

6 A Work in pairs. Discuss the questions.

1 How often do you use email?
2 What do you use it for?

B Write an email giving news. Go to the Writing Bank.

⇒ page 106 **WRITING BANK**

77

6 REVIEW

GRAMMAR

necessity, prohibition and permission

1 A Choose the correct words to complete the descriptions of some of the world's strangest jobs.
1. Pet food tasters taste tins of pet food. Imagine having a plate of cat food that **needs to be eaten / needs to eat**.
2. For mosquito researchers, **allowing / being permitted** themselves to be bitten is part of the job.
3. Imagine being **forbidden / permitted** to play computer games all day and all night. Gold farmers earn in-game currency which can be sold for real money.
4. Professional queue standers stand in queues for other people. Obviously, you're **permitted / not allowed** to leave the queue once you're there.

B Work in pairs. Which of the jobs in Ex 1A would you like to do? Why?

reported orders, requests and advice

2 Report what the people said using *ask*, *tell* or *advise*.
1. Last week an interviewer said, 'Can you talk about your biggest weakness?'
2. The other day a ticket inspector said, 'Get off the train!' because I couldn't find my ticket.
3. My sister said, 'I suggest you start looking for a job'.
4. This morning a complete stranger said, 'Can you carry my suitcase for me?'
5. The concierge in the hotel said, 'You should leave early because there might be traffic'.

VOCABULARY

3 Complete the words in the sentences with a suitable prefix.
1. Sorry, I must have .... understood the instructions.
2. I don't enjoy waiting. I get very .... patient.
3. It was very .... honest of him to lie to us.
4. Perhaps your expectations are a bit .... realistic.
5. I couldn't live in .... zero temperatures. I hate the cold.
6. I'm going to start again and .... do it all.

4 A Complete the questions with the correct form of the verbs in the box.

| accuse admit apologise refuse remind suggest |

1. Where would you .... visiting in your town/city?
2. Do you find it easy to .... making mistakes?
3. Have you ever .... to pay a bill? Why?
4. Do you ever have to .... people to do things?
5. Would you always .... for being late?
6. Have you ever been wrongly .... of something?

B Work in pairs. Ask and answer the questions.

5 Correct one mistake in each sentence.
1. I often find it hard to take my mind on work.
2. Sometimes I just need to tell someone about a problem and get it on my chest.
3. If someone says something negative to me, I try not to take it personal.
4. I'm not very good at taking anyone else's advices.
5. I tried talking to Jo, but I couldn't put through to her.
6. I hate it when people just don't keep the message.

6 A Choose the correct options (A–C) to complete the text.

Burnout – and what you can do about it

We all have days when we feel we can't keep up with everything that ¹......... . But what if your job starts to feel like an ² .... possible struggle?

If you're suffering from burnout, three things might be happening. Firstly, you're probably feeling emotionally exhausted. You might find it difficult to ³ .... yourself to do all the jobs that ⁴ .... Secondly, you're starting to produce ⁵ .... standard work. Thirdly, perhaps you feel ⁶ .... connected from your work. Maybe you feel resentful or angry about your co-workers and have started to take things ⁷ ....

⁸ .... , there are plenty of things you can do to help yourself. Here are two things you could try.

Take care of yourself. Do more exercise and get enough sleep. Go out for lunch instead of staring at a screen. Do things to try and take your mind ⁹ .... work.

Look to the future. The opposite of job burnout is job engagement. Imagine what it would be like to be engaged in your work. Is there something else you would prefer to do? Could you ¹⁰ .... train or switch companies?

If you're close to burnout, act fast and make a change.

1 A needs to do	B needs doing	C was needed
2 A im-	B un-	C in-
3 A persuade	B admit	C threaten
4 A forbid to be done	B need to be done	C aren't permitted
5 A mis-	B sub-	C un-
6 A dis-	B mis-	C im-
7 A personally	B serious	C yourself
8 A Disappointingly	B Fortunately	C Unfortunately
9 A away	B from	C off
10 A dis-	B re-	C mis-

B 🔊 R6.01 | Listen and check your answers.

talent 7

GSE LEARNING OBJECTIVES

7A READING | Read an article about *The accidental pianist*: compound adjectives; chance
Speculate about a story: past modals of deduction
Pronunciation: connected speech: past modals of deduction

7B LISTENING | Understand a discussion about missed opportunities: idioms: regrets
Talk about regrets: *wish, if only, should have*
Pronunciation: chunking in idioms
Write a personal essay

7C HOW TO … | describe a process: phrasal verbs: explaining
Pronunciation: stress in phrasal verbs

7D BBC STREET INTERVIEWS | Understand street interviews about hard work vs. talent
Talk about talents: adverbials of concession
Write a social media post

VLOGS

Q: Do you have any hidden talents?

1 ▶ Watch the video. What talents do the people mention?

2 Work in pairs. Discuss your hidden talents. Demonstrate them if possible.

Unit 7 | Lesson A

7A An unexpected passion

GRAMMAR | past modals of deduction
VOCABULARY | compound adjectives; chance
PRONUNCIATION | connected speech: past modals of deduction

READING

1 A Work in pairs. Discuss the questions.
1 What are your passions and interests in life?
2 How did you become interested in these things?
3 In what other ways can people discover a new interest?
4 Have you ever suddenly developed an interest in something new? What happened?

B Read about Tony Cicoria. What is his passion? How did he develop it?

2 Complete the article with the missing sentences (a–g). There is one sentence that you don't need.

a The weather was often changeable at that time of year.
b He got out of bed and started trying to play the music on the piano, even though he didn't know how to.
c However, by the time the police arrived, Cicoria was conscious, although disorientated, and refused to be taken to hospital.
d His friends and family were amazed at his sudden interest.
e He started taking lessons and practising in every spare moment of the day.
f He would regularly work long hours, often twelve or fourteen hours a day, seven days a week.
g He played it day and night, in his car, at home and at work.

3 A Work in pairs. You are going to retell the story of Tony Cicoria. Read the prompts and try to remember the main events of the story. Make notes.

hard-working surgeon / Sleepy Hollow Lake / phone / struck by lightning / incredible desire to hear classical music / piano / sheet music / a dream / day and night / *The Lightning Sonata*

B Read the Future Skills box and do the task. Then retell the story in pairs.

> **FUTURE SKILLS**
> **Communication**
>
> When you tell a story, try to add descriptions to make it more interesting.
>
> You can describe background details ('It was a beautiful autumn day …') or specific details related to the main events ('He noticed a few rain drops …'). Go back through the story and think of some descriptions to include when you retell the story.

4 A Work in groups. If you could suddenly develop any skill or ability, what would it be and why?

B Scan the article again. What meaning do the words and phrases in bold all share?

C Learn and practise. Go to the Vocabulary Bank.

▶▶ page 141 **VOCABULARY BANK** chance

The accidental pianist

Michelle Ionova | Saturday 8 April | 11.01 GMT

Inspiration a bolt from the blue for world-famous surgeon

How do we develop our passions in life? For most of us, our interests start slowly, maybe beginning as a childhood hobby or teenage pastime and gradually developing as we get older. But in the case of Tony Cicoria, it happened in an instant, and changed his life forever.

In the 1990s, Tony Cicoria lived with his family in New York State. He trained at medical school and went on to become a successful surgeon. [1] .... However, he also tried to make time to spend with his children in the evenings whenever he could.

One weekend in August 1994, he travelled with his wife and children to Sleepy Hollow Lake to attend a family reunion. It was autumn and the leaves on the trees were a beautiful red. Children ran around playing as the family enjoyed a barbecue by the lake. At one point, Cicoria remembers noticing a few drops of rain, but he wasn't worried. [2] .... When he went to a pay phone to call his mother, something **unexpected** happened. He heard a loud crack, and a huge flash of light came out of the phone, hit him in the face and threw him back onto the ground. He had been struck by lightning, and he thought he must have died.

While Cicoria was unconscious, a woman who had been waiting to use the phone started to help him.

He had apparently suffered a cardiac arrest and also had burns to his face and foot. [3] .... Cicoria went home, where he recovered for two weeks before returning to work.

At first, he believed everything was normal. But two weeks after his **freak** accident, he started to feel an incredible desire to listen to piano music. Although he had never been interested in classical music before, he drove to a music shop and bought a CD of well-known piano music. [4] .... He also shared his new-found passion by making his family and work colleagues listen, too.

He soon realised that listening to music was not enough – he had to be able to play it, too. At that time, he didn't have a piano, but **by chance**, an old babysitter asked if she could store her piano at his home for a while. Cicorica bought sheet music of famous pieces, but realised he had no idea how he would ever play them. Then, one night, he had a dream in which he was playing a piece of music in a concert hall. When he woke from the dream, he realised that the melody was his own creation. [5] .... The music didn't go away, but stayed in his head day and night.

He decided he had to learn how to play this music. [6] .... He would get up at four o'clock in the morning in order to play the piano before going to work. When he got home from work, he would have dinner, put the children to bed and play the piano again.

Cicoria continued with his new passion night and day, and in 2008, he played his own composition, *The Lightning Sonata*, in a concert hall in New York, and it was shown on television all over the world.

Unit 7 | Lesson A

GRAMMAR

past modals of deduction

5 A Read the comments about the story (a–d). Match the past modals in bold with the meanings (1–3).

a It **must have been** strange for his family to watch him change so completely.
b It **can't have been** easy for his neighbours if he was playing the piano in the middle of the night!
c He **might have had** the talent since he was a child, but just not known about it.
d His brain **could have been affected** by the lightning strike.

1 It's almost certain that this happened or is true.
2 It's possible that this happened or is true.
3 It's almost certain that this is not true, or impossible.

B Read the comments (a–d) again and complete the rules.

1 We use .... + *have* + past participle to say we are sure something happened because there's strong evidence.
2 We use .... / .... + *have* + past participle to say we think something is possible, but we aren't sure.
3 We use .... + *have* + past participle to say we are sure something did not happen because there's strong evidence.
4 We use a modal + *have* + ... + past participle in the passive.

C Learn and practise. Go to the Grammar Bank.

▶▶ page 129 **GRAMMAR BANK**

PRONUNCIATION

6 A 🔊 7.01 | connected speech: past modals of deduction | Listen and complete the sentences.

1 His medical colleagues .... wondered if he would give up his job as a surgeon.
2 It .... been easy learning to play the piano whilst working full time.
3 He .... known that he'd end up becoming a concert pianist.
4 His family .... got fed up with his piano playing sometimes.

B 🔊 7.01 | Listen again. Which words are connected in each sentence? Is the pronunciation of *have* strong or weak?

C Work in pairs. Take turns speculating about what it was like for Tony Cicoria and for the people that knew him, using the prompts in the box.

> his wife   his children   his neighbours
> his work colleagues   his piano teacher
> the doctors who examined his brain
> the woman who helped him   other musicians

It must have been very scary for his wife when he was struck by lightning.

VOCABULARY

compound adjectives

7 A Work in pairs. Read the sentences and think of a different way to express the words in bold.

1 Tony Cicoria was a fit and healthy **forty-two-year-old** surgeon. Tony Cicoria was forty-two years old.
2 He was a **widely respected** surgeon.
3 His job was very **time-consuming**. He often worked twelve to fourteen hours a day.
4 Being struck by lightning was a **life-changing** event.
5 The accident left him with **long-lasting** effects.
6 He acquired a **second-hand** piano from a friend.
7 He developed an **all-consuming** determination to learn to play the piano.
8 Now, he is a **world-famous** musician.

B Which is correct, a or b? Why?

a a ten-year-old boy   b a ten years old boy

C Work in pairs. Student A: Go to page 143. Student B: Go to page 144.

SPEAKING

8 Work in groups. Read the stories and speculate about what chance event might have happened in each. Try to think of three possibilities. Then turn to page 143 to find the answers.

The story of Shariah Harris

Sharia Harris grew up in inner-city Philadelphia and had never ridden a horse. Then one summer, when she was eight years old, a chance event changed her life and she ended up becoming a top U.S. polo player.

The accidental artist

Jon Sarkin is a contemporary artist who has been featured in the *New York Times* and whose work is displayed at The American Museum of Visionary Art. However, until he was thirty-five years old, Sarkin was a chiropractor with more interest in golf than art. Then a life-changing event left Jon with an irresistible desire to draw and paint.

7B I wish!

GRAMMAR | wish, if only, should have
VOCABULARY | idioms: regrets
PRONUNCIATION | chunking in idioms

LISTENING

1 Work in groups. Discuss the questions.
1 Who is the most talented person you know?
2 Do you know anyone who is very talented, but hasn't used their talent?
3 Why might someone not use their talent?

2 A 🔊 7.02 | Listen to three people talking about missed opportunities. What were their talents and why didn't they use them?

B 🔊 7.02 | Number the events (a–e) in the correct order for each speaker. Then listen again and check.

Speaker 1
a was asked to play in a professional trial
b became well known locally, appearing in newspapers
c became an excellent player
d started work
e played football with brothers

Speaker 2
a was told she had a talent for acting
b began an office job
c acted while at school
d decided to stay in the north of England
e went to the theatre for the first time

Speaker 3
a local fame, song played on the radio
b band found a new singer and got a contract
c had singing lessons
d left the band
e started going to college, playing music at weekends

C 🔊 7.03 | Listen and complete the extracts with the phrases you hear. What do you think the phrases mean?
1 I carried on playing for a few more years, then, when I was eighteen, I decided to .... and got a regular job, which I've been doing ever since.
2 … I went to drama classes and my tutor said I could definitely make a career out of it. I thought she was .... , but she seemed convinced I had a real talent.
3 I had to decide whether to stick with the band and try to make it, or quit and get an education. I was kind of .... about it until my dad suggested I try and do both.

D Work in pairs. Discuss the questions.
1 Do you think the speakers were right not to follow their talents? Why?
2 What are the risks and rewards of following your talent, rather than choosing a 'safe' job?

GRAMMAR

wish, if only, should have

3 A Read the extracts from the three speakers. Underline the phrases that express or introduce a regret.
1 I should have gone to the trial.
2 If only I'd kept going with it.
3 I wish I'd stayed with the band.

B Read the extracts in Ex 3A again and answer the questions.
1 Which phrases are followed by the past perfect (had + past participle)?
2 Which phrase is a past modal and is followed by a past participle?

C Learn and practise. Go to the Grammar Bank.

▶▶ page 130 **GRAMMAR BANK**

Unit 7 | Lesson B

VOCABULARY

idioms: regrets

4 A Read some regrets from an online forum. Which person was happy in the end?

MikeD
1 day ago
2.4k Comments
Share | Reply

'I wish ...' What's one thing you wish?

Dancing_Girl
2 hours ago
Share | Reply

I'd always been a good dancer, and when I was fourteen, I had an opportunity to join a famous dance group. At the time I just wanted to hang out with friends and go to parties, so I didn't get back to them. By the time I decided that I did actually want to go, it was too late. I'd **missed the boat**. Now I wish I'd taken my chance.

Andrej_the_giant
5 hours ago
Share | Reply

I wish I'd never started learning Italian. I thought it would **be a piece of cake** because I'm quite good at languages and I'd already studied Spanish, which is quite similar. But I found the more Italian I learnt, the more confused I got between Spanish and Italian, and now I can't speak either!

Luca765
3 hours ago
Share | Reply

I wasn't able to get into law school, which had always been my biggest wish. At the time, I was really disappointed. Instead, I did a degree in English. Now I know it was **a blessing in disguise** because that's how I met my partner. He was studying English in the same department.

JakeJ92
6 hours ago
Share | Reply

I'm really sporty, but I wish I hadn't tried skiing! What a waste of money! I spent the whole time face down in the snow. Let's just say, **it wasn't my cup of tea**.

BigMo
4 hours ago
Share | Reply

I loved my old job, and everyone told me I was doing really well. But when I saw an ad for a job in a bigger company, with a better salary, I applied, and was offered it. Unfortunately, I didn't get on with my new colleagues, and the work was so boring! I guess it's true that **the grass is always greener on the other side**. I wish I hadn't left my first job. If only I'd stayed where I was, I'm sure I would have been much more successful!

SallyR
1 hour ago
Share | Reply

When I was thirty, I decided to set up my own business, making and selling wooden toys. I wish I'd known how difficult it was going to be. Everything went wrong – the products didn't sell, the staff weren't happy, and the company made a loss – so it was **back to the drawing board** for me.

B Read the posts again. Match the idioms in bold with the situations in which we use them (1–6).

1 when you have to start something again from the beginning
2 when something at first appears bad or unlucky, but has good results later
3 when you don't like something or aren't interested in it
4 when something is very easy to achieve
5 when you lost a good opportunity because you were too slow to act
6 when a different place or situation seems more attractive, even though it isn't really better than where you are now

C Complete the sentences with the correct form of idioms from Ex 4B.

1 Losing my job turned out to be a .... because it gave me time to think about what I really wanted. Now I have my own business!
2 When I was younger, I always wanted to move to the city. But now I'm here, I miss the countryside! I guess it's true what they say – ....
3 My dad always wanted me to watch football with him when I was younger, but I thought it was really boring. It just wasn't ....
4 I thought being a teacher would be a .... How wrong I was! I now work longer hours than I did before!
5 I really wanted to see my favourite band play live, but I was working when the tickets went on sale and I .... The tickets sold out within ten minutes.
6 Although we spent weeks putting it together, the investors rejected our proposal, so I guess it's .... for us!

PRONUNCIATION

5 A 🔊 **7.04** | **chunking in idioms** | Listen to the sentences. Note how the idioms are said without pauses, as if they are one word.

B 🔊 **7.04** | Listen again and repeat the idioms.

C Work in pairs. Tell your partner about a time when …
- you thought something was a piece of cake.
- you missed the boat.
- something happened to you which was a blessing in disguise.
- you had to go back to the drawing board.
- you thought something wasn't your cup of tea.
- you thought the grass was greener on the other side.

SPEAKING

6 A Complete the infographic on regrets with the headings in the box.

| Character   Education   Relationships   Travel   Work |

B Work in pairs. What other regrets might people have in each of the areas in Ex 6A?

C Make notes about three things you regret. Use the infographic and the questions (1–3) to help you.
1 What decision did you make and why?
2 What was the result?
3 What do you regret now?

D Work in groups. Take turns discussing your regrets. Talk about your own experiences to support your opinions.

WRITING

a personal essay

7 A Work in pairs. Has anything bad ever happened to you or someone you know that turned out to be a blessing in disguise?

B Turn to page 145 and do the exercises.

8 A Work in pairs. Think of a situation in your life that illustrates each of the idioms (1–5).
1 a blessing in disguise
2 a piece of cake
3 miss the boat
4 back to the drawing board
5 not my cup of tea

B Choose one of the situations you discussed in Ex 8A to write a personal essay about. Make notes about the main events and any interesting or useful details.

C Write your essay. Remember to make it clear how the experience relates to the idiom and what you learnt from it.

Top 6 regrets in life

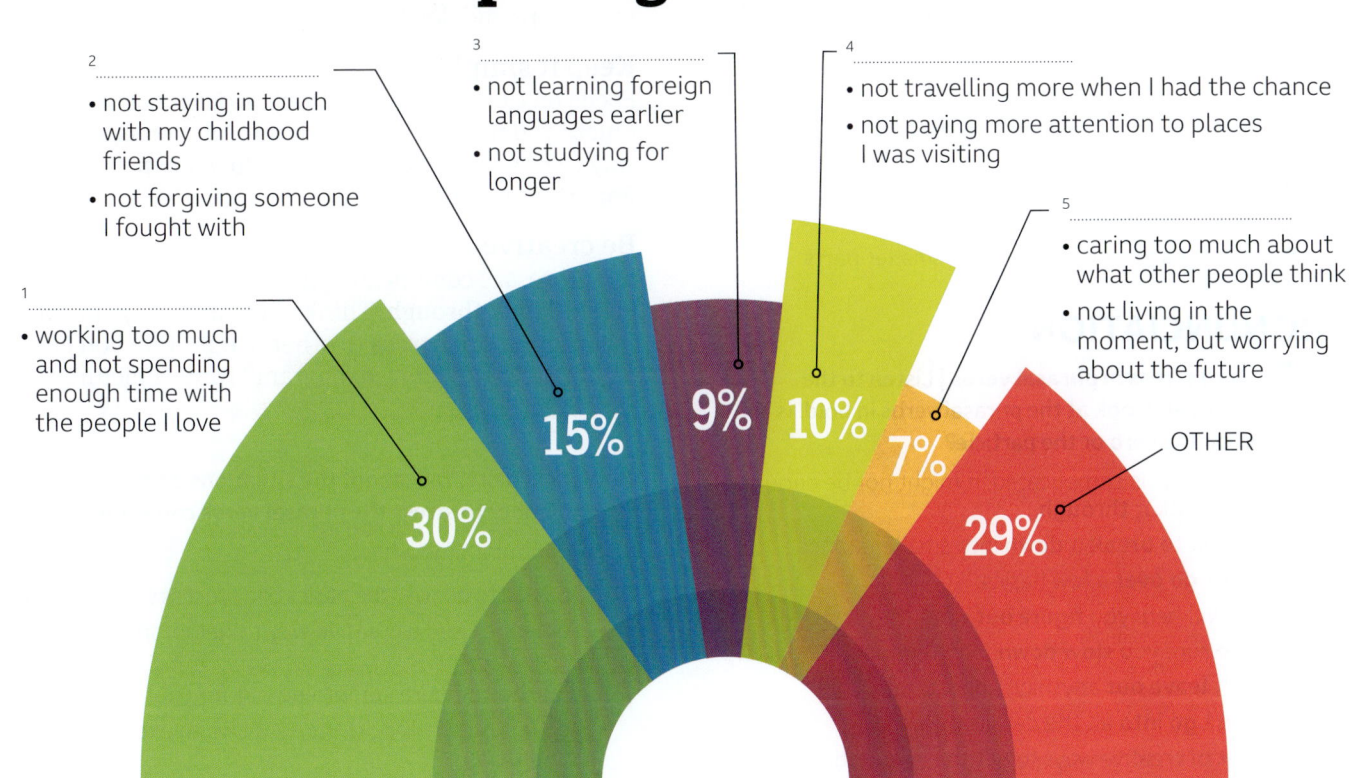

1 — 30%
- working too much and not spending enough time with the people I love

2 — 15%
- not staying in touch with my childhood friends
- not forgiving someone I fought with

3 — 9%
- not learning foreign languages earlier
- not studying for longer

4 — 10%
- not travelling more when I had the chance
- not paying more attention to places I was visiting

5 — 7%
- caring too much about what other people think
- not living in the moment, but worrying about the future

OTHER — 29%

Unit 7 | Lesson C

7C Let me explain

HOW TO ... | describe a process
VOCABULARY | phrasal verbs: explaining
PRONUNCIATION | stress in phrasal verbs

VOCABULARY

phrasal verbs: explaining

1 A Work in groups. Discuss how you do the following activities. Is it important that you do them in a specific way? Do you do them in similar or different ways?
- make tea or coffee
- organise clothes in your wardrobe
- organise food in your fridge

B Read the article about explaining things. Which ideas did you use in your discussions in Ex 1A?

C Scan the article again. Match the phrasal verbs in bold with their meanings (1–8).
1 explain something from beginning to end   talk something through
2 explain something slowly and carefully
3 forget something or not include it
4 speak or do something less quickly
5 communicate information clearly so that other people understand it
6 understand something by thinking about it yourself
7 talk about something in detail
8 separate a longer process into smaller parts

PRONUNCIATION

2 A 🔊 **7.05** | **stress in phrasal verbs** | Listen to the sentences and look at the phrasal verbs in bold. Is the stress on the verb or the particle?
1 If a process is complicated, it might not be enough just to **talk** it **through**.
2 It's best to **break** it **down** into smaller stages.
3 I'll just **go over** a few basics.
4 This will help you **figure out** what they know.
5 Make sure you **slow down** for the important parts.
6 Don't **leave out** anything important.
7 I won't **go into** all the details now.
8 Think of creative ways to **get** the information **across**.

How to explain absolutely anything

Rajeev Khatri | Saturday 29 March | 13.01 GMT

Have you ever tried to explain to a technophobe how to use an app? Or show young children how to cook something? Or even explain to a friend how you like your coffee made? Explaining even the simplest process clearly can be a bit of a challenge, so here are a few tips that might help.

Start right
People have different backgrounds and educational experiences, so don't assume they all know the same things. **Go over** a few basics, to make sure they understand them. This will also help you **figure out** what they know. Then start from there with your explanation.

Take it step by step
Learning a whole new process can be tricky. **Break** it **down** into smaller stages. Make sure you include all the main steps and don't **leave out** any important details.

Keep it simple
Focus on the main points. Don't **go into** all the details unless you have to. Too much information is a sure way to lose your audience. And **slow down** at the most important points.

Be creative
If a process is complicated, it might not be enough just to **talk** it **through**. Think of creative ways to **get** the information **across** to other people. Can you give a demonstration? Show a diagram? Draw a picture?

B Work in pairs. Talk about the situations below. Remember to stress the phrasal verbs correctly.

Talk about a time when:
- you had to go over the basics of a process with someone.
- someone used a creative way to get information across to you.
- you had to figure something out for yourself.
- you left out an important detail when explaining something.

7C

How to ...
describe a process

3 A 🔊 **7.06** | Listen to a YouTuber explaining how to make a vegetable lasagne. Do you think she gives a clear explanation? Why/Why not? What is her secret ingredient?

B 🔊 **7.06** | Listen again and number the pictures in the correct order.

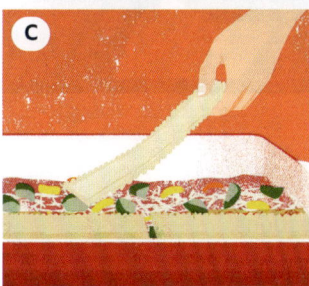

4 A 🔊 **7.07** | Work in pairs. Complete the extracts with the words in the box. Then listen and check.

> begin   careful   essential   involves   optional
> recommend   step   taking   want   you've

1 To .... with, you'll want to get your ingredients together.
2 The next .... is to make the vegetable mixture.
3 I would .... using olive oil.
4 You can also add some fresh herbs, but **this is** ....
5 It's .... that you stir it, so the sauce stays nice and smooth.
6 Be .... not to overcook them.
7 Once .... done that, add a layer of your roasted vegetables.
8 If you ...., you can add my secret ingredient.
9 The final stage .... baking the dish at 180 degrees Celsius.
10 Avoid .... it out too early because it may not be cooked on the inside.

B Complete the table with the phrases in bold in Ex 4A.

describing stages in order	To begin with, you'll want to ... 1 .... 2 .... 3 ....
giving instructions according to necessity	I would recommend using/adding ... 4 .... 5 .... 6 ....
warning about potential problems	Be careful not to ... 7 ....

C Work in pairs. Which phrases in Ex 4A describe:
1 something that is necessary?
2 something that is a good idea, but not completely necessary?

D Learn and practise. Go to the Grammar Bank.

⏵ page 131 **GRAMMAR BANK**

SPEAKING

5 A You are going to teach other students how to do something. Choose an idea from the box or think of your own.

> cooking a dish   creating something (art, objects)
> doing a task in your job or studies
> fixing something   planning a trip

B Make notes on the following:
- things you need
- the main stages/optional stages
- detailed instructions
- potential problems

C Read the Future Skills box and do the task.

FUTURE SKILLS
Communication

When we explain something, we need to predict which parts might be difficult for the listener. Look at your notes again. Which parts of your process are the most complicated? What can you do to simplify them?

D Work in groups. Take turns teaching each other.

MEDIATION SKILLS
making concepts easier to understand

make a concept easier for someone else to understand

⏵ page 154 **MEDIATION BANK**

Unit 7 | Lesson D

7D BBC Street Interviews
Hard work or talent?

GRAMMAR | adverbials of concession
SPEAKING | a discussion about talents
WRITING | a social media post

Constance

Delaney

PREVIEW

1 A Work in groups. Which of the talents in the box do you think are the most and least useful? Why?

> cooking   football   horse riding
> making people laugh   science
> singing   speaking other languages
> telling stories   tennis   writing

B Work in pairs. Discuss the questions.
1 Which of the things in the box are you good at?
2 What other things are you talented at?
3 What things do you have to work hard at? Give examples.

Q1: What are you good at?
Q2: Which is more important – talent or hard work?

VIEW

2 A ▶ Watch the video and answer the questions.
1 Which of the talents in Ex 1A are mentioned?
2 How many speakers think talent is more important than hard work?

B ▶ Watch the first part of the video again. Which speaker would you contact to:
a make you a meal?
b teach you a racket sport?
c treat you if you were sick?
d arrange a party for you?
e perform some music?
f kick a ball around with?
g take you to a football match?

C ▶ Complete the extracts (1–7) with the words in the box. Then watch the second part of the video again to check.

> by   excel   get   in   natural   put   take

1 Delaney: You still need some kind of natural talent to help you .... whatever skill you're doing.
2 Olivia: If you .... enough hard work in, then you're going to succeed.
3 John: You can't get .... on talent alone.
4 Amit: You do need to have some .... ability.
5 Kirsty: Talent is definitely a necessary foundation if you want to .... at something.
6 Flo: You've got to work hard to .... anywhere in life.
7 Constance: Having that drive … will .... you a lot further.

D Work in pairs. Do you agree with the statements in Ex 2C?

3 A Work in pairs. Read the extract from the interview. What do you think the phrase in bold means?

> I'm quite good at cooking. I grew up in Italy, so it **runs in my blood**.

B Work in groups. Which talents run in your blood?

88

GRAMMAR

adverbials of concession

4 A Read the extracts from the interviews. Choose the correct option to complete the rule.

1 I think hard work is more important. **However**, I do believe you still need some type of natural talent to help you in whatever skill you're doing.

2 I personally think that hard work is a lot more important than talent. Obviously, talent is great, **though** when it comes to anything in life, if you put enough hard work in, you're going to succeed.

3 On the one hand, talent is fundamental because I think you do need to have some natural ability. But, **on the other hand**, talent's not enough without hard work.

We can use words like *however, though, on the other hand* to introduce **a contrasting idea / an example**.

B Learn and practise. Go to the Grammar Bank.

⏩ page 132 **GRAMMAR BANK**

SPEAKING

a discussion about talents

5 A Make notes about three talents you wish you had (e.g. speak another language, play an instrument) and why.

B Work in groups. Discuss the talents you made notes about. Use the questions to help you.

1 How could your classmates use these talents to help themselves and others?
2 Who do you know that has these talents already? What can we learn from these people?
3 Are there any negative sides to having these talents?

WRITING

a social media post

6 A Work in groups. Discuss the questions.

1 Do you ever take part in online discussions?
2 Have you ever disagreed with someone online? What happened?

B Write a social media post. Go to the Writing Bank.

⏩ page 107 **WRITING BANK**

7 REVIEW

GRAMMAR
past modals of deduction

1 A Choose the correct words to complete the sentences.
1. He **must / can't** have left yet. His bag is still here.
2. If you'd stayed in that job, you **might / must** have been promoted. You were doing very well.
3. She's been working for months in the same office as you. Surely you **can't / must** have met her!
4. Let's ask in reception if they have your keys. They **might / can't** have been handed in.
5. I can't find my phone anywhere. I **must / couldn't** have left it at home.
6. Where's Angela? She **can't / might** have gone home yet, her bag's here and her computer's on.

B Work in pairs. Read the scenarios and speculate about what might have happened. Then check your answers on page 143.
1. A pianist performed a concert in a famous concert hall. She played perfectly, but nobody clapped when she finished. Why?
2. A girl fell off a seven-metre-tall ladder. She wasn't hurt. How?
3. Two people were playing chess. They both won. How is this possible?

wish, if only, should have

2 A Write sentences about your wishes and regrets. Use the topics in the box and the sentence beginnings.

> dreams   education   family or relationships
> money   possessions   travel   your home

I wish …   If only …   I should have …

B Work in pairs. Tell your partner about your wishes and regrets. Ask and answer questions about each one.

VOCABULARY

3 A Complete the questions with compound adjectives made using a word from each box.

> A | life   long   ~~second~~   time   widely   world
>
> B | changing   consuming   famous
>   ~~hand~~   lasting   respected

1. Do you prefer new or <u>second-hand</u> books?
2. What are your most _____ jobs or duties?
3. Would you enjoy being a _____ actor, musician or sportsperson? Why/Why not?
4. Name three _____ events in your life.
5. If you could choose one profession to be a _____ expert in, what would it be and why?
6. What will be the _____ effects of you learning English?

B Work in pairs. Ask and answer the questions.

4 Complete the sentences using the correct form of the idioms in the box.

> a blessing in disguise   a piece of cake
> go back to the drawing board
> grass is greener on the other side
> not my cup of tea   missed the boat

1. I thought this job would be different. But I guess the _____ .
2. I learnt that song really quickly. It was _____ .
3. That idea won't work. I think we need to _____ .
4. He should have applied for that position weeks ago. I think he's probably _____ .
5. I was made redundant, but it was _____ as I would never have got this job otherwise!
6. I tried learning the trumpet, but it's _____ .

5 Choose the correct words to complete the sentences.
1. There are a few things I would like to talk **to / through** before we get started.
2. With a difficult task, it's important to **take / break** it down into manageable stages.
3. I didn't catch that last bit. Could you slow **up / down** a little, please?
4. Try not to **go / be** into too much detail.
5. Be careful not to **keep / leave** out any important details.
6. This bit is quite difficult, but I'm sure that between us we can figure it **out / up**.

6 A Complete the article with one word in each gap.

What's your talent?

Do you ever think to yourself, 'perhaps I should ¹_____ been an artist' or 'If ²_____ I was a dancer!'? Perhaps you say to yourself, 'I ³_____ I hadn't given up art' or 'If only I ⁴_____ continued to dance'.

You might have given up a passion because you thought you weren't very talented at it. Someone might ⁵_____ made a negative comment about your work. But therein lies a problem. At that time, you were just learning, so you hadn't fully developed your talent. Imagine how things might have been different if that person had said, 'Wow, what a fantastic talent you have. You should do more of that.'

To get really good at anything takes years of practice. It's not a piece of ⁶_____ . But you probably stopped too soon.

Now, years later, you might feel like you've ⁷_____ the boat. You're stuck in an ⁸_____ -consuming job you don't enjoy. Let's talk through the options, to help you figure ⁹_____ what you want to do. Remember, it's never too late to make a life-¹⁰_____ decision and go back to the ¹¹_____ board and discover your true talent.

B 🔊 R7.01 | Listen and check your answers.

community 8

VLOGS

Q: What does 'community' mean to you?

1 ▶ Watch the video. What ideas do the people mention?

2 Discuss what 'community' means to you. Give examples.

GSE LEARNING OBJECTIVES

8A READING | Read about co-living communities: collocations with *go, have* and *make*; describing homes and living conditions; participle clauses

Discuss living in a co-living community

Pronunciation: pitch in participle clauses

Write an application letter/email

8B LISTENING | Understand a presentation on world issues: world issues

Discuss hypothetical ideas: conditionals with conjunctions

Pronunciation: stress in conditional sentences

8C HOW TO ... | develop an argument: prepositional phrases

Pronunciation: sounding persuasive

8D BBC PROGRAMME | Understand a documentary about someone making a difference

Give a presentation on a project: phrases with *get*

Write a mission statement

Unit 8 | Lesson A

8A A new way of living

GRAMMAR | participle clauses
VOCABULARY | collocations with *go*, *have* and *make*; describing homes and living conditions
PRONUNCIATION | pitch in participle clauses

READING

1 A Work in pairs. Discuss the questions.
  1 What are the pros and cons of living with other people?
  2 Do you feel part of a community where you live?

B Read an article about co-living spaces. Which of the following topics is not mentioned?
  - convenience
  - data privacy
  - the high cost of rent
  - loneliness
  - networking
  - rising house prices
  - rules and regulations
  - shared facilities

C Read the article again. What arguments does the writer make for and against co-living? Make notes.

D Work in pairs. Discuss the questions.
  1 What arguments do you find the most convincing?
  2 Would you like to live in a co-living space?

GRAMMAR

participle clauses

2 A Read the sentences (1–3) from the article and answer the questions (a and b) about the participle clauses in bold.

  1 **Having decided to move to a city**, young people face the challenging task of finding somewhere affordable to live.
  2 **Moving into co-living accommodation**, many people find they have a ready-made community.
  3 **Having moved into co-living accommodation two years ago**, Brad Hoffner, twenty-four, found that the people were friendly, but he was shocked at the size of the small 'box' rooms.

Which participle clause(s) suggest(s):
  a someone finished an action before something else happened?
  b two actions happen at more or less the same time?

B Which two verb forms are used at the start of a participle clause?

C Learn and practise. Go to the Grammar Bank.

  ▶▶ page 133 **GRAMMAR BANK**

'Co-living': the end of urban loneliness – or just another way to make a profit?

With huge numbers of young people moving to expensive cities in search of work, lack of affordable housing and loneliness have become big issues. Could co-living spaces be the answer?

Having decided to move to a city, young people face the challenging task of finding somewhere affordable to live. They often end up living alone, working long hours and locked into expensive rental contracts. It can be hard to find opportunities to meet up with like-minded people. Nowadays, many young workers have the opportunity to work remotely and don't need to be in an office from nine to five. These remote workers often move from city to city, which makes it hard to meet people.

Co-living means living with many other people in one space that encourages residents to interact and work together. Co-living residences are appearing in cities all over the world; from Berlin to San Francisco, Tokyo to New York. They offer residents affordable accommodation in a sociable environment. Residents generally have their own small bedroom and bathroom, but they share living spaces, workspaces, kitchen spaces and laundry rooms with other residents. Some co-living companies put residents together with like-minded people, who are around the same age and have similar interests. Moving into co-living accommodation, many people find they have a ready-made community and lots of opportunities for networking. Sharing interests and values, residents are also able to enjoy workshops and events in the communal living spaces.

The Collective Old Oak is a huge co-living apartment block in northwest London. It doesn't market itself as 'apartments'. It calls itself a 'global living movement' and promises a 'dream lifestyle' to young workers who can't afford to buy their own homes. The 550 residents who call this building home pay a monthly rent to live in rooms that are hotel-sized, but which benefit from communal amenities and events. There's a cinema room, a co-working space, a music venue, a library, a restaurant, a roof terrace, a games room and a gym. You can book classes in pasta making, graffiti or yoga. There's a room-cleaning service and you can leave with one month's notice. This kind of accommodation appeals to young people who are looking for a convenient place to live in the city, without any long-term commitment. Benjamin Webb, 37, has lived at the Collective for eight months. He says co-living offered him a sense of freedom after two decades of renting in London. He enjoys the flexibility and feeling like he is part of the community.

However, co-living also has its downsides. Shared living spaces don't offer a lot of privacy. Although some residences try to group people according to their jobs, age and interests, how effective is this in reality? Wouldn't it be better for you to actually choose a group of friends and find a place to live together? There is also concern about the rules which are imposed. Residents in some co-living spaces complain that their lives are being overly controlled. Watched on CCTV, residents are contacted if their behaviour breaks any of the community rules. In addition to that, many co-living spaces require you to download an app, giving you access to messages and chat groups with other residents, all of which has led to concerns about data privacy. Critics argue that property developers are promoting co-living spaces simply to make more money by renting out rooms which are very small. Having moved into co-living accommodation two years ago, Brad Hoffner, twenty-four, found that the people were friendly, but he was shocked at the size of the small 'box' rooms. He didn't think the space was liveable in the long term.

So, are co-living spaces the future? Well, on the one hand, it seems that co-living can suit young people who are looking for somewhere cheap and convenient to live in the city, and need a ready-made social group. On the other hand, it can feel a bit like you're living in a hotel – a space that's just too impersonal for any real sense of community. Perhaps it's all just a matter of perspective.

8A

PRONUNCIATION

3 A 🔊 8.01 | **pitch in participle clauses** | Listen to the sentences in Ex 2A. Does the speaker use a higher or lower pitch on the participle clauses?

B Work in pairs. Take turns completing the sentences with your own ideas. Focus on the pitch you use.
1 Having lived in … , I …
2 Moving to … , I …
3 Having decided to … , I …

VOCABULARY

collocations with *go*, *have* and *make*

4 A Work in pairs. Complete the texts with *go, have* or *make*. Which place sounds the most enjoyable to live in?

Sällbo – HELSINGBORG, SWEDEN
Proposed as a way to tackle loneliness, this community is only for under-25s and pensioners, and residents agree to spend two hours a week socialising with their neighbours. Both groups benefit and rely on each other when things [1]_____ **wrong**. Friendships form as residents [2]_____ **a point** of watching films together, eating together, or just learning what they [3]_____ **in common**.

Coworksurf – CASCAIS, PORTUGAL
Situated in fashionable Cascais, just outside Lisbon, Coworksurf offers residents the chance to enjoy a beautiful, spacious villa with a pool. They also [4]_____ **the opportunity** to do courses in yoga or climbing, and with Guincho beach close by, there's no excuse not to [5]_____ **a go** at surfing. The house is ideal for people looking for somewhere that working on a project can [6]_____ **hand in hand** with leisure pursuits.

Arcosanti – PHOENIX, ARIZONA
In 1970, architect Paolo Soleri decided he couldn't [7]_____ **sense** of modern cities and set out to create Acrosanti, an experimental eco-city. Unfortunately, things don't always [8]_____ **according to plan,** and the project remains unfinished. However, architects keen to [9]_____ **a difference** continue to work and live there today, collaborating on ideas for sustainable cities of the future.

B Complete the questions with the correct form of collocations in Ex 4A. Then ask and answer them in pairs.
1 When was the last time you _____ to do something exciting?
2 When was the last time something you were doing didn't _____ ?
3 When was the last time you _____ at something new?

C Find words for describing homes and living conditions in the texts in Ex 4A. Can you think of any others?

D Learn and practise. Go to the Vocabulary Bank.

>> page 141 **VOCABULARY BANK** describing homes and living conditions

93

Unit 8 | Lesson A

SPEAKING

5 A Work in pairs. Read the Future Skills box and do the task.

> **FUTURE SKILLS**
> **Collaboration**
>
> When you discuss issues as a group, it's important to encourage members of the group to explain their thinking. You can ask questions like, 'Can you go into a bit more detail?' or 'Can you give us an example?' What other expressions can you use?

B Work in groups. Look at the co-living spaces in Ex 4A again. Discuss the questions. Ask other students to explain their thinking.

1 What do you think are the main advantages and disadvantages of each space?
2 Would any of these projects work in your area? Why/Why not?
3 What do you think can go wrong in co-living accommodation?
4 If you had the opportunity to live in any kind of living situation, what would you choose?
5 How does where you live affect your life?
6 What do you have in common with the people you live/work with?

WRITING

an application letter/email

6 A Work in pairs. Read the job advert. What qualities and experience does someone need to apply for this job?

Multiple Roles
WhiteSpace | London / New York / Paris
3 days ago | 9 applicants

WhiteSpace CoLiving is one of the best co-living operators worldwide. We're looking for fun, sociable and outgoing people to join our team! We need people involved in architecture, marketing, finance, events management, sports, sustainability, catering and social media management.

We're looking for people to help build our brand, create a vibrant community of young professionals and help WhiteSpace CoLiving make a real difference!

If you would like to join our team, please get in touch. Email Alice Munroe on A.Munroe@WhiteSpace.com, telling us a little bit about yourself and why you think you would be a good fit for the company. We look forward to hearing from you.

B Read the job application. Do you think Evelina is well suited to the position at WhiteSpace CoLiving? Why/Why not?

To: Alice Munroe
From: Evelina Martuzzi
Subject: Application for role of chef

Dear Alice Munroe,

[1] I am a chef currently working full-time at the Plaza restaurant in Brighton. Having seen your advertisement on social media, I am writing to apply for a position as a chef in your catering team.

[2] I graduated from the renowned Gourmet Institute four years ago, with distinction. Since then, I have held several positions within 4-star restaurants for a leading hospitality group and spent the past two years working as a chef on luxury yachts. Whether I am preparing a meal for a household dinner party, or an event for more than 250 people, I enjoy creating dining experiences that bring people together.

[3] I believe in sourcing local and seasonal produce where possible, and aiming for zero waste. I have a particular interest in plant-based diets and using influences from other cuisines to keep menus fresh and exciting.

[4] Attached is my CV which will provide you with additional information about my experience and qualifications. I have completed your online application and would be happy to provide any further information you require. I can provide references if necessary and I can be available for interview at your convenience. It would be a pleasure to prepare some sample dishes for you to give you a taste of my culinary style.

I look forward to hearing from you.

Yours sincerely,

Evelina Martuzzi

C Scan the email again. Match the paragraphs (1–4) with the topics (a–d).
a attitude
b availability
c basic biographical information
d education and experience

D Find formal phrases in the email that match the informal phrases (1–6).
1 Get in touch soon.
2 I can meet up with you whenever you want.
3 With best wishes,
4 I can give you any other information you need.
5 I have worked in restaurants
6 I would be happy to …

7 A You are going to write an application email for a position at WhiteSpace. Use the questions to help you make notes.
1 What job/area would you like to apply for?
2 What relevant skills or experience do you have?
3 Do you have any interesting specialities or expertise?

B Write your email, using your notes and the model in Ex 6B to help you.

8B If the world ...

GRAMMAR | conditionals with conjunctions
VOCABULARY | world issues
PRONUNCIATION | stress in conditional sentences

VOCABULARY

world issues

1 A Work in pairs. What issues/problems do you worry about in your country?

B Read the comments about world issues. Match the words/phrases in bold with the definitions (1–10).
1 the ability to read and write
2 behaviour/treatment that is fair and correct
3 languages that may soon not exist
4 containing too many people
5 buildings for people to live in
6 the number of people without a job
7 an increase in temperature around the world, caused by pollution
8 the state of not having a place to live
9 the state of being poor
10 the rights that every person in a country has

C Complete the sentences with the words from Ex 1B.
1 An estimated 698 million people are living in .... and have to survive on less than $1.90 a day.
2 As a result of ...., sea levels have risen by nearly 180 mm since 1990.
3 .... rose to record levels last year, with an estimated 3.4 million people out of work.
4 The project aims to tackle .... by helping rough sleepers find a place to stay.
5 .... is a huge issue in the city, with nearly 38,000 residents per square mile.
6 The after-school reading groups help develop the .... of students that are falling behind.
7 Preventing people from voting denies them one of their basic ....
8 A lack of affordable .... means that many young people are simply unable to afford their own home.
9 Basque is one of many .... in Europe, with fewer than 660,000 speakers left.
10 The footballer has used his social media platforms to campaign for social ....

D Work in groups. Rank the world issues in Ex 1B from 1 (the most important) to 10 (the least important).

Overcrowding is a big concern in my country. There just isn't enough space for all the people who live in the cities.

I think **unemployment** is the cause of many other problems around the world, because if you don't have a job, usually you can't have a good standard of living.

Low levels of **literacy** are a serious issue in many countries. If you can't read, you don't have access to higher education and good jobs.

In my country, a lack of cheap **housing** means it's hard for people to find places to live.

I think **poverty** is the world's biggest issue because it means people don't have enough money to buy basic things like food and medicine.

Where I live, there is always a fight for **justice** because the laws aren't always used fairly and people aren't treated equally.

People in my country are really beginning to feel the effects of **global warming**. Rising sea levels, water shortages and extreme weather events are all caused by the increase in the Earth's temperature.

In my country, we're still fighting for **civil rights** to protect people's social and political freedom.

Few people talk about this, but I think allowing languages to die out is a huge issue. There are many **endangered languages** which will probably disappear completely in the next fifty years.

Homelessness is a big problem in my city. There are many people living on the streets.

Unit 8 | Lesson B

If the world were a village of 100 people

There are over 7.5 billion people in the world, and almost 200 countries. Of these countries, 13 have populations larger than 100 million. China and India have well over a billion people each. But imagine the world had only 100 people and they all lived in one village. Imagine each person represented over 75 million people. If we knew these 100 people, what would we learn about the world and ourselves?

Literacy
...... people can't read

Poverty
...... people live on less than $2 per day

Language & endangered languages
14 speak Mandarin Chinese
8 speak Hindi
...... speak English
6 speak Arabic
...... speak Spanish
7,000 other languages
3,000 endangered languages

こんにちは

Higher education
...... go on to college/university

Electricity
...... have no access to electricity

Housing
...... have no access to decent housing

Technology
...... have no access to the internet

Phones
...... own a mobile phone

Transport
...... own a car

Clean water
...... have no access to safe drinking water

Population
...... from Asia
16 from Africa
10 from Europe
...... from South/Central America/Caribbean
5 from Canada & USA
...... from Oceania (Australia, New Zealand and the Pacific Islands)

LISTENING

2 A Work in pairs. Read the infographic and guess which number out of 100 completes each statistic.

B 🔊 8.02 | Listen to the introduction to a talk about world issues and check your answers.

C Work in pairs. Which of the statistics surprised you the most? Why?

3 A 🔊 8.03 | Listen to the next part of the talk. Which issue from the infographic does the speaker discuss and what is the aim of the talk?

B 🔊 8.03 | Work in pairs. Answer the questions. Then listen again and check.
1 According to the speaker, what is the main reason a language becomes endangered?
2 What does the speaker believe dies alongside a language?
3 How does the speaker feel about Cornish surviving?
4 What methods are people using in Bolivia to revive endangered languages?
5 What is the speaker's opinion of Wikitongues' projects?
6 According to the speaker, what will keep endangered languages alive?

C Work in groups. Discuss the questions.
1 Do you think it is important to preserve endangered languages? Why?/Why not?
2 Can you think of any other ways that communities could preserve their language?

GRAMMAR

conditionals with conjunctions

4 Match the extracts from the talk (1–4) with the descriptions (a–d).
1 If we all spoke the same language, wouldn't it be easier to communicate?
2 Simply put, if a language has no native speakers, it dies.
3 If their language dies, part of their culture will die, too.
4 If there hadn't been a conscious effort to keep Cornish alive, it would have disappeared.

a zero conditional: to talk about things that are always/generally true
b first conditional: to talk about the future consequences of a present situation
c second conditional: to talk about imaginary or unlikely situations in the present or future
d third conditional: to talk about imaginary situations in the past

5 A Read the sentences. Do the conjunctions in bold in each sentence have a similar meaning?
1 **As long as/On condition that** we record and document these languages, they'll survive.
2 **Unless/Provided that** things change, over 3,000 languages could disappear in eighty years.

B Learn and practise. Go to the Grammar Bank.

⏩ page 134 **GRAMMAR BANK**

PRONUNCIATION

6 A 🔊 8.04 | stress in conditional sentences |
Listen and underline the word that is given the main stress in each sentence. Why do you think these words are stressed?

1. Provided the language is actually used, it can survive.
2. Unless we make an effort, many languages will die.
3. As long as people speak the language, it will survive.

B Write three conditional sentences using the conditions and results in the boxes.

Conditions

> there are plenty of jobs available
> education is available to everyone
> we build cheaper housing
> we reduce carbon emissions

Results

> fewer people will be homeless
> poverty will decrease
> levels of literacy will improve
> living standards will improve
> global warming will reduce
> unemployment will fall
> there will be less overcrowding

Unless there are plenty of jobs available, poverty will not decrease/unemployment will not fall.

C Work in pairs. Take turns reading your sentences. Remember to use the correct stress. Then, discuss whether you agree with them or not.

A: If education is available to everyone, living standards will improve.
B: That's true. If you have a good education, you can get a better job, and have a better life.

SPEAKING

7 A Read the Future Skills box. In what industries or subjects do you think 'thought experiments' are most useful? Why? Have you ever done anything like this?

FUTURE SKILLS
Creative and critical thinking

A 'thought experiment' involves imagining something and then asking questions about the consequences. Thought experiments are useful for solving problems and finding new ideas.

What if everyone lived to 150? Would the world become overcrowded? Would there be enough housing and food? Would we need more hospitals and care homes?

B Choose five of the 'What if ...' statements below and make notes about the main consequences of each.

What if ...
- everyone spoke the same language?
- everyone lived to 150?
- money hadn't been invented?
- all work was done by robots?
- leaders were chosen randomly instead of through elections?
- electricity hadn't been discovered?
- there was no poverty because everyone earned the same?
- cars were banned?
- rent was abolished and housing was free?
- parents were paid to stay at home and look after children?
- borders had never been invented?

C Work in groups. Take turns discussing your ideas. Explain whether you agree with each other or not and why.

Unless motorbikes were banned as well as cars, we'd still have the same problem in many parts of the world – too much pollution.

Unit 8 | Lesson C

8C Online communities

HOW TO ... | develop an argument
VOCABULARY | prepositional phrases
PRONUNCIATION | sounding persuasive

VOCABULARY

prepositional phrases

1 A Work in pairs. What kinds of online communities are there? Are you a member of any?

B Read the article about building communities. Answer the questions.
1 What did Annie Lorraine do when people were protesting near her home?
2 What happened to Annie's group after the clean-up?
3 Do you use any social media platforms to keep in touch with people in your neighbourhood?

2 A Read the article again and complete the prepositional phrases (1–7) with *in*, *at*, *on*, *by* or *out*.

B Which prepositional phrase:
1 means 'generally'?
2 introduces more information which emphasises a point you have just made?
3 introduces the reason why someone does something?
4 means 'at the minimum'?
5 is used to emphasise a comparison and make it stronger?
6 introduces a contrasting fact
7 describes a situation where you have no power over something?

C Choose the correct prepositional phrases to complete the statements.
1 **In order to / In fact** truly understand someone's point of view, you need to talk to them in person, not online.
2 **At least / By far** the best way to develop a community is to work together on a project.
3 **On the whole / Out of control** it's easier to develop friendships online than face-to-face.
4 **At the same time / By far** social media helps bring people together online and offline.

D Work in pairs. Do you agree or disagree with the statements in Ex 2C? Why?

Building better communities

Amal Singh | Monday 18 January | 08.35 GMT

It seems that ¹............ **far** the most important factor relating to how happy you are to live in an area relates less to your physical surroundings and more to whether you feel connected to your neighbours and part of some kind of local community.

More and more people looking for a strong sense of community tend to go online to connect with like-minded people from around the globe. However, ²............ **the whole**, while people might claim to have hundreds of 'friends' on social networks, they probably find it difficult to name ³............ **least** six people that live in their local neighbourhood.

Can social media help to build better local communities?

In 2011, a series of violent protests took place in London, which left property damaged and mess in the streets. When Annie Lorraine could smell burning near her home one evening, she knew a protest was starting and feared that things would get ⁴............ **of control**. Feeling upset and wanting to show that not all young people felt the same as those protesting on the streets, she set up a Facebook group organising a community riot clean-up for the following day. The next morning, fifty of the 900 people who had joined the group overnight met ⁵............ **order to** clean up the mess that was left in the streets. ⁶............ **fact**, when they arrived, a local volunteer group had already done most of the work so Annie's group wasn't needed. ⁷............ **the same time**, they were happy to have had the opportunity to contribute and many of them stayed in touch and offered to volunteer again on a regular basis.

Social media, which originally seemed to focus on building better online communities, is increasingly contributing towards building better local communities as well.

How to ...
develop an argument

3 A Work in pairs. Read the statement and write two ideas in favour of it and two ideas against.

Online communities are the best way to connect with people like you.

B 🔊 8.05 | Listen to two people discussing the statement in Ex 3A. Do they agree or disagree with it? Why?

4 A 🔊 8.05 | Work in pairs. Complete the extracts. Then listen again and check.

1. I'd like to start off by saying that I completely _____ with the idea that ...
2. This is true for three main _____. Firstly, online communities allow us to connect with _____ all over the world.
3. A good example of this is when I get home from _____ and I'm tired ...
4. As a result, I still manage to have a good _____ even when I'm busy.
5. Secondly, online communities involve people from all types of _____ and cultural experiences ...
6. For instance, one _____ I belong to has people in it from India, Argentina ...
7. The obvious impact of this is to broaden our understanding and widen our _____ of a particular area ...
8. And finally, online communities are more _____.
9. As far as I can see, whilst online communities allow us to _____ with people ...

B Complete the stages for structuring an argument with the headings in the box.

> Describing the impact   Making a claim
> Presenting evidence and examples

1 _____
I'd like to start off by saying ...
The first point I'd like to make is that ...
Secondly, Thirdly, etc.; Most importantly, ...
As far as I can see, ...
One thing we can be sure of is ...

2 _____
This is true for three main reasons. Firstly, ...
A good example of this is ...
For instance, ...
Apparently, ...
The evidence suggests that ...

3 _____
As a result, ...
The obvious impact of this is ...
This would lead to ...

C Learn and practise. Go to the Grammar Bank.

▶▶ page 135 **GRAMMAR BANK**

PRONUNCIATION

5 A 🔊 8.06 | **sounding persuasive** | Listen to some of the extracts from Ex 4A again. Underline the words that are given extra stress and draw a (/) to show long pauses.

1. I'd like to start off by saying that I completely agree ...
2. This is true for three main reasons. Firstly, online communities ...
3. A good example of this is when I get home from work and I'm tired and ...
4. As a result, I still manage to have a good social life.
5. The obvious impact of this is to broaden our understanding ...
6. As far as I can see, whilst online communities allow us to ...

B Work in pairs. Do you agree or disagree that online communities are the best way to connect with people like you? Take turns making sentences using the prompts in Ex 5A.

SPEAKING

6 A As a class, choose a topic to debate.
- Social media has killed the art of conversation.
- The online world encourages us to only mix with people who share our world view.
- Online education is better than being in a physical classroom.
- Social media is the best way to make friends.
- The internet is encouraging us to spend too much time alone.

B Work in groups. Split your group into two teams, A and B. Then follow the instructions to plan your arguments.

Team A: Plan arguments **in favour** of the debate topic. Make notes using the claims, evidence and impact structure.

Team B: Plan arguments **against** the debate topic. Make notes using the claims, evidence and impact structure.

C Hold your debate. The two teams should take turns to present their arguments.

D Hold a vote. Vote with your own personal opinion.

> **MEDIATION SKILLS**
> using direct and indirect quotations
> make a discursive argument on a topic
>
> ▶▶ page 156 **MEDIATION BANK**

Unit 8 | Lesson D

8D BBC Documentary
Second shot

VOCABULARY | phrases with *get*
SPEAKING | a presentation on a project
WRITING | a mission statement

PREVIEW

1 A Work in groups. Discuss the questions.
  1 What situations can lead to people becoming homeless?
  2 What kinds of things could help them back into society?

B Read about the programme. Why do you think Julius chose to employ homeless people?

Amazing Humans
Amazing Humans is a BBC programme that looks at the inspiring achievements of ordinary people. In this episode, we meet Julius, a young man who opened a café in east London designed to help homeless people get their lives back on track – by training them as baristas.

VIEW

2 A ▶ Watch the video and answer the questions.
  1 How did Julius help the man called Edge?
  2 In what two ways does the café help people who are homeless?

B ▶ Work in pairs. Are these statements True (T) or False (F)? Watch again and check.
  1 Julius wanted to change people's ideas about homelessness.
  2 People need to have a lot of confidence before they start work with Julius.
  3 The training helps people to develop different skills.
  4 The 'pay it forward' scheme lets people pay for their own food before they eat it.
  5 The café has given away over 7,000 coffees and 5,000 meals to homeless people.
  6 Julius feels sad when people leave and he never sees them again.

8D

VOCABULARY

phrases with *get*

3 A Read the sentences. Match the phrases in bold from the video with the meanings (a–g).

1 Julius thinks it's easy for people to fall into homelessness and difficult for them to **get out**.
2 When you go into the café, you shouldn't know whether the person serving you has been working in the industry for ten years, or whether it is someone just **getting their life back together**.
3 Julius works with one trainee at a time and tries to help them **get** their confidence **back**.
4 Edge used to think it would be difficult for him to '**get to the other side**'. Now all his dreams are coming true.
5 Even though Julius is only young, he's seen enough to understand. And he's **got a big heart**.
6 Julius showed me a lot of things and helped me **get to where I am** now.
7 One day they come to us and say, 'Oh, Julius I've got a hostel. I've **got somewhere to live** now'.

a have a home
b reach the end of a difficult situation
c be a kind and generous person
d reach the good situation you are now in
e escape from a difficult situation
f change your life so it is organised and under control
g get something again after you have lost it

B Work in pairs. Use the phrases in Ex 3A talk about how the café helps homeless people.

SPEAKING

a presentation on a project

4 A 🔊 8.07 | Listen to someone talking about another project designed to help homeless people. Answer the questions.

1 What is the aim of the project?   2 How does it work?

B 🔊 8.07 | Listen again. Tick the phrases you hear.

KEY PHRASES

A huge problem/issue …
One of the biggest problems/issues …
According to our research, …
At the same time/In addition to this/On top of this, …
There are large numbers (of people) …
One solution to the problem could be …
The project is run by … (volunteers) …
The purpose of (On the Street Food Bank) is to ….

C Work in groups. Plan a project to help people in need. Use the questions to help you.

1 What problem is your project trying to solve?
2 How will the project help to solve the problem?
3 Who will run the project?
4 What do you need to make it happen?

D Present your project to the class. Which is the best idea and why?

WRITING

a mission statement

5 A Work in pairs. Read the definition. Why do you think mission statements are important?

mission statement (n)
a formal summary of a company or organisation's aims and values

B Write a mission statement. Go to the Writing Bank.

➡ page 107 **WRITING BANK**

8 REVIEW

GRAMMAR
participle clauses

1 A Choose the correct options to complete the anecdote.

¹**Having bought / Buying** my ticket the day before, I avoided the queues and went straight to the platform. After a few minutes, my train arrived. I climbed aboard and found my seat. Shortly afterwards, I went to the train restaurant and ordered a meal. ²**Having waited / Waiting** for my food, I saw someone I recognised. It was Petrov. We'd been in Tehran together, and later Jakarta and Brazzaville. ³**Not spending / Having spent** so much time together, we'd become friends. I smiled and walked over. ⁴**Not having seen / Seeing** him for twenty years, I was thrilled to catch up with him. Then I noticed a new scar on his face. ⁵**Not wanting / Not having wanted** to hurt his feelings, I decided not to ask about it. I waited for him to look up from his food and when he did, I said, 'Hello, Petrov.' ⁶**Having been / Being** away all those years, he had understandably forgotten who I was. But when I told him my name, his expression changed immediately.

B Write a few sentences to finish the story. Then compare your endings in pairs.

2 Complete the sentences with the correct participle form of the verbs in the box.

| eat   know   leave   live   look up |
| push   realise   work |

1 .... in the industry for the past three decades, I can assure you that isn't true!
2 .... , she was astonished to see a bull charging straight towards her.
3 .... that they were distracted, he got up and made a run for the door.
4 .... all of his meal, he now started to look enviously at hers.
5 .... which path to take, he decided to call his university professor for advice.
6 .... in Hanoi for eight years, she was now pretty much fluent in Vietnamese.
7 .... her way through the crowd, she wondered why it was so busy that night.
8 .... his wallet at home, he now had no way of paying for the meal.

conditionals with conjunctions

3 Complete the conversations with no more than two words in each gap.

1 A: Have you decided whether to move into that community?
   B: I'm thinking about it. If I move there, it .... be very convenient.
2 A: Do you think I should join that club now?
   B: Yes, I do. You'll miss the opportunity .... you join now.
3 A: I'm thinking of starting my own wiki. What do you think?
   B: Yes, if .... you, I'd do it immediately – it's a really good idea.
4 A: Do you want to join our book club?
   B: Yes, I'll join as .... I don't have to read science fiction!
5 A: Can I borrow your bike?
   B: Yes, I'll lend it to you on .... you clean it before you give it back!
6 A: Are you learning the guitar?
   B: Yes, I .... learnt ages ago if I'd had more time.

4 Rewrite the sentences using the words in brackets.

1 We're going to get stuck in traffic if we don't leave now.
   .... (unless), we're going to get stuck in traffic.
2 If you promise to be back by 5 p.m., I'll let you borrow the car.
   You can borrow the car .... (condition) back by 5 p.m.
3 We should be finished by December if everything goes well.
   .... (provided), we should be finished by December.
4 If you don't pay me the same amount as Felix, I'll leave the company.
   I'll leave the company .... (unless) the same amount as Felix.
5 If you maintain it properly, the washing machine should last for years.
   The washing machine should last for years, ... (providing) properly.
6 If I can work from home three days a week, I'll take the role.
   I'll take the role .... (condition) can work from home three days a week.
7 I'm sure you'll pass all of your exams if you work hard enough.
   .... (providing) enough, I'm sure you'll pass all of your exams.
8 Global temperatures will continue to rise if we don't act now.
   .... (unless), global temperatures will continue to rise.

VOCABULARY

5 A Complete the statements with the words in the box. There are two words that you don't need.

| done | equal | goes | gone |
| have | make | makes | same |

1 Literacy .... a big difference in people's lives. If you can read, you can get an education.
2 Poverty often .... hand in hand with poor health.
3 Civil rights mean that people should have .... opportunities in life.
4 It's hard to .... sense of global warming because the science is so difficult to explain.
5 Lack of housing and high unemployment .... one thing in common: they are the result of too many people chasing after too few opportunities.
6 If large numbers of people are in prison, maybe something has .... wrong with the country's justice system.

B Work in pairs. Do you agree with the statements in Ex 5A? Why/Why not?

6 Complete the sentences with *in, at, on, by* or *out*.

1 Employment opportunities and the cost of living are .... far the most important factors when choosing where to live.
2 I actually had to join several meet-up groups in the area .... order to meet half of my neighbours!
3 .... the whole, most people surveyed said that social media has a positive influence on their sense of community.
4 House prices in this area are completely .... of control! I'll never be able to afford anything around here.
5 I loved living in London. But .... the same time, I always felt a little disconnected from my community.
6 I try to chat to my neighbours .... least once a week. It just helps promote a better sense of community in the area.
7 The local council is actually pretty helpful. .... fact, I'm sure they'd help you organise the event if you asked.

7 A Choose the correct options (A–C) to complete the story.

The artists' colony

For six artists with no regular income, ¹........ was always a problem, as they struggled to find enough money for rent. In order to be able to live in the city, they decided to rent a ²........ but ugly warehouse and live together that winter. It wasn't a fashionable neighbourhood and they learnt they were close to a railway line when the rumbling of passing trains kept them awake all night. Living in ³........ had never been the plan, but at least they had something in ⁴........ – they were artists and they were going to get their lives ⁵........ together and change the world. As ⁶........ as they had enough money to buy materials and eat, everything would be OK.

But everything ⁷........ wrong immediately. While they were out shopping for mattresses, there was a flood that destroyed four paintings. ⁸........ fact, if Jean-Paul hadn't come home early, all of their work ⁹........ lost. But worse was to come. ¹⁰........ up early the next morning, Jackson shivered and saw ice on the window. The heating had broken and now they were freezing.

1 A literacy	B housing	C justice
2 A spacious	B stylish	C character
3 A unemployment	B homelessness	C poverty
4 A together	B common	C shared
5 A back	B on	C up
6 A long	B far	C good
7 A made	B went	C had
8 A In	B The	C For
9 A has been	B was	C would have been
10 A To wake	B Waking	C He woke

B 🔊 R8.01 | Listen and check your answers.

WRITING BANK

1D a letter of recommendation

1 A Read the letter of recommendation. Do you think Jenna would be suitable for the job? Why/Why not?

To	Gómez, Natalia
From	Hillstock, Martin
Subject	Jenna Davison?

Dear Natalia,

You asked for my opinion about whether Jenna Davison would be a good manager. I have known Jenna for ten years. We met when she was a volunteer teacher in our school. As principal of St Mark's School, I have enjoyed working with Jenna for the last eight years. I would say she is a kind, friendly and enthusiastic teacher. I would also add that she's very passionate about her work. She has led several professional development workshops this term and has been mentoring one of our teaching assistants for the past year. In my opinion, whilst she has good communication skills with both students and teachers, Jenna can sometimes be shy or lack confidence when talking in public, or when making leadership decisions. I believe that while Jenna could make a good manager, she will need training and support to take on the role independently.

If you have any further questions with regard to her experience or qualifications, please do not hesitate to contact me.

Kind regards,
Martin Hillstock

B Work in pairs. Answer the questions.
1 What facts does Martin include about Jenna?
2 What opinions does he express about her?
3 Which phrases does he use to introduce his opinions?

C Work in pairs. Read the job advert. Who do you know that would be suitable for the job?

The Rock Café
4 hours ago

We're looking to recruit a new person to join our friendly team. We need someone to work in the café greeting customers, making coffees and serving at tables. The ideal candidate will need to be friendly and welcoming with a chatty personality to engage with customers as well as being organised and reliable. Flexible working hours.

No experience required – full training will be provided.

D Write a letter of recommendation. Include both facts and opinions about the person.

2D a competition entry

1 A Read the information about a writing competition. Answer the questions.
1 What happens to the best entries?
2 What do you have to write about?
3 What's the maximum number of words?
4 What do you have to include?

Get your article published!

If you could meet any person from the past, who would you meet, why and what would you do? Tell us in no more than 200 words and make sure you give it an attention-grabbing title!

The three winning entries will be published in next month's issue.

B Read the competition entry. Which is the best title?
a The biography of Jules Verne
b A visit with Verne
c A sailing trip to the Bay of Biscay

If I could go back in time and meet anyone I wanted, I'd go back to the 1800s and meet Jules Verne. Jules Verne was a French author who is famous for his revolutionary science-fiction and adventure novels like *Around the World in Eighty Days* and *Twenty Thousand Leagues Under the Sea*.

I'd take him for coffee and pastries in a café in Paris, where he lived, and ask him where he got his ideas from. Verne wrote about space travel and underwater travel before air travel and submarines were common, and before space travel existed. I would ask him what life was like for a writer in those times.

Although Verne wrote about travel adventures, he hadn't travelled much himself until the 1860s when he bought a small sailing boat. So, after our coffee, we would take a trip on his boat, perhaps to the Bay of Biscay, and I would ask him to read to me from his books.

C Choose the best tips (1–4) for writing engaging titles.
A good title:
1 shouldn't be too long.
2 should describe everything mentioned in the text.
3 will make someone want to find out more.
4 uses poetic devices like alliteration (words beginning with the same letter) or metaphors.

D Read the competition information in Ex 1A again. Plan your answer and think of a good title.

E Write your competition entry.

WRITING BANK

3D a forum comment

1 A Work in pairs. Read the main post and comments on a music forum. Whose opinion do you agree with? Why?

B Look at the highlighted phrases. Which express a general opinion and which express an opinion that the writer feels very sure about?

C Write your own comment for the forum. Use some of the opinion phrases in Ex 1B.

Music_Man 1 hour ago

How important do you think music is to society in general?

Big question I know, but I'm working on an essay for college on this topic and wanted to get a few opinions to help get me started.

289 Comments | Share

DJ Mikey 58m

==I think that== music is hugely important. I couldn't live without it. While every country has its own language, there's one language that we all understand, and that's the language of music. We don't need the words to understand what the music is saying – we can feel it. I go to festivals all over the world and ==one thing I know is that== when the music starts, everyone understands and they just start dancing.

Reply | Share

Dannygirl 41m

==I don't think== music is that important. It's nice and ==I do enjoy== listening to music sometimes, but ==it's definitely not== as important as food, water and shelter, or even education. ==I'd say== it's a luxury.

Reply | Share

Banodrums 40m

Music has the power to connect people. People can enjoy playing musical instruments together, share an interest in a particular kind of music, dance to the rhythm of a drum beat or sing aloud with friends to a favourite song. ==One thing is for certain==, music brings us enjoyment.

Reply | Share

Adidreams64 39m

Music is essential for society. It gives us a way to relax and enjoy ourselves so that we don't feel too stressed all the time. It can improve our mood, so if we're feeling a bit down, we can listen to music and feel better. I don't play an instrument myself, but ==I do think== music – playing it, listening to it and dancing to it – is really important for society.

Reply | Share

4D a cause-and-effect essay

1 A Read the extract from an essay about changing lifestyles. What reasons does the writer give for the changes?

The effect of urbanisation on modern lifestyles

William Crane | Wednesday 10 October

Over the last fifty years, there has been a huge shift from rural to urban living, which has resulted in some big changes to our lifestyles. Because cities have grown and developed, they have offered work opportunities to people living in rural environments, who previously had little access to this kind of labour.

In addition, there have been many changes due to improvements in education. More people have access to educational programmes than ever before, resulting in younger people growing up with higher ambitions than those of previous generations. Young people have flocked to the city and have had to adapt to a very different lifestyle, often working in a factory or an office, rather than out in the fields. Working long hours, they have little time for home cooking, which has led to poorer diets. As a result, many people now rely on fast food, which is more easily available in the city. Because of this, there has been an increase in health problems, such as …

B Scan the extract and find the phrases (1–5). Which introduce a cause, and which introduce an effect?
1. Resulting in …/which has resulted in …
2. Because … ,
3. Due to …
4. This has led to …/which has led to …
5. As a result, …/Because of this, …

C Plan a short cause-and-effect essay about how modern lifestyles are changing. Make notes about:
- what you see as the biggest changes.
- possible causes (e.g. better technology, changes to work patterns, etc.).
- possible effects of each change.

D Write your essay.

105

WRITING BANK

5D a thank-you message

1 A Read the email and answer the questions.
1 Who is saying thank you?
2 Who are they thanking? Why?

To Southside Team
From Scarmacci, Ali
Subject Thank you!

Dear team,

I would like to say thank you for your efforts on the Southside project so far. The team has met some extremely demanding deadlines and managed to complete the first three stages of the project on time. We have also managed to maintain the highest standards while under a lot of pressure. Everyone has worked extremely hard and your efforts are very much appreciated.

We now move onto the final stage of the project, which will see the completion of the building. It is likely that this stage will also provide challenges. I have no doubt you will all continue to overcome any difficulties that arise. I'll be in touch again very soon.

Kind regards,

Ali
Alison Scarmacci, MA
Project Manager
Fargo Wesson Buildings

B Work in pairs. Which of the tips below should you follow in a formal thank-you message?
1 Make it short and avoid long, descriptive sentences.
2 Say clearly and specifically what you are thanking the other person for.
3 Mention some things that went wrong and explain what happened.
4 Use a neutral phrase to end the email, e.g. 'Kind regards' or 'Best wishes'.

C Imagine you are a team leader. Choose a situation from below or think of your own. Think of more details.
- Your sales team has sold a record number of products this year.
- Your team of designers has found a solution to a difficult design problem on a piece of equipment.
- Your student group has completed a three-month project collecting information on the environment.

D Write a thank-you message to your team.

6D an email giving news

1 A Read the email. Why does Mel want to tell Leah this personal anecdote?

To Sweney, Leah
From Boffey, Mel
Subject You'll never guess who I saw!

Hi Leah,

I hope all's well with you. I thought you might like to know I bumped into one of our childhood heroes yesterday!

I was on my lunch break and I went into a café near my workplace. I ordered my food and sat down and waited. About two minutes later, Laura Marling walked in. At first, I wasn't sure it was her, but then she sat down kind of in my eyeline and it was definitely her. Do you remember listening to her music for hours on end?

I spent the next twenty minutes in a state of muted excitement, trying not to stare and trying to pluck up the courage to speak to her! I was going to ask if I could take a selfie with her. But then I thought she probably has to deal with that kind of attention the whole time and I bet it's really annoying for her. So, in the end I just sat there basking in the glow of her presence! And of course, seeing her made me think of you trying to play along to *Goodbye England (Covered In Snow)*. Happy days!

Lots of love,

Mel

B Read the email again. What details does Mel give about:
- the context (time and place)?
- how she felt?
- what she did or didn't do in the end, and why?
- her reason for writing the email?

C Find the phrases (1–4) in the email. Match them with their functions (a–d).
1 I thought you might like to know …
2 At first, … , but then …
3 I was going to …
4 So, in the end, …

a giving the conclusion to the anecdote
b introducing the anecdote
c describing the main events
d introducing a personal plan that later changed

D Think about a piece of news to email a friend or family member about. Use the questions to help you make notes.
- Where were you?
- What happened?
- How did you feel?
- What happened in the end?
- Why do you want to tell this particular person about it?

E Write your email.

WRITING BANK

7D a social media post

1 A Read the question and two answers in an online forum. What do the people disagree about? Whose argument do you think is better?

Tony567 1 h

Which is more important: talent or hard work?

6 Comments | 1 Share | 29 Likes

Lydia997 43 mins

Anyone can work hard. However, talent is natural. Take sport, for example. You either have it or you don't. If you don't have it, it doesn't matter how many hours you put in or how hard you try. You aren't going to play for Real Madrid or sing at La Scala or show your paintings at the Met in New York. Overall, talent is far more important.

Comment | Share | Like

MJ_3000 39 mins

It must be awesome to be talented. On the other hand, if you just sit on the couch all day, what's going to happen to your talent? The same as what happens to anything that isn't used. It gets rusty! My old tennis coach had a saying: hard work beats talent that doesn't work hard. You can't achieve anything unless you work your socks off. So IMHO, hard work is more important.

Comment | Share | Like

B Work in pairs. Discuss the questions.
1. What phrases do the two people use to introduce their final opinions?
2. What do you think IMHO means?
   a in my honest opinion   b I mean, how obvious!
3. Which of these phrases for introducing a conclusion are formal?
   a take it from me   c so   e to conclude
   b in conclusion   d to sum up   f essentially

C Write a response to the question in Ex 1A or one of the questions below. Make sure you end with a clear conclusion giving your opinion.

LunaLover 1 hr

Should you spend more time on things you are good at, or things you are not so good at?

8 Comments | 3 Shares | 4 Likes

Ravi106 11 mins

Are you born with talent, or is it something you can develop?

2 Comments | 1 Share | 2 Like

8D a mission statement

1 A Read the mission statement. Match the paragraphs (1–3) with their functions (a–c).

ON THE STREET FOOD BANK

Our mission and vision

¹The mission of the On the Street Food Bank is to reduce food waste and help to ensure that everyone, even if they're living on the streets, has access to sufficient nutritious food. We'd like to be part of a community where food waste is kept to a minimum and surplus food is given to those who need it. We believe that access to nutritious food is a basic human right and essential for people who are trying to get their life back together and get out of poverty. Nobody living on the streets should go hungry when good food is being thrown away.

²In our cities today, there is a huge problem with food waste. Shops and businesses regularly throw out food at the end of the day that is perfectly good to eat. At the same time, people sleeping on the streets often don't have enough money to access nutritious food.

³On the Street Food Bank uses an app which local shops and businesses can download to tell us when they have surplus food at the end of the day. The app allows local businesses to work together and collect all the food in one place. Our volunteers collect the food and distribute it to homeless people in need. We are run by volunteers, so if you would like to join our team, please get in touch.

a Clear actions: how you would tackle the problem
b Mission statement: the general aim the project would like to achieve
c The problem: what is going wrong at present

B Choose one of the projects you discussed in Ex 4D on page 101. Plan your mission statement. Use the questions to help you make notes.
1. What is the general aim the project would like to achieve?
2. What problems exist now? What is going wrong?
3. What clear actions will the project take to help solve the problems?

C Write your mission statement.

GRAMMAR BANK

1A present perfect simple and continuous

REFERENCE ◀◀ page 9

We use both the present perfect simple and the present perfect continuous to talk about situations or actions which started in the past and continue into the present.

Sometimes there is no important difference between the two tenses, particularly with verbs such as *work*, *live* and *study*.
Mauro **has lived/has been living** in Bologna since 2010.

However, there are also some important differences between the two.

Focusing on the result of the activity

We use the present perfect simple to focus on the result of a completed activity.
He's **passed** all of his exams. (Focuses on the result – passing the exams)
We use the present perfect continuous to focus on the activity itself.
He's **been studying** for his exams. (Focuses on the activity of studying)

How many? vs. How long?

We use the present perfect simple to answer the questions: 'How many?', 'How much?' or 'How far?'
We've **interviewed** more than 100 applicants (How many?)
He's **raised** €1,000 for charity. (How much?)
They've **driven** over 3,000 kilometres. (How far?)

We use the present perfect continuous to answer the question: 'How long?' and to emphasise that an action has continued for a long time (using *for* and *since* to describe the duration), or is repeated. We often use the present perfect continuous with verbs that describe long actions, such as *wait*, *stay*, *play*, *sit*, *stand*, *write*, etc.
We've **been waiting** for over forty minutes now!
He's **been sitting** on that bench since this morning.

Completed vs. unfinished actions

We use the present perfect simple to describe completed actions.
We use the present perfect continuous to describe actions that are unfinished or in progress.
Oh no, I've **missed** the bus!
(The bus has gone, so the action is completed.)
I'm afraid she's **left** the office.
(She isn't here now, so the action is completed.)
I've **been learning** Mandarin.
(I'm still learning, so the action is not completed.)
She's **been trying** to speak to you.
(She still hasn't spoken to you, so she's still trying.)

State verbs, experiences and habits

We use the present perfect simple, NOT the present perfect continuous, with state verbs, to talk about states or situations that started in the past and are in progress.
How long **have you known** Jessica?
I've **owned** this car since 2009.

We also use the present perfect simple with the words *always*, *ever* and *never* to talk about experiences and habits.
He's **never driven** to work, he always goes by bike.
I've **always baked** my own bread.

PRACTICE

1 Choose the correct word(s) to complete the sentences.
1 I've **watched** / **been watching** this amazing series recently.
2 I've **been** / **been going** to the gym twice already this week.
3 We've **known** / **been knowing** them for about ten years.
4 You've **worked** / **been working** on that report all morning!
5 He's **stayed** / **been staying** with me whilst they finish repainting his flat.
6 I've probably **seen** / **been seeing** that film about twenty-five times!

2 Complete the sentences with the correct present perfect simple or continuous form of the verb in brackets.
1 Oh, no! I think he .... (break) his foot.
2 I .... (cook) all morning, but I've still got a lot to do!
3 I .... never .... (try) skiing.
4 How many invitations .... you .... (send) so far?
5 .... all the guests .... (arrive) yet?
6 I'm worried about Piotr. He .... (work) so hard recently.
7 How long .... you .... (know) Natasha?
8 She .... (study) for her exams for weeks.

3 Use the answers and the verbs in bold to write questions in the present perfect simple or continuous. If both forms are possible, use the continuous form.
1 I **teach** at the university.
   How long .... there?
2 I **know** Johanna really well.
   How long .... her?
3 I'm **developing** a new website.
   How long .... it?
4 I **play** golf on Saturdays.
   How long .... ?
5 I **live** in Krakow.
   How long .... there?
6 He **wins** a lot of awards.
   How many .... ?

GRAMMAR BANK

1B infinitive and *-ing* forms

REFERENCE ◀◀ page 11

Some verbs can be followed by a *to* infinitive or an *-ing* form, but with a change in meaning.

If you *try to do* something, you make an attempt to do it.

If you *try doing* something, you test it to see if it is suitable, useful or works.

I **tried to fix** the roof.
(I attempted it, but I failed.)

Try drinking green tea if you have a stomachache. (Test it to see if it works.)

If you *remember to do* something, you remember it and then do it.

If you *remember doing* something, you have a memory of doing it in the past.

Remember to feed the dog! (Don't forget!)

I **remember going** to school for the first time when I was five.

If you *forget to do* something, you don't do it because you don't remember.

If you *forget doing* something, you have no memory of it.

I **forgot to feed** the dog! (I didn't remember.)

If you *stop to do* something, you pause what you are doing in order to do something else.

If you *stop doing* something, you finish, and no longer do it.

I **stopped to call** my mother. (I stopped doing something so I could call her.)

I **stopped watching** TV two years ago.
(I no longer watch TV.)

Infinitive after the verb *be*

We can use a *to* infinitive after the verb *be*.

My idea is **to build** an app.
The purpose of the call was **to choose** a design.

Infinitive to express a purpose

We can use a *to* infinitive to express a purpose.

To make the perfect cup of tea, leave the bag in the water for three minutes.
You should practise every day **to get** better.

We can use *so as (not) to* as a formal alternative to a *to* infinitive, to express a purpose.

The house was built with big windows **so as to let** in lots of light.
She ran to school **so as not to be** late.

-ing form after a preposition

We use an *-ing* form, not a *to* infinitive, after a preposition.

I passed my exams **by working** hard.

PRACTICE

1 Find the mistakes and correct them. One sentence is correct.
1 For improve your memory, you need to make emotional connections with the subject.
2 The purpose of this article is show how memory is connected to our personalities.
3 She prepared for her exam by revise every day with a friend.
4 I try to remember all my students' names, but it's difficult.
5 He worked all morning except for when he stopped taking a coffee break.
6 If your computer freezes, try to switch it off and on again.
7 I remember to play in the back garden when I was six years old.
8 Don't forget buying snacks for the party tomorrow!

2 Complete the second sentence using the correct form of the verb in brackets and an *-ing* form or a *to* infinitive.
1 Oh no! I didn't switch on the alarm before we left.
    Oh no! I .... the alarm on before we left. (forget)
2 I experimented with drinking more water, but I still get headaches.
    I .... more water, but I still get headaches. (try)
3 It's important that we take our medicine tomorrow.
    We must .... our medicine tomorrow. (remember)
4 I took a break from my work because I wanted to talk to Jack.
    I .... because I wanted to talk to Jack. (stop)
5 The memory of singing on TV will always be with her!
    She'll never .... on TV! (forget)
6 Because of his injury, he doesn't cycle anymore.
    Because of his injury, he .... (stop)

3 Choose the correct verb forms to complete the text.

When professional chess players play against amateurs, they sometimes make it more challenging for themselves by playing several games at once, while blindfolded, so they can't see the boards. Their opponents have to tell them where they are moving their pieces, and the professionals play by [1]**remember / remembering** where everything is on the board. Of course, it's not only chess players who need good memories. Some judges have to remember thousands of laws. Actors must learn their lines but also remember [2]**to take / taking** a step to the left, turn around, and take a pace to the right. How can people like this prepare so as not [3]**to forget / forgetting** the information they need? One technique is [4]**by create / to create** a memory palace. [5]**Remembering / To remember** lists of objects, you can imagine a huge building. Inside it, you put each imaginary object in its special place. [6]**So as not to forget / Not forgetting** the location, you imagine the objects somewhere meaningful. So a hat might hang above a door, a book might be placed by a bed. [7]**Recalling / To recall** the objects, you enter the imaginary building and walk around 'seeing' the objects in the places where you have put them.

Occasionally, teachers ask students to [8]**try creating / try for creating** memory palaces to help them remember important facts. My advice? Try [9]**put / to put** the objects somewhere significant to you. And don't forget [10]**closing / to close** the door to the building. Opening it is a vital part of the remembering process.

GRAMMAR BANK

1C How to … express personal preferences

REFERENCE ◀◀ page 15

We use *really into* something to say we like something a lot.
I'm really into Polish films.

We use *passionate about* something to talk about something we really love.
I'm passionate about Mexican music.

We can use the idiom *It's not my cup of tea* to say that we generally don't like something.
Sorry, football just **isn't** really **my cup of tea**.

Expressing likes and dislikes

I'm really into/I'm passionate about + noun/-*ing* form
I'm (not) keen on/I'm (not) a big fan of + noun/-*ing* form
I love/hate/can't stand + noun/-*ing* form
It's not my cup of tea.
What I like/love about … is …
The thing I love about … is …

We use *would rather* to express a preference. Notice that it is followed by the infinitive without *to*.
I'd rather have rice than pasta.

Would prefer is an alternative to *would rather*. Notice that it is followed by the infinitive with *to*.
We**'d prefer to** travel on Tuesday.

We can use *given the choice* to talk about hypothetical options, to say that you would like to do something, if it was possible.
Given the choice, I'd go to Malawi for my holiday.

Discussing options

I'd rather (not) + infinitive without *to* …
I'd (much) rather + infinitive without *to* …
I'd prefer (not) + infinitive with *to* …
Given the choice, I'd …

When we can't agree completely on what to do, we compromise. This means we agree to do some things that the other person wants to do and some things that we want to do. This keeps both sides happy.

We can use *I'd be happy to …* , *but I don't want to …* to compromise.
We'd be happy to visit the gallery, **but we don't want to** go to the museum.

We can also use *how about if we …/what if we …* , *then we can …* to compromise.
How about we spend the morning shopping, **then we can** go to the castle in the afternoon?

Compromising

I'd be happy to … , but I don't want to …
How about if we … (do your idea), then we can … (do my idea)?

PRACTICE

1 Choose the correct words to complete the conversations.

1 A: I **can't stand** / **rather not** getting caught in traffic jams in big cities. It's awful.
B: Me neither! **What** / **Thing** I like about going by bicycle is you can avoid them.

2 A: I'm not a big **passionate** / **fan** of museums and art galleries.
B: Oh, I'm the opposite. I'm really **keen** / **into** modern art.

3 A: How **about** / **to** if we go to the beach first, then go shopping?
B: I'd much **prefer** / **rather** spend all day on the beach.

4 A: **Thing** / **The thing** I love about this city is the historical monuments.
B: Really? I'm not keen **on** / **about** all those statues myself.

5 A: **If** / **Given** the choice, I'd just wander around the city centre.
B: Oh no. I'd prefer **not to** / **don't** do that because it's too tiring.

6 A: I'm so **keen** / **passionate** about the food! Shall we try the jollof rice?
B: Sorry, I'd rather **not** / **no**.

2 Complete the email with the words in the box.

| about | choice | into | keen |
| passionate | prefer | rather | stand |

Hi Mostafa,

Thank you for the suggested itinerary for my upcoming trip to Cairo. Given the ¹_____ , I'd spend several days with you, but unfortunately I only have twenty-four hours!

I'm ²_____ about history and ancient monuments, so I'm really looking forward to seeing the pyramids. I'm also really ³_____ trying new experiences, so I'd love to sail down the Nile in a felucca! I love all kinds of boats, so that should be interesting.

Normally, I'd much ⁴_____ walk around the city because you see more when you walk, but if it's going to be really hot, as you suggest, I'd ⁵_____ to be driven. How ⁶_____ we see how hot it is on the day?

I agree it would be nice to spend the late afternoon buying souvenirs. I can't ⁷_____ modern shopping centres, so I like your idea of going to Khan el-Khalili. I've heard lots about this market, and of course I'm ⁸_____ on seeing locally made goods.

Thanks again and see you soon,

Dieter Hentschel

GRAMMAR BANK

1D *while, whereas* and *whilst*

REFERENCE ◀◀ page 17

We can use *while*, *whereas* and *whilst* to link two ideas in the same sentence that contrast with each other.

I love listening to jazz, **whilst** my partner can't stand it.
While I used to be quite optimistic when I was younger, nowadays I think I'm more of a realist.
My wife comes from a big family, **whereas** mine is quite small.

We can use *while/whilst* or *whereas* at the beginning of the sentence or in the middle.

If we use *while/whilst/whereas* at the beginning of the sentence, we put a comma at the end of the first statement, before the contrasting statement.

When we use *while/whilst* and *whereas* in the middle of the sentence, we put it directly after the comma.

Whilst Emil enjoys a good steak, I'm a vegetarian.
Emil enjoys a good steak, **whereas** I'm a vegetarian.

Notice that *while* and *whilst* can also be used to introduce a time clause, to describe when two things happen at the same time.

Tim made supper **whilst** I went upstairs for a shower.
While I was stuck in bed, everyone else was enjoying the holiday.

PRACTICE

1 Match the sentence beginnings (1–6) with the endings (a–f).

1 Whilst I like Carl as a person,
2 While Marta is very sociable and outgoing,
3 Whereas the unemployment rate in Spain was fourteen percent,
4 Whilst she generally enjoyed his company,
5 Hiro usually enjoys going out in the evening,
6 While I generally remember where I put things,

a there were times when he made her angry.
b her sister is quiet and shy.
c I completely forgot where my keys were.
d whereas I prefer staying in.
e I wouldn't like to work for him.
f it was much higher in other parts of Europe.

2 A Use the prompts to write sentences using *while, whereas* or *whilst*.

1 an active imagination ✓
   often daydream ✗

   Whilst I have an active imagination, I don't often daydream.

2 always well prepared for things ✓
   good at organising other people ✗
3 enjoy going to parties ✓
   talking to new people ✗
4 like to follow a schedule ✓
   also happy to make changes at the last minute ✗
5 generally feel comfortable around people ✓
   being the centre of attention ✗
6 interested in people ✓
   good at listening to other people's problems ✗
7 usually in a good mood ✓
   sometimes get stressed easily ✓

B Write sentences comparing your own personality to that of people you know. Use *while, whilst* or *whereas*.

Whilst I've always been very arty, my brother Felipe isn't creative at all.

GRAMMAR BANK

2A future probability

REFERENCE ⏪ page 22

We use *will/won't* + infinitive without *to* to make predictions about the future, based on our opinions.

I'm pretty sure Italy **will win** tomorrow.
VR **won't replace** real holidays anytime soon.

We can use adverbs like *definitely/certainly/possibly/probably* with *will/won't*, to say how certain we feel about a prediction.

I'**ll definitely be** there tomorrow.
We **probably won't** come to the party.

Notice that the adverb usually comes after *will* but before *won't*.

We **will probably** come …
We **probably won't** come … ~~We won't probably come …~~

We can also use *will/won't* for things that are sure to happen.

I'**ll be** twenty-two next year.

Use *be going to* for predictions when there is evidence in the present.

It'**s going to rain**! Look at those black clouds!

Use *be certain to* when we are sure that something will happen.

Prices **are certain to rise**.

Use *be likely to* when we think that something will probably happen. We use *unlikely to* or *not likely to* when we think that something probably won't happen.

My team **is likely to reach** the next round.
We **are unlikely to go** on holiday this year.
She **isn't likely to win** that competition.

We use *might*, *may* and *could* + infinitive without *to* when we think that something is possible, but not certain.

Notice that we can use the negative forms *might not* and *may not* to talk about the future, but we can't use ~~could not~~ in the same way.

We **might go** to Japan next year.
They **could make** a lot of money with that.
She **may not be able** to see us today.

We use *be due to* when something is scheduled to happen.

He **is due to retire** next year.
The train **is due to depart** at 6 p.m.

PRACTICE

1 Choose the correct words to complete the sentences.

1 Researchers are due **announce** / **to announce** the findings tomorrow.
2 Virtual reality is unlikely **for** / **to** affect my industry.
3 This ambitious study is **certain to** / **certain** have a big impact.
4 My sister is seventeen now, so she **could** / **will** be eighteen on her next birthday.
5 That tech company **may not** / **could not** invest in VR in the future.
6 Machines **won't probably** / **probably won't** replace human workers for many years.
7 Unfortunately, the lab where I work **likely** / **is likely** to close.
8 We **will definitely be** / **will be definitely** at the conference tomorrow, so see you there.

2 Choose the correct options (A–C) to complete the text.

¹_____ robots likely to replace teachers?
The best teachers have personal qualities and communicative skills that robots ²_____ acquire any time soon. For this reason, robots ³_____ replace teachers completely. But according to futurist Dr Bill Sethers, humans and robots ⁴_____ work well side by side in the classroom of the future. Sethers believes robots ⁵_____ be used more and more as teaching assistants. 'They ⁶_____ be ready to comfort a crying child or laugh at students' jokes, but they are good for boring tasks like cleaning the board and checking homework. Also, they're reliable: they never get sick and they're ⁷_____ ask for a pay rise!' The other surprising advantage of robots ⁸_____ be motivation. Robots that sing and play games are incredibly popular with young children. Several Japanese companies and one Korean company ⁹_____ bring out a new generation of robot language teachers in the near future. Judging by the success of the earlier models, these ¹⁰_____ be a big hit in schools.

	A	B	C
1	Might	Are	Will
2	aren't going to	will	are due to
3	won't probably	could	definitely won't
4	might not	are unlikely to	could
5	are unlikely to	certain to	will
6	may not	might	are going to
7	certain to	unlikely to	due to
8	might	won't	is due to
9	might not	probably won't	are due to
10	definitely won't	will probably	are unlikely to

3 Complete the second sentence using the words in brackets.

1 Some employees will probably work beyond retirement age.
Some employees _____ beyond retirement age. (likely)
2 The rainstorm is predicted to arrive at any moment.
The rainstorm _____ at any moment. (due)
3 I don't think we'll get there tonight because of airport delays.
We _____ tonight because of airport delays. (unlikely)
4 It's possible Jan won't meet us tonight because she isn't feeling well.
Jan _____ us tonight because she isn't feeling well. (might)
5 I'm sure the report will back up the findings of our research.
The report _____ the findings of our research. (certain)
6 Be careful! Don't spill that coffee!
Be careful! You _____ that coffee! (going)

GRAMMAR BANK

2B quantifiers

REFERENCE ⏪ page 23

We use quantifiers with singular, plural and uncountable nouns to specify an amount or number.

	100%	A large amount	A small amount	0%
Uncountable or plural nouns	all any	the majority of in a majority plenty of	hardly any a lack of	no not any
Uncountable nouns		a good deal of	little/a little	
Plural nouns		a large number of	few/a few several a minority of in a minority a handful of	
Singular nouns	every each			no not any

We use *a few* and *a little* to talk about a small amount or number.

There are **a few** tickets left.
I try to spend **a little** bit of time in nature every day.

We use *few* and *little* when there are not as much or as many as we would like.

I have **few** opportunities to get away from the city.
There is **little** chance of me leaving before 6 p.m.

We use *the majority of* to talk about more than 50 percent, and *the minority of* to talk about less than 50 percent. We can also talk about people or things being *in a majority* or *in a minority*.

The majority of people feel more relaxed when they are in the countryside.
I spend **the majority of** my working day sitting at a desk.
Those against the decision were **in a minority**.

We can use *a lack of* to talk about something which there is not enough of, or is missing completely.

There is **a lack of** affordable housing in the city.

We can use *a good deal of* or *plenty of* to talk about when there is a large amount or number of something.

We had **a good deal of** help from the government.
There are **plenty of** opportunities for improvement.

We use *several* or *a handful of* to talk about a small number.

A handful of us went to the concert.
Several of them talked about the importance of downtime.

PRACTICE

1 Choose the correct words to complete the sentences.

1 It was cold, but there was very **little** / **a little** snow.
2 Spending **the little** / **a little** time in a green space can improve your mood.
3 I recently bought **few** / **a few** plants for the office.
4 There are **few** / **a few** things I enjoy more than going for an early morning walk.
5 I spend **a good deal of** / **a handful of** time outdoors.
6 There are **several** / **a good deal of** ways you can improve your mental health.
7 **A few** / **A little** of us are going for a walk later if you want to join us.
8 I would say there has been **a lack of** / **a minority of** focus on the issue.
9 **The majority of** / **Several** people in major cities use public transport.
10 We are so busy that we have **no** / **every** time to just sit and relax.

2 Complete the text with the quantifiers in the box.

> a few (x2)   a little   each   handful   in a minority
> lack of   no   plenty   the majority of

Ways to feel closer to nature even if you live in the city

There are [1]_____ of ways to feel closer to nature, even if you live in a busy city and spend [2]_____ your time working or commuting to work. It only takes [3]_____ minutes [4]_____ day to do something that will help you to feel refreshed. Adapt your routine so that even when you think you have [5]_____ time to spare, you can still enjoy nature. There are a [6]_____ of different ways to do this. Get up [7]_____ earlier and spend [8]_____ minutes outside enjoying the fresh air before you have breakfast or start work. Watch the stars before you go to bed, or go for a walk in your lunch break. Admittedly, people who can spend hours relaxing in nature will be [9]_____. For most people working long hours, there will be a [10]_____ opportunities. Maybe you'll just have to watch a virtual fish tank on your phone instead and see if that makes a difference.

GRAMMAR BANK

2C How to ... speculate

REFERENCE ◀◀ page 27

We use the following phrases when we are speculating, or making guesses about a situation based on the information or evidence we have.

How to speculate

I'd guess …/I'd have thought …/I'd imagine …
I suppose …/I reckon …/I doubt …
There's no way …
She's clearly/obviously …
He/She's bound to …
I'm fairly certain/sure that …
I'm not 100 percent sure, but I'd say …
I know for a fact that …
I bet …
I get the impression that …

When we are very sure about something, we use:
I'm fairly certain that …
I'm fairly sure that …
I know for a fact that … (this is 100 percent)
I'm not 100 percent sure, but I'd say …

I'm fairly certain that living in the Antarctic is tough.
I know for a fact that being at sea on your own is not easy.

We use *There's no way that …* if we're talking about something we think is impossible.

There's no way that they can actually enjoy living there!

If we want to talk about what we think, we can say:
I suppose … , I reckon … , I'd have thought … , I'd imagine that …

I reckon life on the Space Station must be a bit boring.

When we talk about what we think based on the evidence we have, we can say:
I get the impression that …
She/He's clearly …/obviously …
She/He's bound to …
I bet …

I bet the sea's pretty cold at that time of year!

PRACTICE

1 Complete the conversations with the words in the box.

> clearly   impression   reckon   sure   thought   way

1 A: We're thinking of cycling across France.
   B: Really? There's no .... I would even consider doing that!
2 A: When Joe gets back from Chile, he's planning to travel across India on a motorbike.
   B: Wow! He's .... very adventurous, isn't he?
3 A: Did you get that job you applied for?
   B: Well, I'm not 100 percent .... , but I'm feeling pretty confident about it.
4 A: Have you met Tommy's girlfriend yet?
   B: No, but I'm under the .... that she's great company.
5 A: I suggest we call in a consultant to help us deal with the issue.
   B: Really? I'd have .... that we could come up with a solution ourselves.
6 A: Do you know when the meeting is due to end?
   B: I .... we'll be finished by six.

2 Complete the sentences using the prompts in brackets.

1 .... she might be leaving the company next year. (not 100 percent sure / think)
2 .... the temperature in the Antarctic can go as low as -50 degrees Celsius. (know / fact)
3 .... she could have run all the way around the world. (no / way)
4 .... he enjoys being alone. (get / impression)
5 .... life on the International Space Station isn't always as much fun as it looks. (fairly / certain)
6 With all that running, she's .... get through lots of pairs of shoes! (bound)
7 .... wanted to be an explorer since he was a child. (clearly)
8 I'd .... sailing around the Mediterranean would be quite idyllic. (thought)

GRAMMAR BANK

3A relative clauses

REFERENCE ◀◀ page 33

Defining relative clauses

We use defining relative clauses to give essential information about a noun in a sentence. Defining relative clauses tell us which person or thing we are talking about.

I think that's the festival **where Alt-J played years ago**.

We don't use commas before or after defining relative clauses. We can use *that* instead of *who* or *which*.

Fuji Rock uses chopsticks **which/that** are made from local wood.

We can omit the relative pronoun when it is the object of the relative clause.

The organiser **(who)** we usually talk to is not available.

Relative pronouns

We use relative pronouns in relative clauses. We use: *who/that* for people, *which/that* for things, *whose* for possession, *when* for time and *where* for place.

I met some people **whose** tent collapsed in the night!

We can also use *whose* to refer to cities, countries and other nouns which suggest a group of people.

It's a city **whose** ambition is to be more sustainable.

We omit nouns or pronouns which have been replaced by the relative pronoun.

She's someone who I know well. NOT ~~She's someone who I know her well.~~

Non-defining relative clauses

We use non-defining relative clauses to give extra or non-essential information.

The festival, **which was started by a small group of volunteers**, has run for more than twenty years.

We use commas to separate this clause from the rest of the sentence. We cannot use *that* instead of *who* or *which* in non-defining relative clauses.

The concert, **which attracted thousands of people**, was a huge success, NOT ~~The concert, that attracted thousands of people, was a huge success~~.

We cannot omit the relative pronoun.

Splendour in the Grass, **which I attended last year**, will be held in July. NOT ~~Splendour in the Grass, I attended last year, will be held in July.~~

We can use *which* to refer to the whole of a previous clause.

I got sick, **which** meant I could no longer do the job.

Prepositions in relative clauses

In informal English, prepositions usually come at the end of a relative clause.

This is the song **which** she's most famous **for**.

In formal written English, prepositions often come before the relative pronoun. For people, we use *whom*, NOT *who* after the preposition.

He's the person **to whom** I have spoken. (formal)
He's the person **who** I have spoken **to**. (informal)

Where can be replaced by *which … in* in informal English. In more formal English, we use *in which*.

The tent **which** we slept **in** is broken. (informal)
The tent **in which we slept** is broken. (formal)

PRACTICE

1 Combine the sentences using a relative clause. Add commas where the relative clause is non-defining.

1 WOMAD is an international arts festival. It was founded in 1982 by rock musician Peter Gabriel.
   WOMAD .... is an international arts festival.
2 Caterers are invited to the festival. They must use solar power.
   Only .... to the festival.
3 Some plastic is used on site. All of it is recyclable.
   All .... recyclable.
4 We went to a festival last summer. It was the best festival I've ever been to.
   The festival .... I've ever been to.
5 I discussed the problem with someone. She was very understanding.
   The person .... was very understanding.
6 The exhibition features paintings by local artists. The exhibition opened last week.
   The exhibition .... local artists.
7 The hotel overlooks the beach. The hotel was opened in 1886.
   The hotel .... the beach.
8 You should play us a song on your guitar. This is that sort of occasion.
   This is the .... a song on your guitar.

2 Look at the relative clauses in Ex 1. In which can you omit the relative pronoun?

3 Join the sentences with a relative clause. Use the relative pronoun in brackets.

1 You're the person. We always rely on you to sort things out. (who)
2 London is the city. I grew up there. (which)
3 They are colleagues. I spend a lot of time with them. (whom)
4 These are places in Laos. You can ride elephants there. (where)
5 This is the album. The band are most famous for this album. (which)
6 We stayed in a hotel. They recycled a lot there. (where)
7 We stopped at a museum. We had never visited the museum before. (which)
8 This is the lady. I was talking to you about this lady. (who)

115

GRAMMAR BANK

3B cleft sentences

REFERENCE ◀◀ page 36

We can use a cleft sentence to emphasise information. *Cleft* means 'divided'. In cleft sentences, one sentence is divided into two parts, each with its own verb.

Juanita **works** with Magdaleno.
(one verb)

It**'s** Magdaleno that Juanita **works** with.
(two verbs, emphasises Magdaleno)

The following structures are used in cleft sentences.

Cleft sentences with *It*	Cleft sentences with *What*
It is/was … who …	*What* + subject + present tense + *is* …
It is/was … that …	*What* + subject + past tense + *was* …

We can use *It + be + that/who* to emphasise a part of a sentence. In this structure, we emphasise the part of the sentence after the verb *be*.

It was **Jim** who lost his wallet.
(not Paul)

It was **his wallet** that he lost.
(not his bag)

It was **yesterday** that he lost his wallet.
(not two days ago)

We can also use *What* + subject + verb + *be*. In this structure, we emphasise the part of the sentence after *what*, before the verb *be*.

What **I'd like to know** is where it came from!

What **you need to do** is talk to your manager.

Notice that we use the singular form of *be* after *It* and *What* in cleft sentences.

It was my parents I had to thank.
NOT ~~It were my parents …~~

What is most impressive are the songs he recorded at home.
NOT ~~What are most impressive …~~

PRACTICE

1 Match the sentence beginnings (1–8) with the endings (a–h) to make cleft sentences.

1. It was Nikolai
2. What worries me
3. It's singing in public
4. What's interesting is
5. It was in Belgium
6. What you need to do is
7. It was last week that
8. What I like about

a. that really scares me.
b. she went for her interview, not yesterday.
c. London is the music scene.
d. that they got married, not France.
e. speak to your manager.
f. the local culture.
g. who wrote the book, not Fyodor.
h. is the lack of planning for this project.

2 Complete the conversation with one word in each gap.

Luisa: Did you watch *The Loved Ones* last night?
Rejane: Of course! It's my favourite soap opera!
Luisa: Wasn't it brilliant? ¹_____ I want to know is who stole the laptop!
Rejane: Really? But it's obvious! ²_____ was Julio who stole it!
Luisa: No way! It ³_____ Lena who stole it, not Julio! Why do you think it was Julio?
Rejane: Whenever there's a mystery in *The Loved Ones* ⁴_____ you need to do is see who looks the most innocent. Then you know they're the guilty one.
Luisa: But what's strange ⁵_____ that the laptop reappeared at the end.
Rejane: True, but it ⁶_____ Julio who always does clever things like that. He returned it before he got caught.
Luisa: Hmmm, maybe …

3 Rewrite the sentences using the words in brackets.

1. The singer messed up, not the guitarist. (it, who)
   It was the singer who messed up, not the guitarist.
2. You need to practise a lot before performing. (what, do)
   ....
3. Taking deep breaths works for me. (what, is)
   ....
4. I like acting in public the most. (what, is)
   ....
5. I'm studying music, not theatre. (it's, that)
   ....
6. The low salary put me off, not the hours. (it, that)
   ....

GRAMMAR BANK

3C How to ... use vague language

REFERENCE ⏪ page 39

Vague language is very common, especially in spoken English. We often add words and phrases such as *kind of*, *sort of*, *that kind of thing* to make what we're saying sound less factual and direct.

I watch a lot of crime drama **and that kind of thing**.

We use vague language when:
- we are not very sure of the precise details of something.
- we can't remember the exact word or information.
- we are having an informal conversation and want to talk generally and sound less direct.

Vague nouns and phrases

We use *thing/things* to refer to something without saying its name.

There are a few **things** I don't like about that film.

We use *bit* to refer to a small piece of something.

I love the **bit** where the animals escape.

We use *stuff* to refer to more than one object, or an uncountable noun.

In the end, they move all their **stuff** into a new flat.

We use *what's her name?* or *what's it called?* when we can't remember the name of someone or something.

The hero is played by that actress – **what's her name**?

Numbers

We use *around* and *about* to give a vague idea of a number.

There are **around** ten episodes in the series.

We use *-odd* after a number, to mean 'about'.

There are 200-**odd** dancers in the final scene.

We use *or so* after a number, to show that the number is not completely accurate.

The storm lasted for two days **or so**.

Adjectives and ages

We use *-ish* to make either an adjective or an age more vague.

She's about twenty-**ish**.

Making a statement less certain

We use *sort of* and *kind of* to make a statement slightly more vague and less certain.

I **sort of** understood what the film was about. (I didn't understand very well.)

It's **kind of** like a modern version of *Groundhog Day*.

Avoiding a long list

We can use phrases such as *and stuff*, *and everything*, *and so on*, *and that kind of thing*, or *something* instead of finishing a list.

We organised a movie night at home with pizzas, crisps, drinks **and so on**.

He's basically a superhero, so he can fly **and everything**.

PRACTICE

1 Choose the correct options (a–c) to complete the vague statements.

1 I think the films starts at ....
  a around seven-ish
  b sort of seven o'clock
  c seven o'clock and so on

2 There are .... we should discuss.
  a stuff
  b kind of things
  c a couple of things

3 There are .... people coming to the dinner.
  a kind of twenty
  b twenty-odd
  c twenty and everything

4 There's a lot of action and violence and ....
  a that kind of thing
  b something like that
  c sort of that

5 Where have you put .... ?
  a my stuff, or something like that
  b my stuff or so
  c all my stuff

6 I think we should wait for .... before speaking to them.
  a a week or so   b kind of a week   c a week-ish

7 Her hair has turned a .... colour.
  a grey and so on
  b grey-odd
  c grey-ish

8 I watch all kinds of different things, like drama, mystery, comedy, thrillers ....
  a and stuff
  b and kind of
  c and something

2 Complete the sentences with the words in the box.

| bit | four-ish | name | of |
| so | something | sort | stuff |

1 I never usually eat chocolates, or sweets or .... like that.
2 We expect it to take two years or .... to finish the project.
3 They were .... of planning to leave once he'd found a job.
4 Did you turn the lights out, lock all the doors and that kind .... thing?
5 Do you remember the .... near the beginning of the film, where they first meet?
6 We're meeting Justina at ....
7 We need to come up with some kind of a plan or ....
8 You know the film I'm talking about, the one with what's his .... ?

GRAMMAR BANK

3D *do* and *did* for emphasis

REFERENCE ◀ page 41

We can use *do*, *does* or *did* in affirmative sentences to emphasise that what we are saying is true, especially when we are making a contrast with different information or a different opinion.

I **do** really want to go to the concert.
(Perhaps you think I don't want to go.)

I **did** really enjoy their last album.
(I didn't think I would enjoy it.)

He **does** enjoy playing the drums.
(He hates playing the guitar.)

Notice that when we use *do*, *does* or *did* for emphasis, we stress the auxiliary.

I can't stand opera, but I **do** like classical music.

A: He doesn't like jazz music, does he?
B: No, he **does** like jazz, but he doesn't like R&B.

A: You said you would call them.
B: I **did** call them, but they didn't answer.

We can also use *do*, *does* and *did* to emphasise that we feel strongly about something.

I **do** love eating out in expensive restaurants.

He **does** look amazing in that new suit.

We can also use *do*, *does* and *did* to confirm something we think is true, by adding a question tag.

You **do** like spicy food, **don't you?**
He **doesn't** still work there, **does he?**
You **did** remember the passports, **didn't you?**

PRACTICE

1 Choose the correct options to complete the conversations.

1 A: You **do / don't** really like jazz music, do you?
   B: I **do / don't** like it. I'm just not very keen on this album.
2 A: We're going to see The Underwater Crew this weekend. Do you want to come?
   B: I **do / don't** want to come, but I'm not sure I can afford it.
3 A: I hear Francesco is enjoying his new job.
   B: He **doesn't / does** enjoy it, but he'd like to be paid a bit more.
4 A: You got here on time! I thought you were going to be late.
   B: Yes, I **do / did** have to run a bit though!
5 A: I don't have any plans for the weekend, but I **do / don't** think we should go somewhere. You don't want to watch the football match, do you?
   B: No, I **do / don't**.
6 A: Hey, are you still coming for dinner?
   B: Er, yes. But I **do / don't** have to finish this report first.
7 A: Did you check that the music room is free?
   B: I **did / didn't** send a message, but I haven't heard back yet.
8 A: Have you decided whether to sell your car or not?
   B: We **did / didn't** discuss it, but we're going to keep it for now.

2 Complete the sentences with *do*, *don't*, *does*, *doesn't* or *did*.

1 Nearly everyone had gone by the time I got there, but I .... manage to see Jasmin.
2 I .... play the guitar much now, but I .... play in a few different bands when I was younger.
3 He .... enjoy living in Spain – it's so sunny all the time and the people are so friendly.
4 .... tell me you forgot to bring the passports! We'll have to go home and get them.
5 He's a very difficult manager to work for, but they .... all try to keep him happy.
6 I .... see Angela very often anymore, but I .... see her brother quite a lot.
7 Liv .... have a lot of time for playing music at the moment, but she .... still play the occasional gig at the weekend.
8 Are you still OK to drive us to the festival? You .... offer to the other day.

GRAMMAR BANK

4A future continuous and future perfect

REFERENCE ⏪ page 46

Future continuous

We form the future continuous with *will* + *be* + *ing*. We use it for an action or event that will be in progress at a specific time in the future.

I can't meet at 1.00 because I**'ll be taking** Tom to the airport.

This time next week you**'ll be swimming** in the Caribbean Sea.

Don't call me at 8.00 because the band **will be playing**.

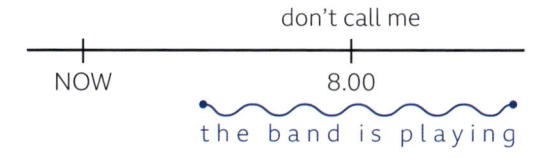

```
                    don't call me
        |                |
       NOW             8.00
              ~~~~~~~~~~~~~~~~~~~
              the band is playing
```

Future perfect

We form the future perfect with *will* + *have* + past participle. We use it for an action or event that will be finished before a specific time in the future.

We often use the future perfect with *by* + a time, meaning *at some time before*.

You can borrow the book next week. I**'ll have finished** it by then.

You can't come at 2.00 because we**'ll have left** by then.

We**'ll have eaten** by 3.00, so we can meet you after that.

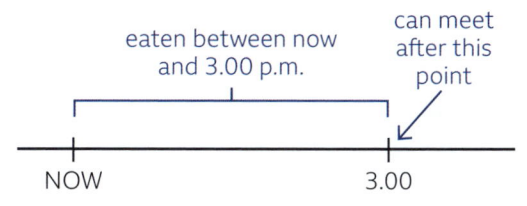

```
     eaten between now      can meet
       and 3.00 p.m.        after this
                              point
        |------------------|  ↙
        |                  |
       NOW               3.00
```

It is possible to use other modal verbs instead of *will* with the future continuous and future perfect.

She **might be travelling** at that time.

This time next week I **could be relaxing** on a beach in Thailand!

I'll call again tomorrow. He **may have forgotten** we'd arranged to meet now.

We **should have completed** the project by the end of next week.

PRACTICE

1 Choose the correct verb forms to complete the sentences.

1 Don't call me at 5 a.m. I'll **be sleeping** / **have slept**!
2 No, I can't do 2 p.m. I won't **be finishing** / **have finished** by then.
3 The driver will **be waiting** / **have waited** for you at the airport.
4 Good luck tomorrow. I'll **be thinking** / **have thought** of you.
5 Call me on Friday. I'll **be speaking** / **have spoken** to Amy by then, so I'll know her plans.
6 He can't meet at 7 p.m. because he'll still **be travelling** / **have travelled**.

2 Complete the second sentence so it has the same meaning as the first. Use the future perfect or continuous form of the verb in brackets.

1 The meeting ends at 3.30.
   The meeting _____ by 3.45. (end)
2 This time next year we'll be in Germany permanently.
   This time next year we _____ in Germany. (live)
3 Come over on Saturday, as I'll be free.
   Come over on Saturday as I _____ anything. (do)
4 Do you need the car later or can I borrow it?
   _____ the car later, or can I borrow it? (use)
5 We can't go to the gym at 5 a.m. It will still be shut.
   The gym _____ by 5 a.m. (open)
6 Their football match starts at 2 and finishes at around 4.
   The girls _____ football at 3.30. (play)

3 Look at the information and complete the sentences (1–6) with the future perfect or future continuous form of the verb in brackets.

> 4 p.m. – Jack's train arrives. Get there a few minutes before to meet him on the platform. Drive back.
>
> 4.10 p.m. – Home!

1 At 3.55, we _____ on the platform. (wait)
2 By 4.30, we _____ back at the house. (arrive)

> 10 p.m. bed time!
>
> (the next day) 6 a.m. early start! 6.45 leave for airport.

3 At 11 p.m., I _____ . (sleep)
4 By 6.45 a.m. the next day, I _____ breakfast. (had)

> This afternoon – meet Jack and his new girlfriend!
>
> Tomorrow morning – go to British Museum.

5 By tonight, I _____ Jack's new girlfriend for the first time. (meet)
6 Tomorrow at 10, I _____ the British Museum. (visit)

GRAMMAR BANK

4B passives

REFERENCE — page 48

Passives

In general, we use the passive to focus on the person or thing affected by an action rather than the person or thing doing the action.

We use the passive when the person or thing that does the action:
- isn't obvious.
- is unknown.
- isn't important.

The theory **has** since **been disproven**.
(We don't know who disproved it and it isn't important.)

General beliefs and opinions

We can also use the passive to talk about general beliefs and opinions. This use is more common in formal writing.

To talk about present beliefs, we use *It is* + *thought/expected/believed/reported* + *that* + clause. We can omit *that* in less formal English.

It is thought (that) a lack of sleep can lead to health problems.

It is believed (that) many children do not get enough sleep nowadays.

To talk about beliefs in the past, we can use the same structure with the past simple or present perfect form of *be*.

In the 4th century BCE, **it was thought** that the Earth was at the centre of the solar system.

It was expected that she would be made CEO within the next year.

It has been suggested that people who have a varied diet have a lower risk of getting cancer.

It has been reported that a huge number of people regularly sleep fewer than six hours a night.

PRACTICE

1 Put the words into the correct order to complete the sentences.

1. the / has / population / It / that / reported / thirty percent / been / of
   _____ suffers from poor sleep.
2. need / thought / most / is / that / It / people
   _____ about eight hours' sleep a night.
3. get / if / is / you / It / expected / too little / that / sleep
   _____, you will not be able to work effectively.
4. 1800s / is / the / that / It / believed / in
   _____ people used to sleep in two blocks of four hours.
5. company / suggested / has / the / that / It / been
   _____ should allow people to start work later in the morning.
6. reported / it / Last / that / children / week / was
   _____ had started the fire.
7. In / that / it / Ancient Egypt / believed / was
   _____ wearing a necklace protected you from bad health.
8. is / It / proportion / that / a / reported / large
   _____ of people are now out of work.

2 Complete the article with *it* and the correct passive form of the verbs in brackets.

Sleep habits from around the world

Siestas
¹_____ (think) that the Spanish tradition of having a sleep in the afternoon dates back thousands of years. In the past, ²_____ (believe) that a siesta was necessary to give farmers time to rest and restore their energy in the hot climate. Nowadays, ³_____ still _____ (expect) that many people will go home and enjoy a long lunch and rest with their family.

Late bedtimes for kids
⁴_____ (report) recently that parents in countries like New Zealand and Australia put their young children to bed by about 7 p.m., whereas in countries like Spain and Argentina it's common to see young children staying up until late in the evening, after 11 p.m. ⁵_____ (think) that children in Asian countries sleep less on average that children who live in the USA, Canada and New Zealand.

Alfresco naps
In a recent study, ⁶_____ (report) that in Scandinavian countries including Norway and Sweden, parents often leave their babies outside to sleep, even in the middle of winter. In these countries, ⁷_____ (believe) that the fresh air is good for children's health and being outside helps to prevent them from getting sick.

Napping in public
The Japanese practice of *inemuri*, or 'sleeping while present', allows people to multitask. In many Japanese companies, ⁸_____ (expect) that people will work long hours and might be tired. As a result, ⁹_____ (considered) quite normal that workers might fall asleep on a park bench or a commuter train, at a dinner party or even during a work meeting.

120

GRAMMAR BANK

4C How to ... express agreement and disagreement

REFERENCE — page 51

Giving opinions

We can use a range of phrases for expressing personal opinions, and for expressing agreement and disagreement.

Expressing personal opinions

Personally, I think/feel/believe that …
In my opinion/view, …
From my perspective/my point of view, …
As far as I'm concerned/aware, …
If you ask me, …

Expressing agreement and disagreement.

We use these phrases for expressing agreement and disagreement.

Agreeing

I couldn't agree more.
That's a good/fair point.
I take/see your point.
That makes sense.

Disagreeing

I'm not sure.
But on the other hand, …
I completely disagree with you.

Concession

Sometimes you may agree with part of what someone says, but not all of it.

A: People should be responsible for their own health. It's not up to the government to tell them what to do.
B: **I agree with you up to a point, but** the government also has a duty to look after its people – and health is part of that.

You might also want to show that you acknowledge or understand someone's argument, even if you don't agree with it. This is called concession.

A: Yoga is fun, but it doesn't help you with cardio.
B: **I understand what you're saying, but** it does help you with strength and flexibility.

We use these phrases to express concession, or to partially agree with someone.

Partially agreeing

I agree (with you) up to a point, but …
I agree to some extent, but …
I suppose so, but …
I understand what you're saying, but …
That's a fair point, although it could also be argued that …

PRACTICE

1 Match the sentence beginnings (1–8) with the endings (a–h) to make phrases for agreeing, disagreeing or partially agreeing.

1 I couldn't agree
2 In my
3 I agree with you up
4 That's a fair point, although
5 I see your
6 As far as I'm
7 I completely
8 True, but on the other

a disagree with you.
b concerned, you're right.
c opinion, he's correct.
d to a point, but …
e it could be argued that the opposite is true.
f hand, they could be right.
g point.
h more.

2 Complete each conversation with the words in the box. There are two extra words in each box.

| disagree   opinion   perspective   point   sense   suppose |

Conversation 1

A: In my ¹........., to coach a team you need to know everything about the sport.
B: I completely ²......... with you. Your relationship with the players is more important.
A: I take your ³........., but you need to know the game.
B: I ⁴......... so, but it's not the most important thing.

| agree   ask   fair   hand   perspective   point |

Conversation 2

A: If you ⁵......... me, it's important to have a new challenge in your life.
B: That's a ⁶........., point, although it's good to take it easy, too!
A: True, but on the other ⁷........., life is about expanding your horizons.
B: I couldn't ⁸......... more, as long as it's not too much effort!

3 Complete the second sentence so it has the same meaning as the first. Use the word in brackets.

1 I think it's good to be active.
   In ...., it's good to be active. (opinion)
2 The opposite view is that running is bad for your knees.
   ...., running is bad for your knees. (hand)
3 I agree with that.
   That .... (sense)
4 You're 100 percent correct!
   .... more! (couldn't)
5 My point of view is that sport should be free to watch.
   ...., sport should be free to watch. (perspective)
6 You might be right.
   Yes, I .... (suppose)
7 I partly agree with you.
   I agree with you up .... (point)
8 In my view, , it's easy to get motivated to exercise.
   As ...., it's easy to get motivated to exercise. (concerned)

GRAMMAR BANK

5A past perfect simple and continuous

REFERENCE ◀◀ page 56

Past perfect simple

We form the past perfect simple with *had* + past participle.
We use the past perfect simple to talk about a completed action in the past that happened before another action.
When I got to the airport, the plane **had already left**.
By the time we arrived, the party **had finished**.

```
the party finished     we arrived
       ✗                   ✗
───────────────────────────────────────
                                    NOW
```

We often use the past perfect simple after 'thinking' verbs such as *realise*, *remember*, *forget*, *think* and *find out* when we thought or learnt about something that happened earlier.
I suddenly **remembered I hadn't called** my mother.
I **found out they had offered** the job to someone else.

Past perfect continuous

We form the past perfect continuous with *had* + *been* + *-ing* form.
We use the past perfect continuous to talk about actions or situations which started before a specific time in the past and were still in progress up to that point.
She retired last year. She**'d been working** at the company since 1972.

We often use the past simple with the past perfect continuous to show that one action interrupted or stopped another.
She**'d been waiting** for two hours when Joe appeared.
He**'d been living** there for three months before he met his neighbour.

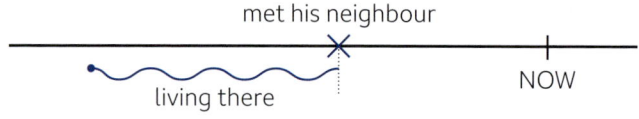

```
                    met his neighbour
                           ✗
───────────────────────────────────────
       ～～～～～～～～            NOW
         living there
```

We can also use the past continuous to described an action which started before a specific time in the past and has finished, but the effects or results were still important.
I was exhausted because I**'d been studying** all night.

Notice the difference between the past perfect simple and past perfect continuous.
I was proud of myself because I**'d cleaned** the whole flat. (The action was completed.)
I was tired because I**'d been cleaning** the flat. (The action was not completed.)

Notice that we use the past perfect simple, NOT the past perfect continuous, with state verbs such as *like*, *love*, *hate*, *know*, *own*, etc.
I**'d known** Sam since we were at college.
I**'d always loved** sailing.

PRACTICE

1 Choose the correct verb forms to complete the story.

Last day at work

When I finally retired three years ago, it was both a sad and a happy day. I [1]**had worked / had been working** at the same rugby club for forty years as the team physiotherapist. I [2]**had treated / had been treating** some of the most talented athletes in the world and, in a few cases, seen their children become professional players and treated them, too. The day itself was special. I [3]**had looked / had been looking** after one of our injured players, as usual, when there was a knock on the door. It was the coach. He asked me to come to the changing room for a moment. I [4]**hadn't finished / hadn't been finishing** working with the player, so I told the coach I'd be there in ten minutes. When I got to the changing room, I realised the whole squad – over forty players – plus fifteen members of staff [5]**waited / had been waiting** for me! The coach [6]**made / had been making** a speech thanking me and presented me with the shirt our captain had worn the day we won the cup in 1997. Then the players [7]**sang / had sung** a song. I was so surprised! I [8]**didn't expect / hadn't expected** any of this. It was a great way to finish, and I'm still in touch with many people at the club.

2 Complete the sentences using the correct past simple, past perfect or past perfect continuous form of the verbs in brackets.

1. Mohamed was very excited because he .... (never / visit) Paris before.
2. She was tired because she .... (paint) the dining room all day.
3. I didn't go to the theatre with them because I .... (already / see) the play twice.
4. What .... (you / think) of the new biology professor yesterday?
5. When I opened the door, everything was white; it .... (snow) all night.
6. As soon as Marta saw the teacher, she realised she .... (meet) him before.
7. We .... (drive) across Australia for eight weeks when the car broke down.
8. They .... (not / know) each other for long before they got married.
9. It was clear he .... (run) because he was sweating and out of breath.
10. Jack made fish for dinner because his guest .... (not / eat) meat.

GRAMMAR BANK

5B past plans and intentions

REFERENCE ◀◀ page 60

We use the following phrases and past verb forms to talk about past plans or intentions which changed and didn't come true.

Compare:

I **had arranged to meet** Stefan after the show, and we went for a meal together.
(I had a plan, and it didn't change.)

I **was planning to meet** Stefan after the show, but I was too tired, so I went straight home.
(I had a plan, but it changed.)

Forms followed by the infinitive

We can use *I was meant to …* , *I was supposed to …* , *I was going to …* , *I was planning to …* , *I was hoping to …* , *I was expecting to …* + infinitive without *to*. The plural form uses *were* instead of *was*.

We **were meant to** meet in the park, but it was raining, so we met in a café instead.

I **was supposed to** call her to arrange an appointment, but I forgot.

I **was going to** study law, but I switched to history instead.

He **was planning to** meet us at the venue, but his car broke down.

Martina **was hoping to** study physics at university, but her grades weren't good enough.

Raj **was expecting to** join his father's company, but his father took on someone else instead.

Forms followed by the -ing form

We can use *I was thinking of …* , *I was considering …* and *I was planning on …* + -ing form. The plural form uses *were* instead of *was*.

I **was thinking of applying** for that job, but I didn't think I had the right qualifications.

She **was considering switching** careers, but she changed her mind.

They **were planning on staying** in a hotel, but they found a holiday cottage instead.

Notice the difference in form between:
I **was planning to meet** some friends.
I **was planning on meeting** some friends.

PRACTICE

1 Complete the sentences with the correct form of the verbs in brackets.

1 She was supposed .... (check) all the details before we left.
2 Arjun was thinking of .... (join) us this evening, but he's not feeling great.
3 I was meant .... (go) to Art School, but my parents didn't approve.
4 I've been considering .... (retrain) as a physiotherapist.
5 I was planning .... (tell) you as soon as I had confirmation.
6 We were expecting .... (see) you at the conference.
7 Jason was planning on .... (stay) for an extra couple of days.
8 We were supposed .... (sign) the new contract today.
9 I've been thinking of .... (apply) for a new position.
10 We were going .... (visit) Canada, but we couldn't get a visa.

2 Cross out the option that is NOT possible in each sentence.

1 What are you doing here? We were **meant to meet** / **supposed to meeting** / **going to meet** you at 8 p.m.
2 He was **thinking of** / **supposed to** / **hoping to** set up his own business, but then the economic crisis made it impossible.
3 I was **thinking of inviting** / **planning to invite** / **meant to inviting** a few people to dinner, but I don't know what to cook.
4 We were **expecting to have** / **going to having** / **meant to have** the appointment on Friday but it's been cancelled.
5 She was seriously **considering to resign** / **considering resigning** / **thinking of resigning** when they offered her a transfer.

3 Complete the responses using the prompts in brackets.

1 A: I thought he was going to be a doctor.
   B: He .... (think / study) medicine, but now he's decided to do biology instead.
2 A: I thought you were going to stay in and have an early night.
   B: Yes, I .... (plan / stay in), but then Anna invited me to a house party.
3 A: Didn't you meet Jeremy?
   B: No, we .... (hope / see) him at the restaurant, but he never showed up.
4 A: Congratulations! I heard you won a prize at the exhibition.
   B: Thanks. I was so surprised. I wasn't .... (expect / win) anything.
5 A: Have you seen Gabriella? She's not here yet.
   B: No, she .... (suppose / meet) us at 3 p.m., but she hasn't arrived yet.
6 A: Have you decided where to go on holiday?
   B: Yes, we .... (consider / take) a trip to Hawaii, but in the end we decided on Thailand.
7 A: I can't believe you didn't tell me Juan was coming to dinner.
   B: I .... (plan on / tell) you, but I must have forgotten.
8 A: Did you make it to the beach?
   B: No, we .... (going / have a swim), but then it started to rain.

123

GRAMMAR BANK

5C How to ... describe problems and suggest solutions

REFERENCE ◀ page 63

Describing problems

We use *I can't get the ... working/to work* to say we don't know how to start using a machine.

I can't get the webcam **to work**.

We use keep + *-ing* form to say that a problem happens repeatedly.

The image **keeps disappearing**.
The sound **keeps cutting out**.

Describing problems
I can't get the ... working.
There seems to be a problem with ...
There's something wrong with my ...
The ... isn't working.
It keeps + *-ing* form (crashing/disappearing/stopping).
Every time I ... , it ...

Suggesting solutions

We use *perhaps + you could* and *maybe + you could* to make suggestions. They have the same meaning.

Maybe you could open a new window.
Perhaps you could log off and on again.

We use try + *-ing* form to suggest a solution.

Try switching off your camera.
Why don't you **try using** different headphones?

Suggesting a solution
Perhaps you could try + *-ing* form.
Maybe you could + infinitive without *to*.
Why don't you try + *-ing* form?
It might be worth + *-ing* form.
Have you checked the .../(tried + *-ing* form)?

Explaining why a solution would work

We use *that might work* and *it's worth a try* to suggest that it's possible a solution will work.

Shall we switch hosts? **It's worth a try** because it worked yesterday.
Shall we try logging in again? **That might work**.

We use *It sometimes helps if you* + infinitive without *to* to show an action has been tried successfully before.

It sometimes helps if you turn down the volume.
It sometimes helps if you move away from the mic.

Explaining why a solution would work
That might work because ...
It's worth a try because ...
It sometimes helps if you + infinitive without *to* because ...

PRACTICE

1 Match the sentence beginnings (1–10) with the endings (a–j).

1 My laptop keeps
2 It might be worth
3 There seems to be a problem
4 Have you
5 There's something
6 I can't get the
7 It's worth a try because it
8 Maybe you could log
9 It sometimes helps if
10 Perhaps you could

a checked the microphone?
b wrong with my picture.
c off and on again.
d checking your internet connection.
e try sending a link.
f you turn off the video.
g sometimes fixes itself.
h crashing.
i sound working.
j with your sound.

2 Complete the conversations with the phrases in the boxes.

| every time   have you tried   maybe you could   there seems to be   worth a try |

Conversation 1

A: ¹_____ a problem with my washing machine. ²_____ I switch it on, it overflows.
B: Oh. ³_____ unplugging it and plugging it in again?
A: Yes, I tried that. It still didn't work.
B: Well, ⁴_____ call Steve and tell him about the problem.
A: Yes, that's ⁵_____ . Thanks.

| I can't get   it keeps   it sometimes helps if   there's something wrong |

Conversation 2

A: ⁶_____ with my phone.
B: Oh dear. What's the issue?
A: ⁷_____ the camera working. ⁸_____ shutting down.
B: ⁹_____ you restart the phone.
A: Really? I'll try that.

| isn't working   it might work because   why don't you try |

Conversation 3

A: My TV remote ¹⁰_____ . I can't seem to change channel.
B: That's annoying. ¹¹_____ replacing the batteries?
A: Do you think that'll work?
B: ¹²_____ you probably haven't changed them for years!
A: Yeah, that's true.

GRAMMAR BANK

5D non-defining relative clauses for comments

REFERENCE ◂◂ page 65

We use defining relative clauses to explain exactly which person or thing we are talking about.

The team that I work with has won several awards.

We use non-defining relative clauses to give extra, non-essential information.

The building, which was built in 1882, is due to be redecorated next month.

(We don't need to know when it was built – this is extra information.)

To introduce a non-defining relative clause, we use the following relative pronouns – *which* (for things), *who* (for people), *whose* (for possession), *where* (for places) and *when* (for times).

Yuki, who joined the company last year, has had a really positive impact on the team.

Poland, where our next meeting will be held, is one of our fastest-growing markets.

Non-defining relative clauses are often used in the middle of a sentence. However, we can also use them at the end of a sentence to make a comment or give an opinion about what we've just said.

I worked with Tim on the Greenway project, which was an absolute pleasure.

(We don't need to know the speaker enjoyed working with Tim – this is an extra comment/opinion.)

They introduced me to Nicky Laird, whose books I've loved for years.

(We don't need to know the speaker likes Nicky Laird's books – this is an extra comment/opinion.)

The company just appointed Felix Schulz, who is a really nice guy.

(We don't need to know the speaker likes Felix – this is an extra comment/opinion.)

PRACTICE

1 Match the main information (1–6) with the comments (a–f) to make sentences.

1 They've just returned from Cambridge,
2 I spent the weekend with my cousins,
3 They cooked some home-made pizzas,
4 He left the company without telling anybody,
5 Let's get together in the summer,
6 If you want ideas for recipes, talk to Matt,

a who live in Scotland.
b which were delicious.
c whose cooking skills are amazing!
d which was quite a shock.
e when the weather's usually better.
f where they had a lovely week's holiday.

2 Read the sentences and the comments in brackets. Rewrite them using a non-defining relative clause as a comment.

1 Thank you for the T-shirt. (lovely!)
   Thank you for the T-shirt, which is lovely!
2 We worked in a small office. (not very comfortable)
3 I've got a new boss. (great to work with)
4 When I told her my plans, she was very understanding. (didn't expect that)
5 My first year has gone really well. (quite a relief)
6 I'm much happier working on my own. (quite surprising)
7 He offered everyone a promotion except Dennis. (seems a bit unfair)
8 He sits around all day doing nothing. (drives me crazy)
9 The worst part of the job is over. (really pleased about this).
10 We were delayed on the way to the airport. (I found this really annoying)

GRAMMAR BANK

6A necessity, prohibition and permission

REFERENCE ◀ page 70

Necessity

We can use structures with *need* to express necessity, when the focus is on the action, not the person who does the action.

We can use *need* + *-ing* form. This is often used to talk about chores or things we haven't had time to do yet.

The lightbulb in the kitchen **needs changing**.
Your nails **need redoing**.

We can also use *need* + the passive infinitive.

The TV **needs to be repaired**.
The meat **needs to be cooked** for a bit longer.

We can also use *must*, *need to* and *have to* to express necessity, when the focus is on the person who does the action.

You **need to apply** for a visa before you travel.
You **have to speak** to the manager if you want a refund.

Prohibition

We use *be* + *not* + *allowed to* when someone does not have permission to do something or it is against the rules or illegal. We can use it with different forms of *be*, to talk about the present or the past.

You**'re not allowed to** park there.
We **weren't allowed to** stay out after midnight.

We can use *forbid* or *be forbidden* in formal sentences. It is often used in the passive form.

The museum **forbids** photography.
Feeding the animals **is forbidden**.

We can also say that something *is not* or *was not permitted* in formal sentences.

Liquids **are not permitted** inside hand luggage.
Phones **were not permitted** in the classroom.

We can also use *mustn't*, *can't* and *couldn't* to express prohibition.

You **mustn't talk** during the exam.
Without a credit card, you **can't** rent a car.

Permission

We use *allow* and *be allowed to* to express permission. In the active form, we use *allow* + object + infinitive with *to*.

I **allowed her to borrow** my car.
We **were allowed to retake** the exam.

We can use *permit* and *be permitted to* in more formal sentences. In the active form, we use *permit* + object + infinitive with *to*.

The rules **permit players to take** a ten-minute break between games.
Dogs **are permitted** inside the building.

PRACTICE

1 Read the pairs of sentences. Does each pair have the same (S) or a different (D) meaning?
   1 a Your passport needs to be renewed this year.
      b You have to renew your passport this year.
   2 a You aren't allowed to use a dictionary in the exam.
      b Dictionaries are permitted in the exam.
   3 a Mobile phones were forbidden.
      b You mustn't use your mobile phone.
   4 a We could do what we wanted in our free time.
      b We were allowed to do what we wanted in our free time.
   5 a The law forbids graffiti on public buildings.
      b The law allows graffiti on public buildings.
   6 a The clothes needed ironing.
      b The clothes needed to be ironed.

2 Choose the correct words to complete the sentences.
   1 Were you **allowed do / allowed to do** experiments in the lab?
   2 Our employees didn't need **retraining / being retrained**.
   3 They **permitted us to enter / permitted that we enter** the gallery and we loved it.
   4 With that visa, having a part-time job **is forbid / is forbidden**.
   5 The essay is fine and doesn't **need be rewritten / need to be rewritten**.
   6 The children are **forbidden to play / forbid to play** outside.
   7 We **couldn't go / couldn't going** inside the museum without a ticket.
   8 Food **isn't allow / isn't allowed** in the library.

3 Complete the second sentence so it means the same as the first sentence. Use the word in brackets.
   1 We must do several tasks this morning.
     Several tasks .... this morning. (doing)
   2 We had to replace our pipes.
     The pipes .... replaced. (need)
   3 The teacher didn't let us use our phones in class.
     We .... our phones in class. (allowed)
   4 The document has already been edited.
     The document doesn't .... (edited)
   5 You can't play ball games here.
     Ball games .... here. (permitted)
   6 She let me stay in her flat.
     She .... in her flat. (allowed)
   7 You aren't allowed to take photos in this building.
     Taking photos .... in this building. (forbidden)
   8 The law says that parents can make decisions for their children.
     The law .... decisions for their children. (permits)

GRAMMAR BANK

6B reported orders, requests and advice

REFERENCE → page 71

Reported orders, requests and advice

We can use *order*, *tell*, *ask* and *advise* to report orders, requests and advice. The verb pattern for all the verbs is the same: verb + object + infinitive with *to*.

We use *order* and *tell* to report orders.

'Shut the door!' → She **ordered me to shut** the door.
'Sit down!' → He **told us to sit** down.

We use *ask* to report requests.

'Can you open the door?' → I **asked him to open** the door.

We use *advise* to report advice.

'You should change jobs.' → He **advised me to change** jobs.

Tense changes, pronouns and time references

When we report speech, the verb often goes back further into the past. Pronouns and time references, etc. also change.

Direct speech	Reported speech
present simple	past simple
'I'm really tired!'	She said she **was** really tired.
present continuous	past continuous
'I'm working on a new project.'	She told us she **was working** on a new project.
past simple	past perfect
'I enjoyed reading your book.'	She said that she **had enjoyed** reading my book.
past continuous	past perfect continuous
'I was hoping to apply for the job.'	He said that he **had been hoping** to apply for the job.
will/would/can/could/should	would/could/should
'We'll help you find somewhere to stay.'	They said they **would** help me find somewhere to stay.
'You can stay with me.'	She said I **could** stay with her.
now/yesterday/here	then/the day before/there
He arrived yesterday.	He arrived **the day before**.

We don't need to change the verb form into the past when we are reporting something that is still true now, or was said recently. We use the present form of a reporting verb.

'I think the meeting is finishing now.' → Paolo **says** he thinks the meeting **is finishing** now.

Reported questions

When we report questions, we keep the word order the same as for statements.

We don't use the auxiliary verb *do/does/did*, and we don't use a question mark.

'What does Imogen think?'
They asked me **what Imogen thought**.
NOT ~~They asked me what did Imogen think.~~

With *yes/no* questions, use *if* or *whether*.

'Are you coming to the party?'
She asked me **if I was coming** to the party.

PRACTICE

1 Put the words into the correct order to complete the reported sentences.

1 'Complete the report by Monday.'
   Monday / report / to / me / the / ordered / by / He / complete
2 'Do you think you could open the door for me?'
   door / me / for / open / her / the / She / to / asked
3 'Can you arrange a meeting for Wednesday?'
   for / They asked / arrange / me / Wednesday / a / meeting / to
4 'Could you please organise a taxi to collect me?'
   taxi / to / a / asked / her / me / to / She / organise / collect
5 'I think you should try not to work at the weekend.'
   weekend / work / me / She / to / at / the / not / advised

2 Read the comments (1–5). Then complete the reported speech (a–e). Use the pronoun in brackets.

1 'Do you think you could help me move the chairs?'
2 'I think it would be a good idea for you to leave early.'
3 'Put the files on my desk and leave immediately.'
4 'Can you give me a lift to the station?'
5 'I suggest you take some time off work to recover.'

a He <u>asked me to move</u> the chairs. (me)
b She .... early. (him)
c He .... the files on his desk and leave immediately. (me)
d She .... her a lift to the station. (me)
e She .... some time off work to recover. (them)

3 Complete the stories with the correct form of the pairs of verbs in the box.

> advise/arrive   order/wait   advise/not call
> ask/allow   tell/go   ask/stop

I was interviewing a candidate when she [1]............ the interview for a few minutes because she had forgotten to lock her car. I said yes. She left and never came back.

I once had an interview with a twenty-two-year-old student who turned up with his mother! Even worse, he [2]............ her to answer any questions he wasn't sure about! I [3]............ back home and grow up!

A young woman came into my office for an interview. She arrived late and was wearing dirty jeans and a ripped T-shirt. She told me she'd had a lot of interviews but nobody had given her a job. I [4]............ on time and dress smartly for her next interview.

I flew from San Francisco to New York for a job interview. When I arrived, the manager [5]............ in the hotel lobby while he finished his game of solitaire on his laptop because he was about to win!

One interviewee gave me a list of references but then [6]............ two of them because they would say bad things about him.

127

GRAMMAR BANK

6C How to ... ask for advice and give advice tactfully

REFERENCE ◀◀ page 75

Asking for advice

What do you think I should do?
What would you do?
What do you think?
Can you give me some advice about … ?
What would you recommend/suggest?

Giving advice tactfully

When we are giving sensitive advice (which could be embarrassing for the person who receives it), we use phrases to prepare the listener. These help to soften the message. Several of these phrases focus on how the listener should view the advice.

I hope you don't take this the wrong way, but you can sometimes come across as slightly rude.
I don't want you to get the wrong idea, but I'm not sure I want to be in the band anymore.
Don't take it personally, but the clothes you wear to work aren't always suitable for the office.

Preparing the listener for sensitive advice

I hope you don't take this the wrong way, but …
I don't want you to get the wrong idea, but …
Don't take it personally, but …
I'm telling you this as a friend.
To be honest, …

When giving advice tactfully, we often use modal verbs like *could* and *might* to soften the message.
It **might** be a good idea to spend a bit more time preparing before you go for interviews.
You **could** try paying a bit more attention in meetings.

We also use *perhaps* and *maybe* to make it clear that our advice is only a suggestion, not an order.
Maybe you should go to bed earlier.
Perhaps you should talk to your manager.

Giving advice tactfully

My advice would be to + infinitive without *to*
If you want my advice, you should …
You should definitely …
Perhaps you should/ought to …
It's probably/It might be a good idea to + infinitive without *to*
Have you thought about/considered + -*ing* form
If I were you, I'd …

PRACTICE

1 Complete the second sentence so it has the same meaning as the first using the words in brackets.

1 Get rid of it!
   My .... be to get rid of it. (advice)
2 You ought to write to him.
   Have .... to him? (consider)
3 Listen to what she's saying!
   I think you .... her advice. (ought)
4 I've told you this before: your dad was right!
   Please don't take this .... your dad was right. (wrong)
5 I completely disagree.
   I don't want you to get .... I disagree. (idea)
6 What should I do?
   What .... ? (recommend)
7 You should ask for help!
   It might be a .... ask for help. (idea)
8 No doubt about it – you got this wrong.
   .... , I think you got this wrong. (honest)

2 Choose the correct words to complete the conversations.

1 A: I can't believe the teacher gave me a B. I'm the best student in class!
   B: Look, I hope you don't ¹**consider / get / take** this the wrong way, but you aren't. You're always forgetting to do your homework.
   A: Not always!
   B: My ²**advise / advice / reason** would be to not take it personally. Just study more next time!

2 A: My flatmates are so messy, I don't know what I can do about it.
   B: I don't want you to ³**make / get / do** the wrong idea, but it isn't only them.
   A: What do you mean? Are you saying that *I'm* messy, too?
   B: Look, if I ⁴**were / would be / am** you, I'd draw up a schedule so everyone shares the cleaning.

3 A: I accidentally texted my boss instead of my partner. What do you think I ⁵**would / will / should** do?
   B: It ⁶**might / must / should** be a good idea to just admit you made a mistake.
   A: But it's so embarrassing!
   B: ⁷**When / If / As** you want my advice, you should apologise and hope they forget about it.

GRAMMAR BANK

7A past modals of deduction

REFERENCE → page 82

We use modal verb + *have* + past participle to speculate or make deductions about past actions or situations.

I **must have left** my phone in the café.

We use *must have* to say we feel certain that something happened or is true, based on the evidence.

I **must have deleted** the email. I can't find it anywhere.

We use *might/could/may have* to say we think it is possible that something happened or is true, based on the evidence.

They **may have missed** their train. The traffic near the station was terrible.

We use *can't/couldn't have* when we are almost certain that something is not true, or impossible, based on the evidence.

He **can't have taken** the car because I've got his car keys.

We use modal verb + *have* + *been* + *-ing* form to speculate or make deductions about continuous actions or states.

They **can't have been living** there very long.
You **must have been waiting** for ages!

We use modal verb + *have* + *been* + past participle to speculate or make deductions using the passive.

Her bag **must have been stolen** while we were sitting at the bus stop.
Their flight **might have been delayed** because of the bad weather.

PRACTICE

1 Choose the correct verb forms to complete the sentences.

1 You're very good on the violin. You must have **practise / practised** a lot!
2 She's very good at painting. I guess she **might / can't** have gone to art college, but I'm not sure.
3 He **can't / must** have finished all that work already. It's impossible!
4 It's a very old building. It might have **built / been built** in the early 1800s.
5 Her bag must **have stolen / have been stolen** while she was in the marketplace.
6 Try calling again – they **might / can't** not have heard you the first time.

2 Rewrite the sentences in bold using a past modal of deduction.

1 He's a highly talented musician. **It's possible that he got the talent from his mother.**
   He <u>might have got the talent</u> from his mother.
2 He's a world-famous author. **It's almost certain that you've read his books.**
   You .... his books.
3 I lost all the work that I did yesterday. **It's impossible that I saved it properly.**
   I .... properly.
4 She fell down the stairs and broke her foot. **I'm quite certain than it was painful.**
   It .... painful.
5 We haven't heard back from Frank yet. **It's possible that he phoned while we were out.**
   He .... while we were out.
6 He built the house entirely by himself. **I'm almost certain it was not easy.**
   It .... easy.

3 Complete the conversations with a past modal of deduction and the correct forms of the verbs in the box.

| be   break   cost   give   look   offer |

1 A: Oh, no! Look what's happened to my necklace.
   B: It .... when you were swimming. I saw a piece like that in the swimming pool.
2 A: Do you like my new coat?
   B: It's gorgeous! That .... you a fortune!
3 A: I've finally finished my novel after years of hard work.
   B: Congratulations! That .... easy.
4 A: What's happened to Giorgio? I haven't seen him recently.
   B: I'm not sure, but I think he .... a new job in another department.
5 A: I've lost my boarding pass!
   B: You .... properly. I saw you put it in your bag just now.
6 A: Where did you get that from? It's lovely.
   B: I can't quite remember, but it .... to me by my sister.

GRAMMAR BANK

7B wish, if only, should have

REFERENCE ◀◀ page 83

	Present	Past
wish	*wish* + past simple or *could*	*wish* + past perfect
if only …	*if only* + past simple or *could*	*if only* + past perfect
should(n't) have		*should(n't)* + *have* + past participle

wish

We use *wish* + past simple or *could* to talk about things we would like to be different in the present, when these things are impossible or unlikely to change.

I wish I had more time. (But I don't have more time.)
I wish you were here. (But you aren't here.)

We use *wish* + object + *would* to talk about something you want to stop happening in the present because it annoys you.

I wish they would be quiet at night.
(But I don't think they will.)
I wish you wouldn't call me at weekends.
(But I know you probably will continue to do it.)

Notice that we don't use this structure to talk about ourselves.
NOT ~~I wish I wouldn't be so poor.~~

We use *wish* + past perfect to talk about things that happened or didn't happen in the past, which we now regret and would like to change.

I wish I'd gone to university when I was younger.
(I didn't go to university and now I regret it.)
I wish they hadn't moved away. I really miss them!
(They moved, and now I feel sad about this.)

if only

We can use *if only* instead of *wish* in the structures above to show more emotion.

If only we lived by the sea!
If only the car **would** start!
If only he **would** be quiet!
If only I'd listened to my mother!

should have

We can also use *should(n't) have* + past participle to talk about things in the past that we regret.

We **should have arrived** earlier. Now there are no seats.
I **shouldn't have spoken** to you like that. I'm sorry.

PRACTICE

1 Match the sentence beginnings (1–6) with the endings (a–f).

1 I wish you would   a learnt it by heart.
2 If only I wasn't   b I'd taken advantage of my opportunities.
3 I should have
4 If only I   c terrified of heights.
5 I wish   d have switched careers.
6 You shouldn't   e be a bit more adventurous!
                            f hadn't taken my friend's stupid advice!

2 Choose the correct options (A–C) to complete the anecdotes.

I wish ¹_____ started learning the piano earlier. I only started when I was in my twenties and I discovered I had a talent for it. My sister already played and she told me I should try it. I ²_____ listened to her. ³_____ I'd taken her advice earlier: I might have become a professional musician. (Pauline)

⁴_____ I hadn't left school at sixteen! That's my biggest regret. I wish ⁵_____ to university. I love studying, but at that age I didn't know any better and I ended up in a boring job instead. I wish I ⁶_____ change career now, but it's too late. (Eugenia)

I don't really have any regrets. Maybe I ⁷_____ gone to so many parties as a teenager, but it was fun at the time and that's how I made a lot of friends. Looking back, there's nothing I really wish I ⁸_____ . (Pavel)

1 A I would   B I   C I had
2 A should have   B should   C wish I
3 A I should   B I should have C I wish
4 A I should have   B I wish you   C If only
5 A I hadn't gone   B I'd gone   C I went
6 A would   B had   C could
7 A shouldn't have   B should go   C would have
8 A would do   B did   C hadn't done

3 Complete the second sentence using the word in brackets.

1 I wish I'd learnt to swim when I was a child.
   _____ when I was a child. (should)
2 I think buying that phone was a big mistake.
   _____ that phone. (wish)
3 I didn't listen to my mother, and now I regret it.
   _____ to my mother. (only)
4 It's so annoying that my car won't start!
   _____ start. (would)
5 She dropped out of university, which was a bad idea.
   _____ of university. (shouldn't)
6 I can't remember her number, and I need it now!
   _____ her number! (only)
7 Unfortunately, I have very little time to work on this.
   _____ more time to work on this. (wish)
8 Alberto talks so much! It really annoys me.
   _____ talk so much! (wish)

GRAMMAR BANK

7C How to ... describe a process

REFERENCE ◀◀ page 87

When we describe a process, it is helpful to break it down into stages. We can use different phrases to introduce each stage. These prepare the listener to focus on the information that comes next.

To begin with, put the ingredients in a bowl.
The next step is to mix the ingredients.
The final stage is to let the dish cool for five minutes.

Describing stages in order	
First stage	To begin with, you'll want to …
Middle stage	The next stage/step is to … Once you've done … , (you) …
Last stage	The final stage involves + -ing form

Some stages in a process are more important than others. It is helpful to indicate which stages are necessary, and which are not completely necessary.

It's essential to book early.
Choosing your seats is optional.

Giving instructions according to necessity	
100% necessary	It's essential that you … It's essential to …
a good idea but not 100% necessary	I would recommend + -ing form
not necessary, but maybe nice to do	This is optional. If you want, you can …

When describing a process, it is useful to give warnings about common problems or mistakes.

Avoid taking selfies with your back to the light.
Be careful not to hold the camera too close.

Warning about potential problems
Be careful not to …
Avoid + -ing form
One common mistake is to …
Watch out for …

PRACTICE

1 Choose the correct words to complete the conversations.

1 A: How can I apply for a work visa?
B: ¹**To begin** / **For begin** with, you'll need to fill out this form.
A: OK. What's the next ²**movement** / **step**?
B: ³**Since** / **Once** you've done that, you send it to the consulate.

2 A: Do I have to buy travel insurance when I book my ticket?
B: No, it's ⁴**essential** / **optional**.
A: But would you recommend ⁵**buying** / **to buy** it?
B: Yes, I'd avoid ⁶**to travel** / **travelling** without insurance.

2 Choose the correct options (A–C) to complete the text.

Writing exams: Tips

¹_____ , make sure you prepare well by practising writing in the weeks before the exam. I'd ²_____ doing at least three timed practice tests. ³_____ this, you'll feel more confident that you can write the essays in the time given.

When you take the real exam, ⁴_____ read the instructions. Go over each point and plan the essay before you write. ⁵_____ that you think of some ideas first and know what points you want to get across. One common ⁶_____ write everything you know about the subject instead of writing to a plan. ⁷_____ doing this because marks are given for organisation, not just content. The ⁸_____ checking your work for silly mistakes and making sure your writing is accurate.

1 A	It's essential	B To begin with	C Be careful
2 A	recommend	B avoid	C want
3 A	To begin	B If you want	C Once you've done
4 A	be careful to	B I'd recommend	C it's essential
5 A	The next step	B It's essential	C If you want
6 A	problem is	B stage is to	C mistake is to
7 A	I'd recommend	B Avoid	C It's optional
8 A	final stage involves	B next step is to	C common mistake is

3 Complete the second sentence so it has the same meaning as the first using the word in brackets.

1 You must buy a ticket before you enter.
It's _____ a ticket before you enter. (essential)

2 It's a good idea to check in early, but not 100 percent necessary.
I _____ early. (recommend)

3 The last thing you do is pour the mixture into a jar.
The _____ pouring the mixture into a jar. (final)

4 Bumps in the road are a potential problem!
_____ bumps in the road! (watch)

5 Don't overcook the pasta.
Be _____ the pasta. (careful)

6 You can bring your own food, but it's not necessary.
You can bring your own food if you want to, but _____ . (optional)

GRAMMAR BANK

7D adverbials of concession

REFERENCE ⏪ page 89

however

We use *however* to introduce information which contrasts with something that has just been said. We put a comma after *however*.

Our house was very comfortable. **However**, it was too small for our growing family.

We usually put *however* at the beginning of a sentence, but it can also go at the end. This sounds a little more formal.

The trip was very long. **However**, it was fun.
The trip was very long. It was fun, **however**.

We cannot use *however* to join two clauses in the same sentence. We need to make two sentences.

She always did really well at school. **However**, she struggled when she went to university.
NOT ~~She always did really well at school, however, she struggled when she went to university.~~

though/although

We use *though* or *although* to introduce a contrasting idea or piece of information. We often use it to introduce another side of an argument or opinion.

We can use *though* or *although* between two clauses. We usually use a comma before them.

The film is never boring, **though** it's really long.
My flat looks nice from outside, **although** it's dark inside.

We can also use *though* or *although* at the beginning of a sentence. We use a comma at the end of the first clause.

Although Jo doesn't practise much, she's good at the guitar.
Though I said 2 p.m. earlier, let's meet at 3 p.m.

Unlike *however*, we don't use *although* at the end of a sentence. Use *though* instead.

Although the weather was bad, we enjoyed the holiday.
We enjoyed the holiday, **although** the weather was bad.
We enjoyed the holiday. The weather was bad, **though**.

Though and *although* are different from *however* in that they join two clauses together in one sentence.

I like swimming, **though** it's not my favourite activity.
I like swimming. **However**, it's not my favourite activity.

on the other hand

We use *on the other hand* to contrast a second piece of information with the first. We often use it to introduce another side of an argument or opinion. We put a comma after *on the other hand*.

It's difficult. I do think it's important to think about your future. **On the other hand**, you also need to enjoy what you're doing now.

We can use the full phrase *on the one hand … on the other hand …* to give both sides of an argument or opinion.

On the one hand, we'd love to move somewhere greener. **On the other hand**, we love being in the city.

PRACTICE

1 Choose the correct options to complete the sentences.
1 **Though / However** she's a talented musician, she never plays in public.
2 I didn't recognise her. **On the one hand / However**, we'd met before.
3 **Although / On the other hand** there was a loud noise, she didn't wake up.
4 The train was late. **Though / However**, we managed to arrive on time.
5 **On the one hand / Though** it was freezing, I wasn't wearing a coat.
6 It's true you'd have to move away. **On the other hand / Although**, it's a great opportunity.
7 **Although / However** both his parents are scientists, he hates physics and chemistry.
8 I don't usually watch horror films. **On the one hand / However**, I enjoyed this one.

2 Match 1–8 with a–h.
1 I've known Chen for twenty years.
2 Though the picture is frozen,
3 On the one hand, this flight time looks good.
4 I broke my foot.
5 It's a lovely house,
6 Her paintings are brilliant.
7 His first two films were amazing.
8 Though we could try that restaurant,

a On the other hand, this one is cheaper.
b although I wish it were nearer the sea.
c However, we aren't close friends.
d I think it's usually closed on Sundays.
e I can hear you fine.
f However, the rest were terrible.
g However, it was a blessing in disguise.
h On the other hand, I don't think much of her sculptures.

3 Complete the article with one word in each gap.

The talented Mr Robeson

It's hard to say which of Paul Robeson's many talents was his finest. On the ¹_____ hand, he was a world-class singer; on the ²_____ hand, his most important work was arguably his human rights activism.

³_____ he is best known as a singer and actor, Robeson was also incredibly talented in other fields. He was outstanding at American football, winning an athletic scholarship to Rutgers University. He also earned a law degree from Columbia University Law School, ⁴_____ he didn't work as a lawyer for long.

At the time, few Americans spoke more than one or two languages. ⁵_____, Robeson was familiar with over a dozen, including Mandarin Chinese, German, Spanish and Arabic, several of which he picked up on his many travels.

For decades, he was one of the world's most famous men. ⁶_____, after a series of illnesses, he retired in his sixties and died in 1976, largely forgotten by the public.

GRAMMAR BANK

8A participle clauses

REFERENCE → page 92

We can use participle clauses to join two actions together in the same sentence.

She was sitting in the waiting room. She thought about her father.

→ **Sitting** in the waiting room, she thought about her father.

They finished their meal. Then they left the restaurant.

→ **Having** finished their meal, they left the restaurant.

We use a present participle (-*ing* form) when the two actions happen at more or less the same time.

I walked into the room, and I noticed everyone was busy.

→ **Walking** into the room, I noticed everyone was busy.

We use a past participle clause (*having* + past participle) when one action happened before the other.

I read through all the information, then I decided to sign the contract.

→ **Having** read through all the information, I decided to sign the contract.

The two actions in the sentence must have the same subject.

Ana finished her talk, then she left.
(same subject)

→ **Having** finished her talk, Ana left.

Ana finished her talk, then everyone left.
(different subjects)

NOT ~~Having finished her talk, everyone left.~~

PRACTICE

1 Choose the correct verb forms to complete each second sentence.

1 She was working long hours. She usually felt tired in the evening.
   Working / Having worked long hours, she usually felt tired in the evening.

2 He finished his exams and then he considered whether to apply for university.
   Having finished / Finishing his exams, he considered whether to apply for university.

3 They visited all the important sights and then went back to their accommodation.
   Visiting / Having visited all the important sights, they went back to their accommodation.

4 She was standing at the window as she watched the cars drive past.
   Standing / Having stood at the window, she watched the cars drive past.

5 She read all the books in the house and then went to the library for more.
   Reading / Having read all the books in the house, she went to the library for more.

6 As she opened her office door, she saw Max disappearing down the corridor.
   Opening / Having opened her office the door, she saw Max disappearing down the corridor.

2 Complete the sentences with the correct participle form of the verbs in the box. More than one answer might be possible.

| clean   complete   leave   move   promise   sit   visit   work |

1 .... several co-living spaces, she eventually decided to look for an apartment of her own.
2 .... to the city for the first time, he found that it was difficult to meet people.
3 .... at her desk, she tried to focus on her essay.
4 .... her degree, she was keen to find her first job.
5 .... with an experienced artist every day, Sara had the confidence to try new techniques.
6 .... the entire apartment, he sat down to enjoy a cup of tea.
7 .... for work in the mornings, they often bumped into each other.
8 .... to take Natalia on holiday, he searched for a suitable villa.

3 Rewrite or combine the sentences using participle clauses.

1 Young people start new jobs and often find they need to work long hours.
   Starting new jobs, young people often find they need to work long hours.

2 He is living in Lisbon. He enjoys his job and has the chance to surf.

3 They considered the various options and then they decided to move into the co-living space.

4 She was walking through the park when she realised that she had forgotten her laptop.

5 He'd lived with someone who didn't pay the rent, and was now looking for a different solution.

6 They cooked meals together and got to know each other better.

7 They looked at the available workshops and then they chose the pizza-making course.

8 She finished her work and then she went to the beach to swim.

GRAMMAR BANK

8B conditionals with conjunctions

REFERENCE ◀◀ page 96

Zero conditional

We use the zero conditional to talk about things that are always or generally true.

We form the zero conditional with *if/when* + present simple + present simple.

When you mix blue and yellow, you get green.

First conditional

We use the first conditional to talk about the future consequences of a present situation.

We form the first conditional with *if* + present simple + *will/won't* or *could/can/may/might*.

We might go to the cinema if there's a good film showing.

Second conditional

We use the second conditional to talk about imaginary or unlikely situations in the present or future.

We form the second conditional with *if* + past simple + *would/wouldn't*.

If I was a billionaire, I'd buy a private island.

In the second conditional, we can use *were* instead of *was* when the subject is singular. This is slightly more formal.

If I were taller, I'd be better at basketball.

Third conditional

We use the third conditional to talk about imaginary situations in the past.

We form the third conditional with *if* + past perfect + *would/wouldn't have*.

If we'd left on time, we wouldn't have been late.

Conjunctions

We use *provided (that), providing (that)* and *as long as/so long as* to mean *only if*.

I'll buy the food **as long as** you do the cooking.
(I'll **only** buy the food **if** you do the cooking.)

We'll be there in ten minutes **provided that** the traffic is OK.
(We'll **only** be there in ten minutes **if** the traffic is OK.)

The car will last for years **providing** you maintain it properly.
(The car will **only** last **if** you maintain it properly.)

We use *on condition that* with a similar meaning. The meaning is stronger, and it is often used to talk about rules.

You can work from home **on condition that** you attend online meetings.
(We agree that you can work from home, but **only if** you attend online meetings.)

Unless means *if not*.

We'll miss our flight **unless** we leave at 6.
(We'll miss our flight **if** we do**n't** leave at 6.)

I won't go to the party **unless** you go with me.
(**If** you do**n't** go with me, I won't go to the party.)

PRACTICE

1 Read the pairs of sentences. Does each sentence have the same (S) or a different (D) meaning?

1. a You'll get the job provided that you have the right qualifications.
   b If you don't have the right qualifications, you won't get the job.
2. a We won't have a picnic outside unless it's sunny.
   b We'll have a picnic outside as long as it's sunny.
3. a You can borrow the money on condition that you promise to pay it back.
   b You can borrow the money unless you promise to pay it back.
4. a If he doesn't get here soon, we'll have to go without him.
   b Unless he gets here soon, we'll have to leave without him.

2 Complete the text with the words in the box.

| condition | don't | provided |
| that | unless | will | wouldn't |

¹_____ that trends remain the same, India will overtake China as the country with the largest population sometime in the 2030s. This will be the big demographic change in the future, and ²_____ India builds huge numbers of skyscrapers, it will lead to more overcrowding.

Many issues, such as housing, literacy and civil rights, are connected to poverty. Generally, if your country is poor, your numbers ³_____ be worse in all of these categories. Providing ⁴_____ the world comes together to fight poverty, these figures can change for the better.

Many global issues are closely tied together. If you ⁵_____ have a functioning education system, you don't have widespread literacy. You only manufacture large numbers of cars on ⁶_____ that your government invests in building roads. This has been the case for centuries. If the Romans hadn't known how to build bridges and roads, they ⁷_____ have conquered the world.

3 Rewrite the sentences using the word in brackets.

1. We need to act fast or these languages will die out.
   These languages _____ fast. (unless)
2. Do your best and you'll be OK.
   You _____ your best. (long)
3. To accept the job offer, I require a company car.
   I'll _____ get a company car. (condition)
4. We'll be there at midday unless our plans change.
   We _____ change. (providing)
5. If we keep quiet, we won't get into trouble.
   We _____ quiet. (unless)

GRAMMAR BANK

8C How to ... develop an argument

REFERENCE ◀◀ page 99

When we structure an argument, we usually use the following structure:
1 Make a claim, stating that something is true.
2 Present evidence and examples to support our claim.
3 Present ideas or information that show the impact of what we are saying.

We can use the following words and phrases to help structure an argument.

Making a claim

I'd like to start off by saying …
The first point I'd like to make is that …
Secondly, Thirdly, etc.; Most importantly, …
As far as I can see, …
One thing we can be sure of is …

Presenting evidence and examples

This is true for three main reasons. Firstly, …
A good example of this is …
For instance, …
Apparently, …
The evidence suggests that …

Showing the impact of what we are saying

As a result, …
The obvious impact of this is …
This would lead to …

PRACTICE

1 Choose the correct words to complete the sentences.

1 I'd just like to start off **to say** / **by saying** that I completely disagree with that comment.
2 The first point **I like** / **I'd like** to make is that it really depends on the situation.
3 **This** / **One** thing we can be sure of is that social media is here to stay.
4 This is true for three main **reasons** / **arguments**. Firstly, everybody is busy.
5 The obvious impact **of** / **on** this is that prices would go up.
6 This would **lead** / **leads** to mass disruption.

2 Choose the correct options (A–C) to complete the argument.

¹……… that ²………, social media has killed the art of conversation. If you look at a group of teenagers who get together, the first thing you'll see is that they're all looking at their screens instead of having conversations with each other. I think this is really sad. Furthermore, ³……… it's making people feel lonely, too.

⁴………, we can see that people often choose to text or message each other, rather than using the phone and talking to someone. Nowadays, people even finish their relationships by text. ⁵……… is in companies. Lots of office workers talk to their colleagues through messages even when they work in the same office. Some companies even use text messages to fire their staff! I think ⁶……… that the more we use messaging instead of talking to people, the harder it becomes to have real conversations because we simply can't remember how to do it. We haven't had enough practice. And ⁷……… the younger generation never even learning the art of conversation in the first place.

1 A This would lead to
  B I'd like to start off by saying
  C The evidence suggests
2 A as far as I can see
  B as a result
  C the obvious impact of this is
3 A this is true for three main reasons
  B the evidence suggests
  C as a result
4 A This is true for three main reasons
  B As far as I can see
  C Secondly
5 A As a result
  B Another good example of this
  C Apparently
6 A the obvious impact of this is
  B a good example of this is
  C as a result
7 A the first point I'd like to note is that
  B I'd like to start off by saying
  C this leads to

3 🔊 **GB8.01** | Listen and check your answers.

VOCABULARY BANK

1A suffixes
◀◀ page 8

1 A Look at how we can form adjectives from verbs and nouns by using different suffixes, e.g. *-ed, -ous, -ful*. What is the root word for each of the adjectives in the table? How has the spelling changed?

experienc**e** – experienc**ed**

-ed	-ic
experienc**ed**	optimist**ic**/pessimist**ic**
relax**ed**	realist**ic**
1	2 ....

-ous	-able
gener**ous**	reli**able**
3	5 ....
4	

-ful	-al
thought**ful**	practic**al**
cheer**ful**	music**al**
6	8 ....
7	

B Complete the table in Ex 1A with adjectives formed from the verbs and nouns in the box.

adventure   ambition   artist
emotion   help   hope   like   talent

2 A Complete the sentences with the correct adjective form of the words in brackets.

1 We can depend on Sam to be here on time. He's very .... (rely).
2 Melissa became quite .... as she was watching the film. (emotion).
3 Al will need some help setting up the new printer. He's not very .... (practice)
4 I love the fact that Leo is always so .... about life! (optimist)
5 Sasha is a really .... musician. (talent)
6 Thanks for moving those boxes – it was really .... (help)
7 It was very .... of you to send those flowers to cheer me up! (thought)
8 I don't think I'll go to the party – I'm not feeling very .... today. (social)
9 I'm not .... enough to go paragliding! (adventure).
10 I'm sure she'll be prime minister one day. She's incredibly .... (ambition)

B 🔊 **VB1.01** | Listen and check your answers.

C Work in pairs. Take turns describing adjectives for your partner to guess.

Student A: This describes someone who plays the guitar and sings, and loves going to watch bands.
Student B: Musical?
Student A: That's right.

1B idioms: memory
◀◀ page 12

1 A Complete the idioms in bold with the words in the box.

bell   ~~ear~~   memory   mind   tongue   tricks

1 He never remembers anything I tell him. Things go **in one ..ear.. and out the other**!
2 Oh no! I forgot to buy vegetables for the curry. Sorry, it totally **slipped my** ....
3 Hmm ... I'm not sure. I'll need to look at my notes again to **refresh my** ....
4 I'll remember it in a minute. The answer **is on the tip of my** .... !
5 I'm sure I've heard that name before. It definitely **rings a** ....
6 Oh, yes. You were there too, weren't you? My **memory is playing** .... **on me**.

B 🔊 **VB1.02** | Listen and check. Do you have similar idioms in your language?

C Work in pairs. Think of an idiom to use in each situation. More than one may be possible.
1 You went shopping and forgot to buy milk.
2 You're doing a quiz. You know the answer but can't quite remember it.
3 You're discussing a friend's son. The boy is a bad listener and forgets everything.
4 You recognise someone at a party but can't remember their name. You ask your friend.
5 A friend is telling you about a new book. You think you've heard about it before.
6 You and a friend are trying to find a restaurant. You went there years ago. You thought you knew the address, but you were wrong.

D Now roleplay a short conversation with your partner about each situation, using the idioms.

A: So, you went shopping and forgot to buy milk?
B: Yes, sorry. It slipped my mind.
A: Well, how am I supposed to make tea now?

VOCABULARY BANK

2A word families
◀◀ page 20

1 A Work in pairs. Complete the table with the correct form of each word.

verb	noun/person	adjective	adverb
research	research/¹.........		
predict	prediction	².........	predictably
		virtual	virtually
		³.........	remotely
analyse	⁴........./analyst	analytical	analytically
	science/scientist	scientific	⁵.........

B Complete the news headlines with the correct forms of words from Ex 1A.

1. Scientist makes alarming new **predictions** about global warming

2. GAMING CEO OFFERS $1,000,000 FOR GAMERS TO DESIGN ² .... WORLDS

3. Astronaut says moon rocks were never .... in space lab

4. Most workers prefer .... working to being in the office

5. BIOLIST .... LOSS OF OVER 100,000 ANIMAL SPECIES IN NEXT 10 YEARS

6. NEW THEORY ABOUT GRAVITY CANNOT YET BE PROVED ⁶.........

7. Documentary shows what we learnt from 50 years of ⁷ .... into octopuses

8. New car can be controlled ⁸........., from over a mile away

3A the environment
◀◀ page 32

1 A Match the words in the box with the meanings (1–8).

> carbon emissions   carbon footprint
> clean-up   (natural) resources   recycling
> renewable   solar power   sustainable

1. Electricity produced using energy from the sun. ....
2. Things that a country, person or organisation has that they can use. ....
3. An event which is organised in order to make a place clean. ....
4. When gases responsible for global warming are released into the air. ....
5. Used to describe an activity that you can continue without causing damage to the environment. ....
6. Used to describe something which can replace itself naturally, or be easily replaced. ....
7. The process of treating paper, glass, plastic, etc. so it can be used again. ....
8. A measurement of the amount of carbon dioxide that an individual, company or organisation produces. ....

B 🔊 **VB3.01** | Listen and check.

C Complete the sentences with the words and phrases from Ex 1A.

1. We only use wood from forests that are managed in a .... way.
2. We've taken all the paper and glass to the .... centre.
3. We're organising a beach .... to try and get rid of all the plastic.
4. The problem with fossil fuels like coal and gas is that they are not ...., like other energy sources (solar, water and wind).
5. The country is rich in ...., such as wood and minerals.
6. We need to reduce .... by more than 20 percent.
7. It's important for people individually to make changes to reduce their ....
8. .... is very suitable for domestic water heating.

D Work in groups and discuss the questions.

1. What could you do to reduce your carbon footprint?
2. Which sources of renewable energy would work well in your country (e.g., solar power, wind power, etc.)?
3. Is it important to you that the products you buy are made from sustainable materials? Why/Why not?

VOCABULARY BANK

3B phrasal verbs: communication
⏪ page 35

1A Read each conversation and study the phrasal verbs in bold. Then choose the correct words to complete the sentences (1–8).

Ana: Can you hear me or do I need to **speak up**?
Leo: Your microphone's off!
Ana: Thanks for **pointing** that **out**!

1 Ana thinks she needs to speak **louder / more quietly**.
2 Ana thanks Leo for **giving her useful information / fixing her microphone**.

Sam: Do I need to **spell out** the message again?
Jo: No, it's clear. You can **move on** to a new topic.

3 Sam offers to **keep quiet / explain something**.
4 Jo suggests he can **say more about the topic / talk about a new topic**.

Maria: Can I **bring up** a new topic: our finances?
Stefan: Our finance director isn't here yet, so we'll **come back** to that later.

5 Maria wants to **start / stop** talking about a new topic.
6 Stefan suggests that they **forget about that topic / return to that topic later**.

Juan: That speaker **comes across** well. She communicates her ideas clearly.
Mia: Yes, she **got her message across** very well.

7 Juan thinks the speaker speaker created a **positive / negative** image of themselves.
8 Mia thinks that the speaker **explained her ideas clearly / gave too much information**.

B Choose the correct phrasal verbs to complete the advice for giving a presentation.

1 Always start with a joke, so you **come across / come back** as friendly.
2 Make sure you **point out / speak up** so everyone can hear you.
3 When you **bring up / spell out** a new topic, speak more slowly to emphasise it.
4 To **get your message across / speak up** clearly, use visuals like photos or pictures.
5 Only **point out / move on to** a new topic when you know the audience has understood the previous point.
6 If someone asks a difficult question, say you'll **come back / come across** to it later.

C Work in pairs. Which advice in Ex 1B do you agree with? Why?

4A illness and treatment
⏪ page 44

1 A Work in groups. Complete the sentences (1–8) with the words in the boxes.

illness

| allergies ~~asthma~~ food poisoning run-down |

1 If you have _asthma_, you find it difficult to breathe in some conditions.
2 You can get .... by eating something that has gone bad.
3 If you're ...., you feel tired and ill.
4 If you have ...., certain things make you sneeze or make your eyes water.

treatment

| ~~antibiotics~~ first aid medication vaccine |

5 You take _antibiotics_ if you have an infection that is caused by bacteria.
6 You can get a .... to protect you from the flu.
7 You need .... to treat things like small cuts and bruises.
8 You might take regular .... if you have a long-term health problem.

B Work in groups and discuss the questions.

1 Have you ever had food poisoning?
2 Have you ever taken antibiotics? What for?
3 Do you own a first aid kit? Have you ever used it?
4 Do you suffer from asthma or allergies? Do you take medication for them?
5 What do you do to build up your health when you feel run-down?
6 Have you ever had to have a vaccine to travel to another country?

VOCABULARY BANK

4C sport: motivation and benefits

◀◀ page 50

1 A Read the article. Then match the words in bold with the meanings (1–9).
1. the feeling that you are able to do something
2. something which is difficult to achieve
3. working together with other people
4. an advantage of doing something
5. something that you do regularly
6. the feeling of wanting to do something
7. gently persuading someone to do something
8. something which makes you want to do or achieve something
9. the ability to continue doing something, even when you don't really want to do it

B Choose the correct words to complete the sentences.
1. I took up diving because I wanted a new **challenge / encouragement** in my life.
2. It takes a lot of **habit / discipline** to get up early every morning to train.
3. The thought of getting a medal was a great **challenge / incentive** to keep training hard.
4. I don't have the **motivation / challenge** to do exercise every day.
5. You can't win a football match without good **incentive / teamwork**!
6. My parents always gave me a lot of support and **encouragement / incentive** when I was younger.
7. Winning the competition really helped my **discipline / confidence**.
8. The main **benefit / motivation** of joining a gym is being able to use the equipment.
9. I think it's important for children to develop healthy **habits / benefits** at a young age.

C Work in groups and discuss the questions.
1. What activities do you do that involve teamwork?
2. Who gives you encouragement when you find something difficult?
3. What activities do you do that give you confidence?
4. What do you think are the main benefits of joining a gym?
5. What is your motivation for studying English?
6. What do you think is the best way to develop good exercise habits?

Six reasons to do sport

We can't all be sporty, but even if you aren't, there are good reasons to get into the **habit** of doing sport.

Learn **teamwork**
Team sports require cooperation, a skill that may be useful at work and in other situations.

Maintain fitness
Fitness is the most obvious **benefit** of exercise. If you need more of an **incentive** to get you started, remember that people who exercise tend to live healthier lives. Many sports, like running and cycling, help us to build stamina.

Give yourself a **challenge**
Can you run around the track in two minutes or swim the length of a pool underwater? It isn't always about beating your opponent; sometimes, it's about pushing yourself.

Develop **discipline**
Athletes who never give up or who still go to practice when it's wet, cold and dark develop discipline, the ability to keep going when things get tough.

Boost your **confidence**
Many shy kids discover themselves on the sports field: they realise they can run fast or score goals. This gives them a chance to excel, and is a good reason why all children should be given **encouragement** to take part in sports.

Play competitively
For some people, the **motivation** to do sport is to win trophies. This competitive spirit can also be useful in other areas of life.

VOCABULARY BANK

5B areas of work
◀◀ page 59

1 A Complete the sentences with the words in the box.

accountancy	agriculture	banking
construction	consultancy	journalism
medicine	publishing	research	social work

1 My brother is studying .... at university. I think he wants to manage the family farm at some point.
2 The .... company specialises in building residential properties in the Northeast of England.
3 I have a degree in .... and have recently started a new job supporting elderly residents in the area.
4 Looking for a role in .... ? Join our new personal finance team to help people with loans and savings.
5 She works in .... I think her company manages the accounts of a few local businesses.
6 You have to study .... for up to seven years before you can get a job as a doctor.
7 .... is a difficult industry to get into. You have to work long hours and have a real passion for news.
8 Our .... team is developing new methods for scientific analysis of medical data.
9 The shift from print to digital has had a huge effect on the .... industry.
10 We have a small .... business specialising in providing support for telecommunications projects.

B 🔊 VB5.01 | Listen and check your answers.

6A prefixes
◀◀ page 68

1 A Add the correct prefixes to the words in bold. Use the same prefix twice in each sentence. Add a hyphen where necessary.

| dis | im | mis | re | sub | un |

1 Our plan was **perfect**. It took too long, and we were too **patient** to wait.
2 The employees had to **train** for new jobs and the company **wrote** their contracts.
3 The **heading** of this article about the North Pole is 'Life in **zero** temperatures'.
4 The instructions were **helpful** because they were **realistic**. No one could follow them.
5 It turned out he was **honest**: he **appeared** with all our money!
6 I **heard** Seb when he invited me, and then I **read** the invitation. I thought the party was today!

B Write three sentences using other words that use the prefixes in Ex 1A.

C Rewrite your sentences from Ex 1B with the words removed. Then work in pairs. Swap sentences and try to complete your partner's sentences.

6B reporting verbs
◀◀ page 72

1 A 🔊 VB6.01 | Listen to four conversations. For each conversation, choose the correct words to complete the sentences.

1 a Rob apologised for **stealing** / **breaking** Dan's phone.
   b Dan accepted that is was **deliberate** / **an accident**.
2 a Ahmed accused Samira of **using** / **deleting** the files.
   b Samira denied **deleting** / **accessing** the files.
3 a Max doubted that he would be able to **do the job well** / **get the job**.
   b Rose insisted that he would **get the job** / **be very good at it**.
4 a Hannah reminded Julia to **leave** / **arrive** at 10 a.m.
   b Julia regretted not leaving **earlier** / **later**.

B Complete the table with the reporting verbs in Ex 1A.

verb + -ing form
propose, recommend, suggest, admit, ¹............, ²............ She admitted taking the money.
verb + preposition + -ing form
boast about, insist on, ³............ He insisted on driving me to the station.
verb + that
admit, suggest, boast, claim, ⁴............, ⁵............, ⁶............ They claimed that the story wasn't true.
verb + infinitive with to
refuse, threaten, claim She refused to leave.
verb + object + infinitive with to
persuade, ⁷............ He persuaded her to apply for the promotion.
verb + object + preposition + -ing form/sth
criticise someone for, question someone about ⁸............ She criticised him for being late.

C Complete the reported speech. Use the correct form of the verbs in the box.

| accuse | apologise | bring | doubt |
| insist | regret | remind | tell | wake | waste |

1 'You told Tom about us!'
   He .... her of .... Tom about them.
2 'I don't think anyone will notice if we arrive late.'
   He .... that anyone would notice if they arrived late.
3 'I'm so sorry we woke you up.'
   She .... for .... them up.
4 'Don't forget to bring your laptop.'
   He .... her .... her laptop.
5 'You must stay with us. We have a spare bedroom.'
   She .... that we stay with them.
6 'I wish I hadn't wasted so much time.'
   He .... so much time.

VOCABULARY BANK

7A chance
◀◀ page 80

1 Match 1–7 with a–g. Use the words in bold to help you.

1 The selection was completely **random**.
2 There was some **accidental** damage to the car.
3 It was **unfortunate** that their flight was cancelled.
4 I've been **fortunate** to find a career that I love.
5 Marek's decision to leave the band was completely **unexpected**.
6 I bumped into Dave **by chance** on Oxford Street.
7 There was a **freak** storm when we arrived.

a I'm so lucky that I enjoy my job.
b They never usually have such bad weather here.
c Somebody bumped into it by mistake in the car park.
d We only found out a week before the tour was due to start.
e We hadn't arranged to meet.
f They were unlucky – all the other flights were OK.
g They chose the names out of a hat.

2 A Choose the correct words to complete the sentences.

1 The winner was chosen at **random / accidental**.
2 We met on holiday **fortunate / by chance**.
3 My cousin arrived from the USA to visit me. It was completely **unfortunate / unexpected**.
4 **Unfortunately / By chance**, we arrived late and missed the show. I was so upset!
5 I feel so **unfortunate / fortunate** to have this wonderful opportunity.
6 He was struck by lightning in a **freak / by chance** accident.
7 She broke your phone, but it was **accidental / fortunate**.

B 🔊 **VB7.01** | Listen and check your answers.

8A describing homes and living conditions
◀◀ page 93

1 A Read the sentences and match the words in bold with their meanings (a–h).

1 The house had been well maintained and was in excellent **condition**.
2 The room was full of **stylish** furniture and expensive paintings.
3 The house was **elegant** and well kept.
4 The house isn't very **secure**. We need to change the locks.
5 It's an old house with a lot of **character**.
6 The rooms are very **spacious** with large windows opening out onto balconies.
7 Bel Air is an **exclusive** suburb of Los Angeles.
8 The area near the harbour has become very **fashionable**.

a beautiful, attractive or graceful
b in a particular physical state, e.g., clean, dirty, messy, etc.
c attractive in a way that is modern and popular
d large, with plenty of space to move around
e a combination of qualities that makes a place different to others
f so expensive that most people cannot afford it
g protected so that people cannot get in or out
h popular at the moment

B 🔊 **VB8.01** | Choose the correct words to complete the text. Listen and check.

Marmalade Lane – Cambridge, UK

Cambridge is one of the most ¹**fashionable / character** cities in the UK to live in. But price increases have meant the city has become quite ²**stylish / exclusive** and it can be difficult for young people to afford to buy or rent properties which are ³**in good / of good** condition. Marmalade Lane is Cambridge's first co-housing community project, and its residents include families with young children, retired couples, single-person households and young professional couples. The architects have designed ⁴**stylish / exclusive** houses of different sizes and the houses have their own ⁵**character / stylish**. The architecture is ⁶**in terrible condition / elegant** and even the smaller houses feel ⁷**spacious / fashionable**. Residents live in their own houses, which are ⁸**secure / exclusive**, but they share communal spaces and facilities, like a gym and a laundry. There is also a shared garden and a 'common house' where the community can eat together and socialise.

C Work in pairs. Use the words in Ex 1A to describe different areas of your town or city.

COMMUNICATION BANK

Lead-in Ex 1A

It is William Shakespeare.

3A Ex 3A Student B

Fuji Rock

Where: Japan   When: July/August

Fuji Rock is the biggest music festival in Japan, with between 100,000 and 150,000 people attending every year. The festival is held in a stunning ski resort which is about a 90-minute train ride from Tokyo. It has been running since 1997 and the international crowd has been steadily increasing over the years. Because the festival is held mostly outdoors (with only one indoor stage), attendees must be well prepared for rain and shine. Reflecting its Japanese roots, the festival venue has hot springs where you can relax and also plenty of nature walks.

Fuji Rock is also one of the world's most eco-friendly festivals. The festival organisers put effort into conservation and try to achieve a good balance of music and nature. For example, all the plastic bottles which are collected after the event are recycled to make rubbish bags for the following year's festival. Plastic bottle tops are used to make benches for people to sit on. Paper cups are recycled to make toilet paper and the wooden chopsticks, which are made from wood in the local forest, are recycled to make wooden furniture. Through the Fuji Rock Forest Project, the festival runs a number of schemes that focus on the maintenance and protection of the area around the festival site. One such project is Fuji Rock Paper, which uses the wood cut during forest maintenance that would otherwise go to waste. They use this wood together with the recycled cups and plates from the festival to make branded flyers and pamphlets for the festival. Additionally, every year more than 300 volunteers build and maintain a natural path through the forest, made with wooden boards, to help people with wheelchairs who are attending the festival.

4 Review Ex 2B

1 Myth – Drinking coffee does not stop you from growing.
2 True – There is evidence that vegetarian diets are becoming more popular.
3 Myth – 10,000 steps a day is not necessarily enough to maintain your fitness. We probably need around 15,000.
4 Myth – Sugar is sugar and all sugar can cause health problems.

4B Ex 5 Student A

1 Read the following (true) beliefs about sleep. Add a third belief, which is false.
   a It's thought that alternating work and rest (working intensely and then resting) helps us to be more productive.
   b It has been suggested that people who don't check their phone or their emails before they go to sleep tend to fall asleep more quickly.
   c ....

2 Read your statements to your partner (in a different order). Can they guess which is the false belief?

4B Ex 6B

1 Myth – Sleeping fewer than seven hours a night can lead to health conditions such as Alzheimer's and cardiovascular disease. It has been suggested that former British Prime Minister Margaret Thatcher only needed four hours' sleep, but it was a myth invented to intimidate her political opponents.
2 Myth – It's been shown by research that people who work at night and sleep during the day often feel less rested and have poorer health than those who sleep at night.
3 True – Sleepwalking may include simply sitting up and appearing awake, or it may involve complex activities, such as moving furniture, going to the bathroom, cooking or sometimes even driving.
4 Myth – If you are already tired, then being bored will help you to notice it.
5 Myth – Poor sleep is not a normal part of aging. As we get older, we often get less sleep because our ability to sleep for long periods of time and get into the deep restful stages of sleep can decrease. Older people are lighter sleepers and their sleep is more easily interrupted by light, noise and pain or illness.
6 True – Sleeping more at the weekend is a good way to ensure rest.
7 Myth – Many studies have been conducted which show that people who watch TV in bed tend to sleep less.
8 Myth – Exercising at any time during the day will probably help you to sleep better.
9 True – The blue light emitted by your phone screen (or other devices) reduces the production of melatonin (the hormone that controls your sleep cycle) and this makes it more difficult for you to get to sleep or wake up the next day.

COMMUNICATION BANK

6A Ex 6C

1 Read the article and the notes. Cross out the bullet point that repeats the same idea as the previous note.
2 Edit the other notes to make them more concise. The first has been done for you. Use the ideas you discussed on page 70.
3 Compare your notes with other students.

Deadlines and limitations

To focus on a task, some people need deadlines. Given too much time, many of us produce nothing of value. This is because without any pressure we can't get motivated or focused enough to do the work. One reason for this is procrastination – the habit of delaying a task until the last moment. Another reason is that pressure means we simply have to focus. When something needs doing by a certain time, we take responsibility; we cannot delay or get distracted because then we risk failure.

Similarly, creative activities are sometimes easier when there are limitations placed on us. Complete freedom allows us to dream big, but it doesn't always help us to focus. Sculptor Juan Ignacio Hernandez says, 'I work with stone. The limitations of this material mean I'm always thinking practically: what type and size of stone can I buy locally? What kind of figure does the natural shape of the stone suggest? How much can I cut out of the stone before it breaks? These limitations are part of the creative process.'

< Notes ...

- Deadlines can be really useful for some people when they are doing tasks. **Deadlines – useful for doing tasks**
- The author says that without deadlines, some people don't do the work.
- Procrastination, which is delaying a task until the final moment before it's due, is a problem for some people.
- Pressure often means we have to focus.
- When we do creative activities, if we're given limitations, it can sometimes be useful because limitations help people to focus.

7A Ex 8

The story of Shariah Harris

Her mother took a wrong turn driving home and they came across some stables that provided riding lessons to inner-city kids. Shariah started taking lessons and soon became passionate about riding horses and playing polo.

The accidental artist

In 1989, Jon developed tinnitus (a condition which causes ringing in the ear), which led to brain surgery. Complications from surgery led to a stroke, which left him with long-lasting physical and mental changes. During his therapy, he was given some colours and he started to draw. What started as a way to relax turned into a new way for Jon to communicate and he started to draw and paint obsessively in abstract ways, often using words as well as images. When he was on holiday, his sister suggested that he send one of his drawings to the *New Yorker*. It was published and Jon started to receive worldwide recognition as an artist.

7 Review Ex 1B

1 The concert was being recorded by a record company, so they had asked the audience not to clap at the end.
2 She fell off the bottom step.
3 They were playing different opponents.

7A Ex 7C Student A

1 Read the sentences in black to your partner so they can rephrase them using a compound adjective. The answers are in blue.

   1 The journey is 30 kilometres. **It's a thirty-kilometre journey.**
   2 The doctor has a lot of qualifications. **He/She is a well-qualified/highly qualified doctor.**
   3 It's an opportunity that will change your life. **It's a life-changing opportunity.**
   4 He is famous all around the world for his art. **He's world-famous for his art./He's a world-famous artist.**
   5 The effects of the medicine last a long time. **The medicine has long-lasting effects.**

2 Listen to your partner's sentences and rephrase them using a compound adjective.

143

COMMUNICATION BANK

3A Ex 3A Student C

Splendour in the Grass

Where: Australia   When: July

One of the largest family-friendly music festivals in Australia, Splendour in the Grass is held in Yelgun, New South Wales, and always features an exciting line-up of performers from a range of different genres. As well as great music from all around the world, Splendour in the Grass has a huge array of entertainment to keep everyone happy, from science tents where you can learn from some of Australia's top scientists to dance lessons and an eye-catching arts festival. Splendour in the Grass has something for everyone.

This festival has a great attitude when it comes to the environment and is one of the most sustainable festivals around. It does its best to protect the local area and encourages festival-goers to do the same. The festival appointed Damon Gameau, who is a world-renowned filmmaker and environmental activist, as their Eco Ambassador. One initiative tried to reduce carbon emissions by encouraging people who are attending the festival to catch the bus or share a ride with others. The organisers promote ideas for reducing waste like using your own water bottles and reusable cups, instead of buying disposable plastic. When you buy your festival ticket, you can also choose to offset your carbon footprint by donating extra money, which is used to promote solar energy. Finally, the festival organises a tree-planting session on the Saturday.

6C Ex 5 Student B

Read the information below and take turns to ask for and give advice.

1 Start a conversation. You always get overlooked for promotion even though you are a good worker. Ask your partner for advice about this.
2 Listen to your partner's problem. You know that your partner leaves bags of rubbish in the hall for days. They eventually take them out but there's always a bad smell in the hall. The neighbours are angry about it. Give tactful advice.
3 Start a conversation. Your classmates used to study with you after class. Now they don't want to work with you. Ask your partner for advice about this.
4 Listen to your partner's problem. Student A used to give rides on their motorbike to another friend. But you know that Student A drives too fast and dangerously. The other friend is too scared to do this anymore.

7A Ex 7C Student B

1 Listen to your partner's sentences and rephrase them using a compound adjective.

2 Say the sentences in black to your partner so they can rephrase them using a compound adjective. The answers are in blue.
   1 The training course lasts for five years. It's a five-year training course.
   2 The shop is full of books which have been owned by other people. It's a second-hand bookshop.
   3 The job takes up a lot of time. It's a time-consuming job.
   4 The building is twenty metres high. It's a twenty-metre-high building.
   5 She is a politician who is respected by a lot of people. She's a well-respected/widely respected politician.

4B Ex 5 Student B

1 Read the following (true) beliefs about sleep. Add a third belief, which is false.
   a It's believed that having an afternoon sleep can help you to be more creative.
   b It's known that missing even an hour of sleep every night can have serious health consequences.
   c ....

2 Read your statements to your partner (in a different order). Can they guess which is the false belief?

COMMUNICATION BANK

7B Ex 7B

1 Read the essay. Why do you think the author called it 'A blessing in disguise'?

A blessing in disguise
Ayodele Aiyegbusi | 24 August

¹Often in life we find ourselves going through tough times. We struggle and struggle and see only the negative side. But when we look back, maybe years later, we realise things weren't so bad after all. Maybe our difficulties turned out to be a blessing in disguise.

²I remember it as if it were yesterday. The rain was falling like needles and a cold wind lifted the dead leaves from the earth. I was eleven years old, waiting for the school bell to ring so I could cycle home. When it finally did, I climbed onto my bike and barely noticed that the road was wet from the rain. I hadn't been cycling more than two minutes when I skidded, fell off and broke my leg.

³It was quite a bad break and I had to spend a month lying down. I'd been quite an active child and the worst thing wasn't the pain; it was having to stay in that same position the whole time. I was miserable. I wished I'd paid more attention to the road conditions. I kept thinking, if only I hadn't used my bike that day.

⁴One morning, seeing that I was bored, my mother brought me a drawing pad and some coloured pencils. I started drawing everything around me. One of my earliest pictures was a pair of pigeons on the windowsill. They were walking in circles in a little dance. Another was the rubber plant in the corner of the room. Once, I drew the moon peeking behind the curtains. I had seven brothers and sisters and I drew portraits of them, one every day from Monday to Sunday. And that's how I learnt to draw.

⁵Now, years later, I'm an artist. I work from life, sketching the things around me. I carry pencil and paper everywhere: in cafés, on trains, in hotel rooms. I draw everything, including pigeons dancing on windowsills.

⁶I'll always remember with mixed feelings that time I broke my leg. It was a miserable month, but it showed me that disasters can be opportunities if you look closely enough.

2 Read the essay again. Complete the description of each paragraph (1–6) with the words in the box.

| consequence   details   event   good   summary   theme |

1 a general introduction and the main _____ of the essay
2 a description of the main _____ that led to a change
3 more _____ about the event and its immediate consequences
4 a description of something _____ that happened during a bad time
5 a present _____ of the event
6 a _____ of the story, and a general message about life

3 Work in pairs. Answer the questions.
1 In paragraph 2, the author describes the weather. What details does he use?
2 In paragraph 3, he says 'I was miserable'. What wishes and regrets did he have?
3 In paragraph 4, he says he 'started drawing everything around [him].' What examples does he give?
4 In paragraph 5, he says he carries 'pencil and paper everywhere.' What examples does he give of 'everywhere'?
5 What lesson did the writer learn from this experience?

MEDIATION BANK | SPEAKING

1C Top five

SPEAKING OUTPUT | an informal discussion
GOAL | create tourist recommendations for your town/area
MEDIATION SKILL | organising a group task

WARM-UP

1 Work in pairs. Discuss the questions.
1 Is your town or area popular with tourists?
2 Do you think your town or area is a good place for a holiday? Why/Why not?
3 What do you like most about your town or area?

PREPARE

2 Read the Scenario. What decisions do you need to make?

SCENARIO

The editor of a local magazine that you contribute to has got touch in with you and some of the other writers.

To	Hyde, Billie; Blyth, Pete; Wood, Campbell
From	Andersson, Leif
Subject	Next feature

Hi everyone,

Local Culture Week is coming up and we'd like to do a little feature on the top five places to visit in our town/area, both for visitors from abroad and from our country.

I'd like you to list your top five in order and give brief reasons why each is good to visit.

Can you guys get something back to me in the next week or so?

Thanks,

Leif

3 A 🔊 **MB1.01** | Listen to the conversation. How does the group decide to organise the task?

B 🔊 **MB1.01** | Read the Mediation Skill box. Listen to the conversation in Ex 3A again and tick the phrases you hear.

MEDIATION SKILL
organising a group task

When deciding how to do something as a group, it's important to clarify the objective and involve everyone in the process.

Make sure the goal is clear
So, they want us to …
OK, so what we have to do is …

Involve people in the process
OK. So how do you want to do this?
Shall we each come up with [a list/some ideas] and then compare?
How about going through [them/everything] one by one?

Give opinions about the best way of doing things
It would be easier if we …
It's going to take too long if we …
It's better to … first, then later we can …
Let's take about five minutes each to …
Let's just … first.

4 Number sentences a–e in the correct order to make a short conversation.
a Right. So, how shall we start? Shall we pick a couple of ideas and focus on the costs? ....
b Hmm, let's just get a big list of ideas together first and worry about the costs later. ....
c Fine, we can always add more ideas later I guess. ....
d OK, so Maria wants us to come up with some ideas for the party and give her an idea of how much everything would cost. ....
e Making a big list will take too long. Let's just focus on a couple of ideas first. ....

MEDIATE

5 A Work in groups. Read the Scenario again and decide how to organise your group. Then create your top five list, explaining your choices.

B Read your lists to the other groups. How similar are they?

MEDIATION BANK | WRITING

2C Micro gigs

WRITING OUTPUT | an informal summary
GOAL | summarise an informal interview
MEDIATION SKILL | note taking and summarising

WARM-UP

1 Work in pairs. Discuss the questions.
1. How often do you go to gigs or concerts?
2. Do you prefer big or small venues? Why?
3. What are the possible advantages of a very small venue?

PREPARE

2 A Read the Scenario. What do you think a 'micro gig' is?

SCENARIO

Your friend Jez sends you this message.

> Hey! I've got to work tonight, so I won't be able to listen to that interview before class. Could you take some notes for me? I'm actually really interested in this whole micro gig idea. I might even set one up myself! 🙂
>
> 3.52 p.m.

B 🔊 **MB2.01** | Listen to the first part of the interview and check.

3 🔊 **MB2.01** | Listen again. Use the prompts to make sentences about Sam's micro gigs.
1. micro gig / small concert / people's homes
   A micro gig is a small concert which happens in people's homes.
2. Sam / living room / concerts / three years
3. artists / stay / bed and breakfast / part of fee
4. solo artists / fifteen people / big instruments and groups / fewer

4 Read the Mediation Skill box. What type of words are usually 'key' words?

MEDIATION SKILL
note taking and summarising

When taking notes, you don't need to write down every word you hear. Instead, note down the key words (i.e., the ones that give you the most important information). For example, if you heard:

A micro gig is a very small concert, but perhaps the biggest difference is that they happen in people's homes rather than big concert venues.

Your notes might look something like this:

micro gig/small concert/biggest difference/people's homes/not concert venues

Sometimes it's easier to paraphrase certain words rather than writing down exactly what somebody says. Notice the word 'not' is included in the notes above instead of 'rather than', which appears in the interview.

You can then use the notes to summarise the information for someone else. These sentences can be shorter and simpler than what was originally said: *A micro gig is a small concert, but the biggest difference is it happens in people's homes, not in concert venues.*

Also, you don't need to write down notes for every sentence you hear. Listen for sections that give you the most important information.

5 A Look at the transcript of the next section of the interview. Underline the key words in Sam's answers.

Interviewer: How did you get started with all of this?

Sam: I guess it was a bit of an accident really. I had a friend who was a musician, and she wanted to play a gig in the area, but she wasn't really interested in the local venues, as, well, I guess she thought they were a little bit old fashioned, you know? All the bands just sounded the same – there was nothing new or inspiring about any of it.

Interviewer: So, you offered her your place?

Sam: Basically, yes. I said she could use my living room, and I put a couple of posts on social media to promote the event. I came up with the name 'micro gig' to make it sound a bit different, something special, unique.

Interviewer: And was that first gig a success?

Sam: It was a disaster! Very few people came, and it turned out that my living room wasn't great for live sound, but I could still see the potential for it to be a success. I decided I needed to buy better equipment to make the sound better, and that for the next gig I needed to be less lazy about promoting the event. The second gig was a lot better, and I got great feedback. From then on, I was hooked.

B Work in pairs. Compare the key words you underlined.

6 🔊 **MB2.02** | Listen to the final part of the interview and make notes. Remember to only include the key words.

MEDIATE

7 A Read the Scenario again. Write a short summary of the last part of the interview for Jez. Use your notes from Ex 6 to help you.

B Work in pairs. Compare your summaries. Is there anything they mentioned that you didn't?

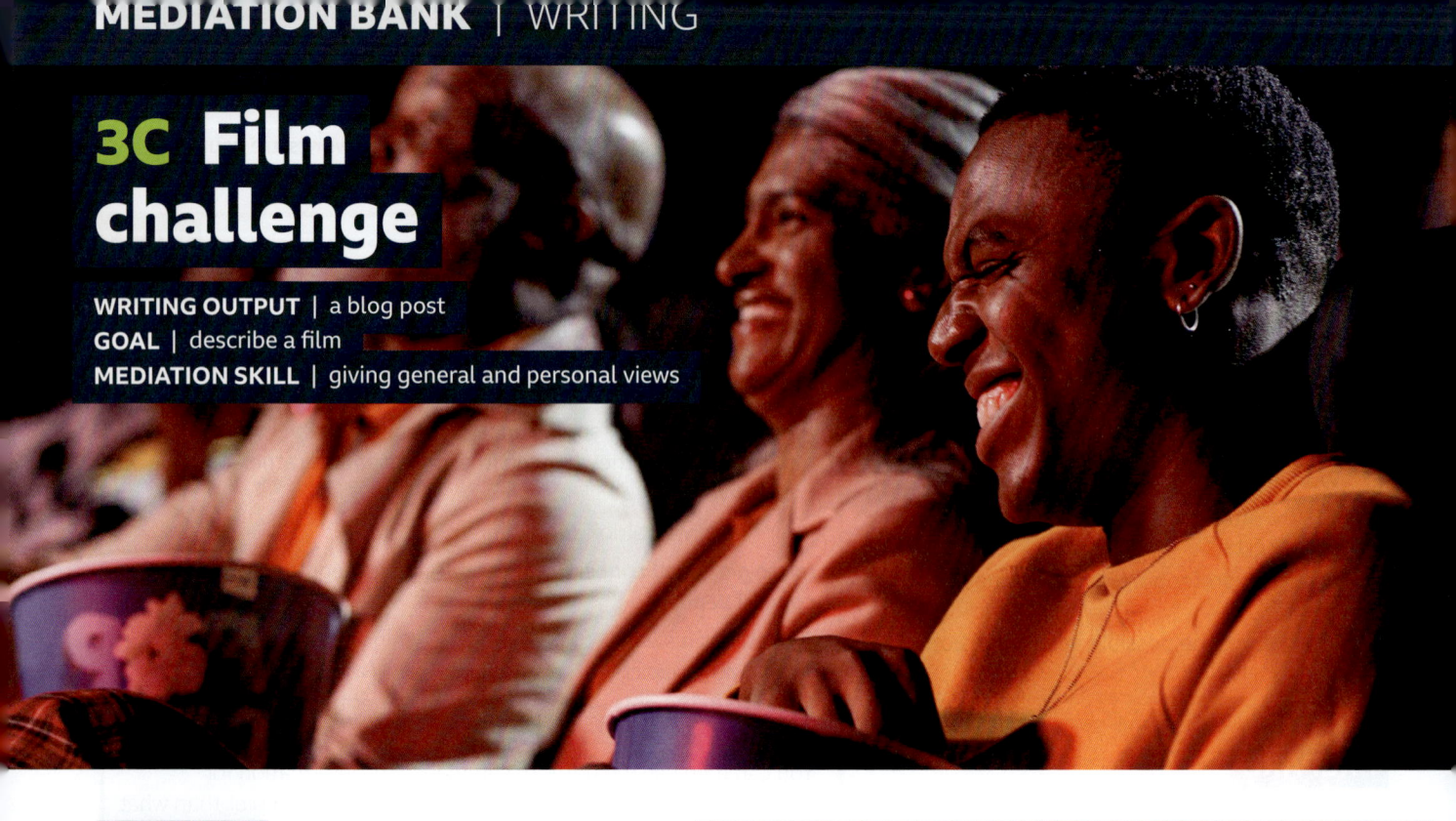

MEDIATION BANK | WRITING

3C Film challenge

WRITING OUTPUT | a blog post
GOAL | describe a film
MEDIATION SKILL | giving general and personal views

WARM-UP

1 Work in pairs. Which of the following sentences are true for you and why? Give examples.
   1 I usually like the most popular films.
   2 I often like films other people don't like.
   3 I have very specific tastes in films.

PREPARE

2 Read the Scenario. What do you think an 'underrated' film is?

3 Read the Mediation Skill box. Underline the phrases in the Scenario that the writer uses to give personal opinions and general opinions.

MEDIATION SKILL
giving general and personal views

When giving your own interpretation of a story, novel, film or play – especially when you think it is under- or overrated – you might want to contrast your own opinions with what other people think.

Giving personal opinions

For me, it's …
Personally, I …
As far as I'm concerned, it's …

Contrasting general opinions with your own

A lot of people say … , but I …
I've heard people say … , but I think …
It's regarded as … , but I think …

SCENARIO

You are tagged in a social media post.

Maya Lewin
Yesterday at 13.36

Thanks for nominating me for the underrated film challenge, @Nickky Blu! Here are three films that are much better than you think …

My first pick is *Jaws*. Yes, it's regarded as one of the best horror films of all time, but I also think there's another level to it; it's about the value of human life – the choice between making money and looking after people – and that's still an important theme today.

My second choice is a film called *Waterworld*. It got mixed reviews when it was released, but personally I think it's great! The basic plot is that the polar ice caps have melted, which has caused sea levels to rise, so most of the world is underwater. Everyone thought it was ridiculous at the time but given everything that's happening with the environment at the moment, maybe it's not so crazy after all! For me, it's well worth a watch!

My last pick is one of Scarlett Johansson's early films – *Ghost World*. On the surface it's another typical American teen film, but what makes it great for me are the two main characters. They were best friends in high school, but now they've graduated, they start to realise that they're very different people. It's a very real relationship and one I think we can all relate to. I've heard people say it's nothing special, but what do people know?

Anyway, that's my list. Now I nominate @you!

20 Likes | 5 Comments

MEDIATION BANK | WRITING

4 Complete the posts with the sentences (a–f).
  a For me, it's more than just a comedy.
  b some people would say it's not an underrated film
  c It's regarded as a complicated film
  d I've heard people say it's badly acted
  e A lot of people say *Star Wars* is the best sci-fi film ever.
  f as far as I'm concerned, it's one of his best performances

Wilco4
20 February at 13:03

Some people say that *Police Academy* is just a funny film. ¹_____ It shows how important friendship is at work, and how true friends will stand by each other in difficult times, even when the situation is completely desperate. ²_____, but for me it's probably the highlight of Steve Guttenberg's career as an actor.

♥ 27   💬 11   ↪

Neko_Desu
28 February at 14:14

³_____. I agree that it's a good film, but personally I think that title should go to *Moon*. While *Star Wars* tells a very simple story, basically a good vs. evil children's story, *Moon* has a complex plot that keeps you guessing till the end and asks serious questions about scientific development. ⁴_____, but you just need to be a little patient and all of the answers appear by the end.

♥ 30   💬 9   ↪

You_Can_Call_Me_Mal
4 March at 09:31

If you ask people to name the best Tom Cruise films, not many people would say *Vanilla Sky*, but ⁵_____. He's really believable as David Aames, a man who has it all and loses it all. While ⁶_____, I find that it rarely gets mentioned when people talk about Cruise's greatest films.

♥ 16   💬 4   ↪

5 Number sentences a–e in the correct order to make a blog post.

  a … but for me, *Hot Fuzz* is one of the best comedy films made in the last thirty years, if not more. ____

  b A lot of people say it's not even as good as other films by Simon Pegg and Edgar Wright, like *Shaun of the Dead*. ____

  c Personally, I find it far funnier than any of his other films, as the chemistry between him and his co-star Nick Frost is just magical in this film. ____

  d I hear a lot of opinions about the best comedy films, some say *The Wedding Singer*, others talk about *The Hangover* … ____

  e As far as I'm concerned, they're the best double act appearing on the screen today. ____

6 Work in pairs. Take turns completing the sentences with your own ideas.
  1 … is regarded as a very funny film. For me, it's …
  2 A lot of people say … is a talented actor. Personally, I think …
  3 Everyone thought … was a terrible film. In my case, I …
  4 Some people think … films are great, but I think …

7 Make a list of films that you think are underrated. Think about what other people say about these films, and what you think about them. Make notes about:
  • the characters.
  • the plot.
  • the themes.

MEDIATE

8 A Write your blog post about three underrated films. Try to contrast what most people think about each film with your own opinion where relevant.

  B Work in pairs. Show your post to another student. Ask and answer questions about the films you've chosen.
  A: Do you really think *Die Hard* is underrated?
  B: Yes, lots of people think it's just an action movie, but for me …

149

MEDIATION BANK | SPEAKING

4C Active week

SPEAKING OUTPUT | a group discussion
GOAL | decide how to contribute to an event
MEDIATION SKILL | making group decisions

WARM-UP

1 Work in groups. Discuss the questions.
   1 Does everyone have a responsibility to have a healthy and active lifestyle? Why/Why not?
   2 Is it the government's responsibility to encourage people to be more active? Why/Why not?
   3 How much do you enjoy exercise? How do you make it enjoyable?

PREPARE

2 Read the Scenario. Why can you only choose one activity for Active Week?

SCENARIO

To Community Group
From Garcia, Abe
Subject Re: Active Week

Hey guys,

It's national Active Week again soon, so we need to come up with an event to encourage people in our community to exercise and be active. I've had a quick brainstorm and this is what I've got so far:
- organising a marathon and inviting people from all over the country to take part.
- organising a football tournament featuring local celebrities.
- organising a walk for the whole town to do together.
- organising a talk from a famous sports star to encourage people to get involved in sport.
- organising a day where people can talk to experts to find the best sport/activity for them.

Can you add this to next week's agenda? We'd probably only be able to do one event as we don't have much time or budget.

Anyway, let me know what you decide.

Abe

3 🔊 **MB4.01** | Listen to a meeting about Active Week. Do the group manage to choose one activity?

4 🔊 **MB4.01** | Read the Mediation Skill box. Then listen to the conversation again. Tick the phrases you hear.

MEDIATION SKILL
making group decisions

Making decisions as a group can be difficult because we often disagree. There are three things we can do to help move the conversation forward.

Ask questions
Find out what everyone thinks and get everyone involved.
So, how does everyone feel about … ?
[Tom] – what do you think about [Sarah's] idea to …

Identify areas of agreement
Highlight areas of agreement. This encourages the people to see what they have in common.
[I think] we all agree that …
None of us want to …

Invite solutions and compromises
We also need to help people resolve things that they don't agree about, either by asking them to come up with a solution, persuading them to change their minds or by offering a compromise.
So, what's the solution?
Is there a way we can do both?
Would that work, [Bruna]?

5 A Work in groups. Read the Scenario again and choose one of Abe's suggestions or think of your own idea. Make sure you each choose something different.

B Make notes about the advantages of your suggestion.

MEDIATE

6 Get back into your groups. Try to agree on one event for your area. Use the Mediation Skill box to help you to reach compromises where necessary.

7 Tell other groups which event you chose. Did you choose the same event, and for the same reasons?

MEDIATION BANK | SPEAKING

5C Online or offline?

SPEAKING OUTPUT | a group discussion
GOAL | agree on a course of action
MEDIATION SKILL | encouraging people to expand on their ideas

WARM-UP

1 Work in pairs. What kind of things do you prefer doing online? What do you prefer doing in person? Why?

I never buy clothes online because it's really hard to know if they'll fit properly. I much prefer actually trying things on in shops.

PREPARE

2 Read the Scenario. What company-wide change is being suggested? Why is your manager contacting you about it?

SCENARIO

Your manager sends your team a message.

To	Marketing Team
From	Olsson, Felix
Subject	New directive – online-only

Hi everyone, I hope you're all OK. I just wanted to let you know that I've been talking to the senior management team this week, and they are suggesting that we should do all meetings online from now on. Obviously, I'd like your feedback on the idea, as it would be a big change in the way we work. Let's talk about this in our weekly meeting, but in the meantime, have a think about how you feel about the idea.
Thanks,
Felix

3 🔊 **MB5.01** | Listen to colleagues discussing the proposal. What advantages and disadvantages do they mention?

4 🔊 **MB5.01** | Read the Mediation Skill box. Then listen again and tick the questions you hear.

MEDIATION SKILL
encouraging people to expand on their ideas

When discussing something in a group, it's useful to encourage people to talk in detail about their opinions so everyone can understand their position better.

Asking for more detail
Can you talk us through your thinking on this?
Can you expand on that a bit?
In what ways is it different?
Can you give us some examples (of that)?

Asking about positive/negative aspects
What are the (main) benefits of … ?
Can you see any problems with that?

Questioning the facts presented
Is that always an issue?
Is that true for everybody?

Giving feedback
I agree that can sometimes be a problem.
That's an interesting point. How does everyone else feel about that?
That's definitely something to think about.

5 Match the questions (1–5) with the correct responses (a–e).

1 Can you talk us through your thinking on this?
2 In what way is it different?
3 What are the benefits of that?
4 Is that always the case?
5 Can you give us any other examples?

a Well, the main difference is that …
b Well, one of the good things is that …
c Not all the time, but it does happen quite often.
d Well, the other situation that comes to mind is …
e Sure. The main reason I think this is because …

6 Read the Scenario again. Make notes about the advantages and disadvantages of holding every meeting online.

MEDIATE

7 Work in groups. Imagine you work in the company described in the Scenario. Discuss the proposal, using your notes from Ex 6 to help you. Listen and encourage everyone to expand on their ideas.

8 Vote on whether or not to hold all of your meetings online from now on. Then, explain your decision to the class.

MEDIATION BANK | WRITING

6C Problem posts

WRITING OUTPUT | online comments
GOAL | add to posts in a thread, building on the advice of other people
MEDIATION SKILL | building on other people's ideas

WARM-UP

1 Work in pairs. Discuss the questions.
  1 How often do you post on social media?
  2 Do you ever post about things that make you angry? Why/Why not?
  3 Do you ever respond to other people's angry posts with help or advice? Why/Why not?

PREPARE

2 Work in pairs. Read the Scenario and discuss which bits of advice are the most helpful and why.

3 Read the Mediation Skill box. Which of the two people, Pixie or Ralf, is each comment for?

> **MEDIATION SKILL**
> **building on other people's ideas**
>
> When you give advice as part of a thread on social media, it's sometimes helpful to build on what other people have said.
>
> 1 **Like RJ says**, you won't achieve anything by getting angry with the people upstairs.
> 2 **Maybe do what Toni suggests** and tell her how you feel.
> 3 **Ronnie makes a good point about** not wanting to upset them – they are your neighbours, after all!
> 4 I'd ask for a refund, **as Linda says**, but you should also give them some feedback.
> 5 **I see it a bit like Rudy** – you can't solve anything when you're furious.

SCENARIO

You're scrolling through your social media and you see some friends asking for advice, and other people's replies.

Pixie 8 August at 9.17

So, it's the third week of this creative-writing course I'm doing and I'm getting pretty annoyed with it all. I just want to learn some new techniques and get a bit of practice, but the teacher just talks about herself and what a great writer she is. Should I quit?

9   3 Comments

JT 8 August at 11.17

Just drop the course if it's boring and ask for a refund. You're paying good money for it after all.

Like | Reply | 2 days ago

Mikey 8 August at 13.57

I had the same problem with that course last year. I left some feedback, but nothing changed. I just stopped going in the end.

Like | Reply | 2 days ago

SarahM 9 August at 06.31

Why don't teachers ever think about how students feel? It's really annoying, isn't it? I feel for you, @Pixie.

Like | Reply | 1 day ago

152

MEDIATION BANK | WRITING

Ralf 8 August at 10.35

Arghh! The upstairs neighbours are doing it AGAIN! They're making so much noise I can't hear the TV. I know they've got a young kid and everything, and they were so nice about it when I went to talk to them the last time, but it's driving me crazy.

● 4   4 Comments

Mike M 8 August at 12.01

Just go round again, but this time don't be so nice. They'll think twice about ruining your evening next time if you give them a good telling off!

Like | Reply | 2 days ago

D Wand 8 August at 14.03

You won't like this, but I think you've just got to accept it, or move. Young kids are always going to run around. That's part of being a young kid and there's no way you can ask them to sit in silence just so you can watch Netflix. It's not just about you.

Like | Reply | 2 days ago

LisaInLondon 9 August at 11:06

Take them some of those lovely cakes you do, @Ralf, and maybe see if you can get chatting? Better than shouting at them @Mike M.

Like | Reply | 1 day ago

Mike M 9 August at 11.32

DID I SAY SHOUT AT THEM, LISA?

Like | Reply | 1 day ago

4 Match the sentence beginnings (1–5) with endings (a–e).

1 Like Lori …
2 Ana makes a good …
3 I'd talk to them about it, …
4 I see it a bit …
5 As …

a point about trying to stay calm.
b as Dierdra suggests.
c like Tomas, getting angry never helps.
d Kayo suggests, try and see it from his side.
e says, you need to ask for help sometimes.

5 Use the correct form of the phrases in the Mediation Skill box to complete the comments. Make sure you refer back to the original comment.

1 Blossom: Don't worry about it too much.
   Like Blossom says, don't worry about it too much.

2 Ajay: I think you should try and push yourself a bit more.
   _____ about trying to push yourself. Otherwise, you won't learn anything.

3 Stella: Try it! How else are you going to find out?
   As _____ , you won't know unless you try.

4 Obi: There's no way you can do it all by yourself – that's ridiculous!
   I see _____ – they can't expect you to do everything on your own.

5 Percival: I'd try and call them before you go if I were you.
   Maybe do _____ and try to call them first?

6 BB: I know you need the work, but you shouldn't take on more than you can handle.
   BB _____ taking on too much – you don't want to burn yourself out!

MEDIATE

6 A Read the Scenario again and write your own responses to Pixie and Ralf. Build on the other arguments made in the thread where possible.

B Work in pairs. Compare your responses. Who has the best solution to each problem?

MEDIATION BANK | SPEAKING

7C Explainers

SPEAKING OUTPUT | a YouTube-style explainer video
GOAL | make a concept easier for someone else to understand
MEDIATION SKILL | making concepts easier to understand

WARM-UP

1 Work in pairs. Discuss the questions.
1 Do you think watching videos online is a good way to learn about new ideas? Why/Why not?
2 What was the last 'explainer' video you watched online? How useful was it?

PREPARE

2 Read the Scenario. What does Henry want you to do?

SCENARIO

To	Creative_Student
From	Lawson, Henry
Subject	Explainers video

Hey! Thanks for agreeing to be in our next video. As I mentioned, it's part of a YouTube series called 'Explainers'. Basically, in each episode, we give an expert two minutes to try and explain something to me – the presenter. You can talk about anything in your field of interest – a key concept related to your studies, the rules of a game, even something you've read about recently. It doesn't matter. It just needs to be something you're interested in and that you think our viewers might care about, too!

Anyway, have a think about it and I'll call you later to work out the details.

Cheers,

Henry

3 🔊 **MB7.01** | Listen to a guest on the show explaining *ad hominem* arguments and answer the questions.
1 What are *ad hominem* arguments?
2 How does Tyra make the concept easier to understand?

4A 🔊 **MB7.01** | Read the Mediation Skill box. Listen to the explanation in Ex 3 again and tick the phrases in bold that Tyra uses.

MEDIATION SKILL
making concepts easier to understand

There are several ways to make complicated ideas easier for listeners to understand:

Give memorable examples and comparisons
It's like a kid trying to put too many sweets in his mouth at the same time. They won't be able to eat them.
For instance, you accidentally see the time is 11.11 on your phone in the morning, and that evening you look at your phone at exactly the same time.

Give a simple summary of the idea
Essentially, we always think we're better than we are.
Basically, it means we can't be in two places at the same time.

Repeat an idea
So, like I said, it's pretty simple.
Yes, **in other words**, it's a two-way system.

B Work in pairs. Think of other phrases you could add to the box.

MEDIATION BANK | SPEAKING

5 Complete the script from an 'explainer' video with the missing text (a–e).

a Essentially, you do this by touching your opponent's electrified jacket, which is called the Lamé, with your weapon and scoring points.

b For instance, you should salute the officals and your opponent before beginning the fight.

c Basically, there are three disciplines in fencing based around three different weapons, Foil, Épée and Sabre.

d Fencing is like a kind of dance really, more than bloodthirsty combat

e But like I said, remember that it's not quite like how they show sword fighting in the movies!

For my explainer video, I'm going to talk about a sport I love dearly: fencing. When I tell people that I do fencing they immediately imagine scenes from films like *Braveheart* or *Highlander* with lots of violence and shouting. They couldn't be more wrong.

¹ _____, and speed is often much more valuable than strength, although the best fencers will obviously have both.

So first of all, let me tell you about different types of fencing. ² _____ Each discipline requires a different strategy based on the weapon that you are using. For example the Épée is super heavy compared to the Foil and Sabre, and there are different rules, too. With the Épée and Sabre, you can attack your opponent's head, for example, while this is not allowed if you're using a Foil. Most people start with the Foil, and it's actually still my favourite weapon to use.

So, how do you win at fencing?

³ _____. The player who reaches fifteen points first is the winner, or the player who has the most points at the end of the third period of the game if neither player has reached fifteen points. It's usually played in three rounds of three minutes. What I love about fencing is that it's a gentle sport, and showing respect to others is very important. ⁴ _____. You should also shake hands with everyone at the end, and to acknowledge when your opponent has made a good hit, we say *touché*.

So that's about it. That's fencing, my one true love. You should give it a go if you're looking for a way to get fit and if you like competitive sports. ⁵ _____ I'll put a list of fencing clubs in different areas in the comments section under the video. Thanks for watching!

6 Work in pairs. Take turns trying to explain the topics in the box in under thirty seconds. Use the phrases from the Mediation Skill box to help you.

> basketball   charity   climate change   money
> New Year's resolutions   poetry   ~~rugby~~   vaccines

Rugby is a sport played by two teams with an oval ball and H-shaped goalposts. There are lots of complicated rules, but basically, you score points by either putting the ball down over the opposition's goal line or by kicking the ball through the posts.

7 A Read the Scenario again. Make a list of concepts or topics you could talk about (e.g., an interest, a hobby, something connected to your work/studies, etc.).

B Plan your explanation. Make notes about:
- the key points.
- concrete examples you can give for each.

C Complete the notes with things you can say during your 'explainer' video.

Give memorable examples and comparisons.
It's like _____.
For instance, _____.

Give a simple summary of the idea.
Essentially, _____.
Basically, _____.

Repeat the main idea.
So, like I said, _____.
In other words, _____.

MEDIATE

8 Work in groups. Take turns explaining your concepts. Ask and answer questions for more information.

9 Whose explainer was the most interesting and useful? Why?

MEDIATION BANK | WRITING

8C Social safety

WRITING OUTPUT | an essay
GOAL | make a discursive argument on a topic
MEDIATION SKILL | using direct and indirect quotations

WARM-UP

1 Work in pairs. Discuss the questions.
  1 Do you think online abuse is a big issue? Why/Why not?
  2 How easy or difficult do you think it is to deal with online abuse? Why?
  3 Whose responsibility is it to deal with online abuse?

PREPARE

2 Read the Scenario. What homework has your teacher given you?

SCENARIO

Your friend Yuki sends you these messages.

> Hey! Sorry you couldn't make it to class yesterday. The homework was to write a short essay following up on the class discussion. The title is: 'How do we stop people receiving abuse on social media?'
> 10.19 a.m.

> Oh, and Miss Waterstone said we need to describe the issue, say what solutions people have suggested and include our own opinion.

> Anyway, I've emailed you a few articles that might help. Just give me a call if you're not sure about any of it.
> 10.25 a.m.

3 Skim the extracts about online abuse that Yuki sent. Which contain survey results?

---

1 A shocking government report claims that almost half of young people have received abuse online. The recent survey also discovered that 75 percent of the victims of this abuse were female. Social media companies have been criticised for failing to do enough to prevent the bullying.

George Behr, *The London Star*, 2017

---

2 'Social media companies shouldn't need to guess what to do – the government needs to tell them what is legal and illegal, and then the companies need to respect the law.'

Mia Okizawa, Centre for Policy Change, 2021

---

3 Online communication has become more and more 'normal' over the years, and at the same time the rules for communication online have become more like the real world's. Where once it was mostly men who used the internet and defined the rules for what was acceptable to say online, it is now used by everyone, and people who are abusive online are starting to receive the same responses from other people that they would receive if they did the same to someone in 'real life'. Based on this, I think we will see online abuse declining in the coming years.

Dawn Schultz, Professor of Technology Studies, Central University, 2020

MEDIATION BANK | WRITING

4 More than 90 percent of adults believe that social media companies need to do more to deal with online abuse, according to a poll conducted by Protect the Net, a UK charity. The poll also revealed that a large majority of people think that these companies should be fined if they do not deal with these issues.

The founder of the charity, Matt Zanker, thinks the companies need to be forced to act, especially in the case where their users are receiving anonymous abuse. 'These cowards hide behind made-up names and social media companies do nothing about it. They should be made to hand over the account information of anyone being abusive on their platform.'

However, not everyone agrees. Sadie Hinsliff, director of the Keep It Free campaign, says that the ability to be anonymous is important to protect privacy and freedom of expression. She points out that many people do positive things online, such as revealing the bad behaviour of powerful people, companies and governments, simply because they can remain anonymous.

Priya Shah, *Yorkshire Guardian*, 2019

5 Social Media companies are required to remove illegal content when it is discovered on their platforms, and the process most companies use is to encourage their users to report abusive content, which they then review and remove. There are also some systems which review content automatically, searching for key words which are often used in online abuse. This flags the content for review by a person working for the company. In terms of legal procedures, it is usually the victim's job to report the abuse to the police themselves, and most social media companies don't offer any support with this.

Isak Jansen, *Social magazine*, 2017

6 The solution is simple. Make every user of social media register using their passport or ID so the social media companies know who they are. Make everyone responsible for their actions, and if their actions are illegal, prosecute them. Do they have the right to remain anonymous? Not if they're breaking the law, no.

Roger Mallard, *The Seeker*, 2020

4 Read the Mediation Skill box. Then read the extracts again and find examples of direct and indirect quotes.

> **MEDIATION SKILL**
> **using direct and indirect quotations**
>
> It's a good idea to include quotes from your sources where you feel it helps describe the issues or support your arguments.
>
> **Quoting directly**
> Direct quotes use quote marks and include information about who wrote the article, in what publication and when:
>
> 'The number of cases is rising at a really alarming speed and I fear it's only going to get worse.'
> Luke Hallis (*The Tribune*, 2017)
>
> This information can also be included as part of a sentence:
>
> Luke Hallis in *The Tribune* (2017) thinks the issue is getting more serious: 'The number of cases is rising …'
>
> **Quoting indirectly**
> With indirect quotes we don't need quote marks, and we may use reporting verbs such as *explain*, *say*, *state* and *ask*. These are often used in the present tense.
>
> James Duckfield claims in *The Echo* (2021) that there's little evidence to suggest that online abuse is a big problem.

5 Rewrite the sentences as indirect quotations.

1 'It's a problem which is getting more and more serious.' Aaron Flynn, *The Flyer*, 2018
   Aaron Flynn ....
2 Ellie Cooper in *The Legal* (2019) says 'Governments need to do more to help social media companies.'
   Ellie Cooper ....
3 'You would feel differently if you had received abuse yourself. It's easy to say it's OK when it's happening to somebody else.' Helen Sharp
   Helen Sharp ....

6 Read the Scenario again. Make notes under the headings below to prepare for your essay. Use information from the extracts in Ex 3 to support your argument.

Paragraph 1:   Introduce the topic and problem
Paragraph 2:   Possible solutions
Paragraph 3:   Problems with the solutions
Paragraph 4:   Talk about your own opinion

MEDIATE

7 A Write your essay. Use your notes from Exercise 6 to help you.

B Work in pairs. Read each other's essays and discuss any differences in your opinions.

AUDIOSCRIPTS

UNIT 1

Audio 1.01
J = Jamie   G = Gini   M = Matteo   H = Hana

J: Hello and welcome to *Who Am I?* I'm your host Jamie Walker …
G: … and I'm Gini Cox.
J: This week we're focusing on identity – all the different elements that make us who we are.
G: That's right. So, we've been interviewing people out on the street, asking them how they would describe their identity. And we've had some really interesting replies.
J: Tell us a bit about yourself.
M: Hi, my name is Matteo and I'm a journalist. I'm thirty-four years old and I'm Brazilian. My mother tongue is Portuguese, but like many Brazilians, I have mixed roots. I'd say that my identity is made up of lots of different things.
J: What do you mean?
M: So, my mother is half Brazilian, half Italian, and my grandmother was Italian, so, I actually have an Italian passport and I spent some time living in Italy when I was younger.
J: Oh, right. So, do you feel that there is an Italian influence on your identity and your personality?
M: Hmm, I don't know about my personality so much. Is my personality connected to my Italian background? I don't know. But I think there is an influence on who I am as a person, you know, the things I do in my everyday life. Like, Italian families love getting together in big groups. That's not something I really enjoy. I do enjoy cooking Italian food though. And I love going to Italy on holiday and speaking the language. So, yeah, I guess the fact I've got Italian heritage is part of my identity, definitely.
J: And how about the UK? How long have you been living here? And do you think it's influenced your sense of identity at all?
M: So, I've been living in the UK for over twenty years now. But I wouldn't say I feel particularly British. I mean, my wife is British, my kids grew up here and I speak the language pretty fluently, but I guess my identity comes more from the place where I grew up, which is Brazil. I definitely feel more at home with my Brazilian and Portuguese friends. And when I listen to Brazilian music, it goes straight to my heart, you know? Like, it makes me think of everything I grew up with – the food, the language, the people – all of that forms a big part of who I am.
G: So, tell us a bit about yourself. What do you think makes you who you are?
H: So, I'm Hana and I'm originally from Korea, but I've lived in lots of different places around the world – mainly the USA but also Hong Kong, Australia, Germany. Now I'm based in Amsterdam, in the Netherlands, which I love. I've been learning Dutch, but it's really hard! So, I've always worked and travelled a lot around other countries and I would say that, um, all of these different places play a part in who I am, far beyond the idea of nationality or belonging to one single place. All of these places and the languages have contributed to the person that I am now.
G: What do you mean?
H: You know, in terms of how I eat and how I choose to live my life, I think there's a lot of Asian influence there. A lot of my favourite dishes to cook are Korean, for example. But I think my identity comes more from my own experiences – the different jobs I've done, the people I've met. I guess my family probably influenced my personality a lot, too.
G: Can you give me some examples?
H: Yeah, so my father is pretty stubborn and I've definitely inherited that from him. I don't think I've inherited anything from my mum – she's very organised, and a great planner, but I'm really not. They've both had a big influence on my attitude to work and studying, though. When I was at school, they encouraged me to work hard and I suppose, because of that, I've always been really focused on my education and my career, even though none of my siblings are. I guess I've always been pretty ambitious.
G: And how about your career? Would you say that's influenced your identity at all?
H: Yeah, definitely. I'm a journalist and that's a big part of my self-identity. I guess, at the end of the day, we are all different and there are lots of influences. Everyone is an individual with different life experiences and a different stories to tell.

Audio 1.02
1 How long have you been living here?
2 Have you ever lived in another country?
3 What have you been doing recently?
4 How long have you been studying English?

Audio 1.05
N = Naomi   A = Ayo

N: You know Lagos already, right?
A: A little bit. I came here on another business trip a few years ago. The thing I like about it is the street life. There are some really good markets where you can find handcrafted goods.
N: Oh, that sounds interesting.
A: Yeah, in the centre. And fairly close by, there's Victoria Island, which is sort of your more upscale area. It has designer stores and boutiques and fancy restaurants, that kind of thing. It's kind of the posh area. Do you want to check it out?
N: Um, I'd be happy to go there for a bit, but maybe not more than a couple of hours. It's not really my cup of tea.
A: OK, that's fine.
N: Yeah, I'm not a big fan of shopping generally. I'd rather go to a park and just wander about for a bit.
A: Actually, there *is* a park which you might like. It's called Freedom Park. It has life-size sculptures and an art gallery. And the last time I was there, there was live music.
N: Oh wow, I'm really into live music.
A: Yeah, there was a stage with a band and a dance group. It was awesome.
N: That sounds great. You know, I've heard there are some beaches outside the centre that are worth visiting.
A: Yeah, definitely.
N: It might be nice just to hang out on a beach for a few hours. I think I'd prefer to do that than to go wandering around the shops.
A: We can do that. There are a *few* beaches, if I remember rightly. One's called Tarkwa Bay Beach. It's about twenty minutes out of town and you take a boat to get there. It's idyllic, just beautiful.
N: Oh wow. You know, what I really like doing is surfing. I don't suppose they rent out surfboards, do they?
A: I'm pretty sure they do, actually. I didn't know you were into surfing.
N: I love it.
A: Me too.
N: Shall we just spend the afternoon surfing then, I mean after the markets and the park?
A: Fine with me.
N: Are you sure?
A: Totally! We can go to a street market and Freedom Park in the morning and spend the afternoon on the beach. Excellent! And then we'll find a local restaurant where we can eat some local food in the evening.
N: Sounds good.
A: Have you ever tried jollof rice?
N: Nope. Not yet.
A: You're going to love it!

UNIT 1 REVIEW

Audio R1.01
Stormy weather

Since I was very young, I have always loved the outdoors. As a ten-year-old, I read lots of books about explorers and I was extremely adventurous. I was happy wandering into the woods on my own, or exploring abandoned houses. While most children are curious about the natural world, I was obsessed. I have one particular childhood memory of a day with my grandfather. He was really into hiking and one day, when I was ten, he took me with him. The idea was to go up a hill called Gomez Peak, and we needed to go at a good pace so as to be back by dinnertime. Unfortunately, we got caught in a storm. There was no escape. We tried standing under a pine tree to stay dry, but it didn't work; we got soaked. As we stood there, he kept trying to comfort me, saying, 'It's going to be OK.' He thought I'd be terrified of all the noise and wind. But I wasn't scared – I loved it. I'll never forget listening to the rain falling like drumbeats. To this day, I have never had so much fun in my life!

AUDIOSCRIPTS

UNIT 1 VOCABULARY BANK

Audio VB1.01
1 We can depend on Sam to be here on time. He's very reliable.
2 Melissa became quite emotional as she was watching the film.
3 Al will need some help setting up the new printer. He's not very practical.
4 I love the fact that Leo is always so optimistic about life!
5 Sasha is a really talented musician.
6 Thanks for moving those boxes – it was really helpful.
7 It was very thoughtful of you to send those flowers to cheer me up!
8 I don't think I'll go to the party – I'm not feeling very sociable today.
9 I'm not adventurous enough to go paragliding!
10 I'm sure she'll be prime minister one day. She's incredibly ambitious.

Audio VB1.02
1 He never remembers anything I tell him! Things go in one ear and out the other.
2 Oh no! I forgot to buy vegetables for the curry. Sorry, it totally slipped my mind.
3 Hmm … I'm not sure. I'll need to look at my notes again to refresh my memory.
4 I'll remember it in a minute. The answer is on the tip of my tongue!
5 I'm sure I've heard that name before. It definitely rings a bell.
6 Oh, yes. You were there too, weren't you? My memory is playing tricks on me.

UNIT 1 MEDIATION BANK

Audio MB1.01
B = Billie   P = Pete   C = Campbell
B: Hey! Have you read Leif's email yet?
P: Yeah, so they want us to come up with a top five list of places to visit, right?
C: Yep, our top five, in order.
B: OK. So how do you want to do this? Shall we each come up with a list and then compare?
C: It's going to take too long if we do it like that. How about going through our favourites one by one?
P: Yeah OK. Then we can list the reasons later. Who wants to go first? Billie?
B: OK, well the Museum of Modern Art's got to be on there, obviously.
C: Obviously.
P: And is that number one?
B: Hmm … let's worry about the order later. Let's just get a big list of places together first.
P: OK, so the museum, and what next, the nature park?

UNIT 2

Audio 2.01
1 VR is certain to be used more in the future.
2 The new headsets are due to go on sale next week.
3 This game is going to be a big hit!
4 VR is unlikely to replace our summer holidays.

Audio 2.02
I want you to imagine yourself in paradise. Think about what you can see. What sounds can you hear? What do you feel? If you imagined a white sand beach with gently lapping waves, or a woodland alive with birdsong, I'm guessing you also imagined a feeling of serenity and relaxation. The idea that spending time in nature can be good for our well-being isn't new. It's actually an idea that goes back for thousands of years. The word 'paradise' comes from the Ancient Persian term for park or orchard, which is 'pardaiza' and I think if you ask most people to imagine paradise, people would think about a white sand beach with waves lapping or with a woodland maybe that's alive with birdsong. They're probably likely to imagine a feeling of serenity and relaxation. And that's the kind of feeling that medics began to try and promote in the UK as early as … sort of … the 1750s. We had doctors travelling around the country, trying to work out what it was like spending time near the sea and whether that's something that could almost be prescribed. And we had sea-bathing hospitals, the idea being that spending time there could help you overcome some of the sort of minor ailments that were common in the 1700s.

In the last 200 years, we've started to sort of lose our connection with some of the preventative effects that spending time in nature can have for us. We've had these incredible advances in technology, in pharmaceuticals, antibiotics, which have meant that we've saved, you know, millions of lives and improved the quality of life in so many countries across the world, but that shift in focus has meant that we've sort of moved away from our ancient nature-based perspectives, and in many cases sort of forgotten that connection that we have with nature.

So the problem now is that for the first time in history, most of the world's population live in big, busy and noisy cities, and they're so different to the kind of environments that we evolved to live in. And whether we're aware of it or not, cities place, you know, a huge amount of stress on our bodies. We're almost in a constant state of alert because we have to navigate things like crossing the road, busy, crowded spaces, threats from passing bicycles. And also the kind of complicated social interactions that we actually start to take for granted now, but that our bodies are constantly trying to deal with and respond to.

So when we live in demanding environments like cities, our body has this desperate need to be able to switch off for downtime. And the natural environment actually provides the perfect kind of setting to allow that kind of restoration to occur.

What's really interesting is that actually just having a view of nature can be enough to see some of these restorative effects. So there's a famous study from the 1980s where hospital patients were shown to recover faster from surgery if they had a view of trees rather than just a window that looked out at the rest of the hospital.

It also looks like the level of biodiversity could be quite important for well-being. It could be that simply seeing or hearing more plants and animals in an environment makes it more fascinating. Which brings us on to the sounds of nature, and several studies have shown that people prefer listening to natural sounds like birdsong or water flowing, compared to the other kinds of sounds they'd hear in a city, for example. But we don't really have a huge amount of data on what kinds of sounds might work best and whether just listening to them is enough. If you just put on a set of headphones on your commute, would that help calm you down enough, or do you need to see, touch, smell, be in nature for it to have the ultimate effect?

Audio 2.05
A: Hey, so, I've been watching this amazing TV series about women with extreme lifestyles. Have you seen it?
B: Yeah, I've been watching that, too. Last week there was one about a woman who's a sea nomad and has spent her whole life at sea.
A: That's right. Amazing. Did you see the one about the astronaut? What was her name … ?
B: Karen Nyberg? Yeah, I saw that one, too.
A: It was incredible, wasn't it?
B: I know. I mean I'd guess it must be so inspiring to see the world like that, from space. Can you imagine?
A: Yeah, it would be incredible, wouldn't it?
B: Absolutely! Although there's no way I would ever consider doing that. I know for a fact that I couldn't go into space. I don't even like getting on a plane! It must be an amazing experience though.
A: Yeah, it was interesting to find out how they actually live up there, you know, the ordinary things that they have to do every day. A lot of it looked pretty tedious, like checking all of the systems and whatever. And that bit about how they keep fit – it was really fascinating!
B: Yeah and how she washes her hair! Did you see that bit?
A: Yeah, it was really interesting to see how she does, you know, normal, everyday things up there. Must be difficult sometimes though – especially being away from people. I mean, she left her three-year-old son at home, and was away for, like, six months. I mean I'd imagine that was really hard.

AUDIOSCRIPTS

B: I suppose they had video chats, but it's not really the same, is it?
A: Not at all. And what about that woman who runs around the world? Did you see that one?
B: Yeah, Rosie Swale-Pope I think her name was. I can't believe she's in her 70s and she runs all around the world by herself, pulling that little trailer behind her.
A: I know, and she sleeps in it at night, and then just carries on running in the morning. It's pretty impressive!
B: Yeah, I reckon it must be pretty lonely at times, though.
A: Well, you would think so, but she obviously finds it really rewarding, seeing all those amazing places and meeting interesting people along the way. She's written a book about some of the things that have happened to her. And she raises money for charity.
B: She's clearly the kind of person who just has to keep moving, sort of nomadic.
A: Yes, that's right. I get the impression she's so used to this lifestyle that she wouldn't be happy living anywhere for long. Even when she's back home in the UK, she sometimes prefers to sleep outside in her little trailer than stay inside her house.
B: Oh, really? I'd have thought it'd be exhausting to live like that all the time. And pretty frightening, too. She's bound to feel scared sometimes.
A: I bet she does. Anyway, it's not for me. I can't even bear going camping for the weekend, let alone …

Audio 2.07
If I could travel back in time to any place in the world, I'd go back to Paris in the 1920s. To start with, I'm a huge fan of all the artists and writers from that period, like Ernest Hemingway, F. Scott Fitzgerald, Salvador Dalí, Pablo Picasso, and Gertrude Stein. And they all lived in Paris, so it was a really exciting city at that time. I'd love to meet all of them, but especially Hemingway because I really like his books.

So, what would I do? Well, at that time, there were all these nightclubs and cafés springing up all over Paris, with loads of incredible shows. With that in mind, I'd want to go dancing with F. Scott Fitzgerald and his wife Zelda. I can imagine that being a whole lot of fun. What else? I'd have a long chat with Hemingway and Picasso about their creativity and what they were planning to do next. And last but not least, I'd take Gertrude Stein out to dinner and ask her what she really thought of all these artists with their amazing talent, but also their big egos!

UNIT 2 REVIEW

Audio R2.01
Anyone looking for solitude is unlikely to find it in a 21st-century city, but there are still plenty of places one can be alone. In the 19th century, the American writer Henry Thoreau did an experiment in solitary living. He went to live on a patch of woodland owned by his friend Ralph Waldo Emerson. Thoreau built a hut on the banks of Walden Pond. He spent over two years there and wrote a book, *Walden*, about his experiences.

More recently, the Italian writer Paolo Cognetti left Milan and rented a shepherd's hut near the mountains of Valle d'Aosta. There he lived for several months, surrounded by incredible scenery and very little noise besides the wind. While there, he took time to analyse his life and think about what he might do next. Like Thoreau, he wrote a book: *The Wild Boy*.

Few people are able to escape like Thoreau and Cognetti. The majority of us are lucky if we get a few days on a deserted beach. But there will always be quiet places for those with the desire and resources to find them.

UNIT 2 MEDIATION BANK

Audio MB2.01
I = Interviewer   S = Sam

I: Now, anyone that's been listening to the podcast for any length of time will know that I love live music. But it can be difficult to feel any real connection with the artists when you're one of thousands of people in the audience.
So, what's the solution? My next guest may well have the answer. Sam Harrington is one of a small, but growing number of music-lovers hosting 'micro gigs' – an alternative to big concerts.
Sam – welcome to the show.
S: Thanks for having me.
I: So, first things first – what is a 'micro-gig'? Is it just a small concert?
S: Well, yeah, it's a really small concert, but perhaps the biggest difference is that they happen in people's homes rather than big concert venues.
I: Right. And you actually put on micro gigs at your house, is that right?
S: Yeah, I've been using my living room to host concerts for the last three years now. We've probably had about 200 artists play here.
I: Wow, that's a lot!
S: Yeah, and most of them have stayed with us, too. We provide bed and breakfast for all the artists who come and play for us as part of their fee.
I: Nice. And what about the audience? How many people can you actually fit in your living room?
S: Hmmm … It, kind of, depends who's performing. If it's a solo artist with a small instrument, we can probably squeeze around fifteen people in. But with big instruments and groups it's much fewer. We once had someone come with their harp and we only had space for five!

Audio MB2.02
I = Interviewer   S = Sam

I: So, why do you do it? What's the attraction of putting on micro gigs?
S: Well, when you go to a big concert the artist or band is usually so far away. You're often in a crowd, which can be uncomfortable, and of course it's often expensive, too. I think music is great when it's a really personal experience, and I love being able to chat with the musicians about the music they make. It's a much more satisfying experience.
I: Sure, but you're never going to have, say, Elton John in your house, are you? I'm guessing the artists don't get paid that much for doing such a small show, so what's in it for them?
S: Haha! Well, Elton is very welcome! But, yeah, you're right, they don't get paid a lot, but I think most artists we have here find it a very positive experience. It's a great place to interact with your audience and to make a very direct connection with people. Music, and art, doesn't always have to be about numbers. Indeed, some famous artists actually use small venues like ours to try out new songs and get feedback from a small audience.
I: Right. So, do people actually know who's playing in advance or is it a surprise?
S: No, we don't have gig listings or anything, we like to keep it a surprise! People just turn up and hope they can get in.
I: And do they always like the artists you invite?
S: Not always! I remember a very angry, shouty, singer songwriter we had here a couple of years ago. He was pretty rude and some of the people who came along really didn't like him.
I: Oh, really? So, was it a bit of a disaster then?
S: No, not at all. Music isn't always about everyone having fun. Sometimes it's good to listen to something that's not your usual thing, and even if you don't like it, it's an experience, something to talk about with your friends, or something that makes you think. And sometimes you change your mind about things you think you don't like. A lot of our regular customers had never seen live hip hop before, for example, but they loved some of the artists who've come to play here. I mean, yeah, it's great to see your favourite artist, but it's good to be a musical explorer, too.
I: Absolutely. Sam – thanks for coming on the show.

AUDIOSCRIPTS

UNIT 3

Audio 3.01
1 Burning Man festival, which takes place at the end of August, attracts huge crowds.
4 The festival appointed Damon Gameau, who is a world-renowned filmmaker, as their Eco Ambassador.

Audio 3.03
P = Pauline   K = Katherine   R = Rufus   M = Mahmoud

P: We've all been there. You've practised a thousand times. You know your lines and you know how to say them. Yet when the time comes to perform, your legs turn to jelly and you just want to hide in the corner. Stage fright affects even the most experienced performers, and can make or break anyone just starting out. So, how do we cope with it? I'm Pauline Hazany and this week I interviewed a few well-known performers to find out. First up is professional musician, Katherine Sherrell, who I caught up with backstage on the first night of her UK tour.
P: Katherine, you used to get pretty bad stage fright, didn't you?
K: Yeah, I did, for years. Every time I had to go on stage, I could hardly stand up, I was shaking so much. I just got so nervous. It was awful. And my time on stage seemed to go on forever!
P: So, what happened? Did things just improve the more you performed?
K: Well, sort of. It was a couple of things, really. Firstly, I told a friend, a fellow musician, about my nerves, and he said something surprising. He said, it's not about you; it's about the music. He also told me to stop worrying about the audience. You know, they want a great night out; they've paid for their tickets, and they're on my side. From that moment, I had a different approach; I was calmer and more relaxed. And it's served me well ever since.
P: Sounds like good advice. Have you picked up any more tips that could help our listeners?
K: Something else I do is focus on my posture, how I stand, and even how I walk on stage before the gig starts. I remember I've been doing this for years and I imagine I'm ten feet tall and that nothing can stop me!
P: The second person I spoke to was Rufus Gerrard, a stage actor who's played all kinds of roles from Hamlet to Frodo in the theatre version of *The Lord of the Rings*. I caught up with Rufus during a rehearsal for his new play, Arthur Miller's *The Crucible*.
P: Rufus, hi.
R: Hi, Pauline.
P: Tell us about stage fright.
R: It's a real problem, even for experienced actors. You feel as if you're going to die of fright. It can hit you at any time and you have to find a way to overcome it.
P: So how do you cope with it?
R: In my case, I learnt quite early on in my career that what I needed to do was prepare both physically and mentally. So, physically I started doing stretching exercises for about fifteen minutes before every performance. And mentally I started using visualisation. Basically, I'd imagine myself not in front of a big, scary audience, but in front of my friends and family, people who'd supported me all my life, and I'd see them smiling and clapping. I also tried to erase myself and my ego, so I was no longer Rufus Gerrard acting in front of an audience, but I was the character in the play. It's the character that's important, not me.
P: And it worked?
R: Yeah, it made all the difference.
P: My last interview was with motivational speaker, Mahmoud Jalil. Mahmoud regularly gives presentations to hundreds of people around the world, so he knows a thing or two about how to stay cool under pressure. I met up with him in a café a couple of hours before he was due on stage.
    So, you're on pretty soon, aren't you, Mahmoud?
M: Er, yeah. I've got about an hour or so before I need to get ready.
P: So, how are you feeling? Getting nervous yet?
M: Haha! Not really. I used to get incredibly nervous before giving my talks though. I mean like a total disaster.
P: So what changed?
M: Well, it was the build-up beforehand that scared me. I used to spend hours going over the performance in my head. Was everyone going to like it? Would I forget what to say? Every time I had to go on stage, it was like the worst day of my life! And then one day I made a decision to just stop caring so much. I said to myself – what's the worst thing that can happen? That I forget what I'm trying to say? Or the technology breaks down? But if that happens, how much does it matter? Will it be the end of the world if I get lost and have to read my notes? The answer was no. And that was how it all changed for me. I mean, it was so liberating.
P: So you just needed a change of mindset?
M: Basically, yeah. What worked for me was approaching the presentation differently. I still get nervous, but I don't spend hours and hours preparing and imagining all the worst things that can happen. Now it's under control.

Audio 3.05
A = Alice   S = Sam   R = Ravi

A: Hey, have any of you guys seen *The Queen's Gambit* yet?
S: Yeah, I have. It's amazing, isn't it? I binge-watched the entire thing in a couple of days!
R: Really? Wow. It must be good, then. What's it about?
A: So, it's about a woman, Beth Harmon, who is a chess prodigy.
R: Chess?
A: Yeah, but trust me, it's good. Anyway, it's set in the USA around the 1950s and it shows her rise to becoming, like, a world-class chess player, you know, beating all the grand masters and that kind of thing.
R: Is it a true story?
S: Hmm … I don't think so. It's based on a book by Walter Tevis. I'm pretty sure the main character is fictional.
A: Well, yes but she's kind of based on a real person, Vera Menchik, who was a chess star, or something like that. So, the story is sort of real. It's beautifully written though, isn't it? And she's such an intriguing character.
S: Yeah, definitely. It really takes us into her world. The acting is fantastic.
A: Yes, I loved that bit at the end when … well, I won't spoil it for you, but it's really good. And it's beautiful to watch, too. You know, the costumes and stuff. It's done really well.
R: Ah, OK. Well, it sounds good. I'll add it to my watch-list.
A: Yeah, do – it's well worth a watch. What about you then? Have you binged-watched anything recently?
R: Me? Yeah, I'm watching a programme called *Big Little Lies* at the moment. It's amazing!
A: Oh, really? I remember hearing about it, but I don't think I ever watched it. Wasn't it the one about the women, set in California? It's like a murder mystery or something.
S: That's right. Oh, it's brilliant. It's based on a book by … um … what's her name, you know that Australian author … Liane Moriarty. It tells the story of five young-ish women in California who become involved in this murder investigation. And the acting is brilliant, you know, really powerful. So, every episode is sort of incredibly tense and gripping to watch.
A: Sounds good.
S: It's got a fantastic cast, as well – Nicole Kidman, Reese Witherspoon and they give these really powerful, realistic performances.
A: Sounds great. Just my kind of thing.
S: Yeah, I think you'd love it. You get really caught up in the drama and that kind of thing, all the plot twists. But it's also visually stunning to watch. Every scene is beautifully shot. It's perfect for a late-night binge-watching session.
A: Brilliant! The show I'm watching at the moment has got about ten seasons, or something like that. But I'm getting through them really quickly, so now I'll have something to watch when I'm finished.
R: Yeah, good to know …
S: I definitely …

161

AUDIOSCRIPTS

Audio 3.06
A = Alice   S = Sam
A: So, it's about a woman, Beth Harmon, who is a chess prodigy. It's set in the USA around the 1950s and it shows her rise to becoming, like, a world-class chess player, you know, beating all the grand masters and that kind of thing.
A: Yes, I loved that bit at the end when … well, I won't spoil it for you, but it's really good. And it's beautiful to watch, too, you know, the costumes and stuff. It's done really well.
A: It's like a murder mystery or something.
S: That's right. Oh, it's brilliant. It's based on a book by um, what's her name? You know, that Australian author … Liane Moriarty. It tells the story of five young-ish women …
S: Every episode is sort of incredibly tense and gripping to watch. You get really caught up in the drama and that kind of thing, all the plot twists …
A: The show I'm watching at the moment has got about ten seasons, or something like that.

UNIT 3 REVIEW

Audio R3.01
The show goes on
I once took on the challenge of trying to put on a show with people who had never performed on stage before. At first it seemed impossible. People kept messing up their lines. After a few weeks, I really didn't want to continue, but everyone was so enthusiastic that in the end, I did agree to carry on. But then I realised that we were trying to rehearse in the evenings, when everyone was tired. So I came up with the idea of rehearsing early in the mornings instead, which was much more successful because everyone was fresh. What I liked about working with people new to acting was that they were completely free – they had no expectations to live up to.
As the day of the performance approached, I must admit I became more nervous. We had put up posters to attract an audience, but I wasn't sure how many would attend. Thankfully, the theatre was full. My amateur cast ended up giving an incredible performance, and the audience loved it!

UNIT 3 VOCABULARY BANK

Audio VB3.01
1 solar power
2 natural resources
3 clean-up
4 carbon emissions
5 sustainable
6 renewable
7 recycling
8 carbon footprint

UNIT 4

Audio 4.01
1 This time next year, I'll have graduated from university.
2 I hope we'll have cut down on junk food by then.
3 When you next see me, I'll have started working out.
4 I hope you'll have found a new job by the summer.

Audio 4.02
P = Presenter   M = Matthew
TV P = TV Presenter
P: Matthew Walker researches how you spend around a third of your life.
M: I'm a sleep scientist.
P: Actually, one of the world's leading sleep scientists. At the root of sleep science lies a puzzle. All these hours lying down, eyes shut. Why? Why do we sleep? It's not just that it seems a monumental waste of time.
M: Sleep actually seems to be the most idiotic of all things that human beings could do because when you're asleep, you're not finding a mate, you're not reproducing, you're not caring for your young, you're not finding food, and in fact, it's been suggested that if sleep doesn't serve an absolutely vital function, then it's the biggest mistake the evolutionary process has ever made.
P: Managing eight hours' shut-eye is for me just a dream. And it turns out I'm not alone. There's evidence that in many parts of the developed world, we're sleeping less and less. A poll in 1942 found Americans were sleeping eight hours a night.
M: Now, on a recent National Sleep Foundation survey, what they found was that the average adult in America was down to sleeping six hours and thirty-one minutes a night. In the United Kingdom it was six hours and forty-nine minutes. Japan perhaps the worst down to six hours and twenty-two minutes.
P: Only ten percent of Japanese adults, according to this survey, were getting eight hours or more.
TV P: Good morning, this is Diana Speed welcoming you to the network and reminding you that if you've forgotten that the clocks went forward last night so the time is now twenty past five on Sunday the twenty-ninth of March …
P: Researchers have studied what happens in countries after clocks are adjusted in spring and autumn.
M: What they found was that in the spring, when we lose one hour of sleep, there was a twenty-four percent relative increase in heart attacks the following day, whilst in the autumn, in the fall, when we gain an hour of sleep, there was actually a twenty-one percent reduction in relative heart attack rates.
P: When the clocks go forward and we lose an hour's sleep, there are also more hospital admissions and more car accidents.
It also turns out that during sleep, we're able to reorganise information in the brain rather as though we were putting together the components of an IKEA furniture pack. And when we wake up, 'Eureka!' Every language has a variation of the English phrase 'sleep on it', 'sleep on the problem'. 'Dormici su, … la nuit porte conseil,' …
M: Yeah, I think there's probably a reason that no one has ever told you to stay awake on a problem.

Audio 4.03
It's been suggested that if sleep doesn't serve an absolutely vital function, then it's the biggest mistake the evolutionary process has ever made.

Audio 4.06
M = Martin   L = Leah
M: I read this article the other day about how much exercise we should do. It recommended 150 minutes of moderate exercise a week, which sounds about right to me. What do you think?
L: Hmmm, I'm not sure. I agree with you up to a point, but it depends, doesn't it? I mean, it depends on your age, your general health, and whether or not you're sporty. For most people, I'd say about an hour a day is enough to keep you fit and healthy. That's what I do, and I enjoy it.
M: An hour a day?! That's a lot, if you ask me!
L: Do you think so? It depends what kind of exercise, I guess. In my opinion, there's a big difference between, say, walking for an hour and playing football for an hour. So if you're doing a contact sport like football or basketball, you might only want to do that, say, two or three days a week. But you can easily do moderate exercise every day, like walking or jogging or swimming.
M: Yeah, that's a good point. Not all exercise is equal. But I completely disagree with you that everyone needs to do an hour a day. That's way too much for most people!
L: I know what you mean. Most people would find it hard to fit in exercise every day, but I'm talking about an ideal number. So, how much exercise do you do?
M: What, you mean vigorous exercise – sweating and getting out of breath?
L: Yeah.
M: None.
L: Really?
M: Yeah. But remember, I'm on my feet all day at work, aren't I? So I don't have the stamina to spend my evenings running around as well.
L: Oh, I see your point.

AUDIOSCRIPTS

M: I know in theory I should go to the gym and all that stuff, but on the other hand, I think doing too much exercise is just as bad as doing too little.
L: True.
M: I do a physical job, and I'm exhausted by the evening. As far as I'm concerned, if you do physical work during the day, you don't need to go to a gym or do anything else.
L: Hm. That's a fair point, although it could also be argued that you just need a different type of exercise, like stretching or yoga or something to help you relax.
M: No thanks! That's what the TV's for.
L: Well, you could at least kick a ball around every now and then, or walk the dog.
M: I couldn't agree more, but I don't have a dog.
L: Well, walk the cat, then.
M: Ha ha.

Audio 4.08
I would say that my modern lifestyle is quite different from the traditional lifestyle of, say, my grandmother. Especially as a young woman. Nowadays, most young women where I come from get a good education and go out to work, whereas in the past, in my grandmother's generation, that didn't happen so much. My grandmother left school when she was young, and married my grandfather. She never went out to work, although she used to earn money by sewing, and making suits for people. She dedicated her life to looking after everybody, her parents, her aunt, her children, her grandchildren. She cooked and kept the house clean. She would get up early and go down to the market to buy fresh fruit and vegetables from the local farmers, freshly caught fish and seafood from the fishermen. We still have a market that sells local produce. I suppose that tradition is still quite strong. But it's much smaller than it used to be, and people do most of their shopping in the supermarket, so it's much more difficult for the local fishermen and the farmers to make money. Their lifestyle is disappearing, and we only have a small window of opportunity to save it. A lot of farmers are now choosing to run 'Agritourism' businesses instead – essentially providing holidays on the farm – which is something that didn't exist before. Another tradition that is under threat is home cooking. My grandmother made home-made pasta and bread every day. She would spend hours preparing meals for the family. She lived a simple life. Nowadays, I think the expectations of young people are very different. We don't have so much time to spend at home, so a lot of the traditional skills of cooking and making things at home have been lost. These days, it seems like nobody has time for those lengthy recipes. We use a machine or we buy food that is ready-made and put it in the microwave, so I would say that this is another tradition which is in danger of disappearing. Also, when something breaks, we throw it away and buy a replacement, but I remember my grandfather was always repairing things and making them work again. Our modern-day lifestyle is much more focused on consumerism than in the past. Perhaps it's time to make a change.

UNIT 4 REVIEW

Audio R4.01
Health is the new wealth
Tara Williams, Monday 25 February, 13.00 GMT
In recent years, health and fitness has grown into a multi-billion-dollar industry as many of us strive to eat healthily and stay in shape. With modern technology, the average lifestyle has become increasingly sedentary. We are also busier and in general work longer hours than in the past. So, to make up for it, we follow healthy-eating gurus on Instagram, try to vary our diet by drinking fresh vegetable juice and eating superfood salads. We join gyms, buy fitness technology, take online yoga classes and do regular workouts. It is thought that Americans spend more than $40 billion trying to improve their health and fitness every year.
And future trends look even more extreme. Some are predicting that within the next ten years, a lot of fitness training will have moved outside. The benefits of training outdoors include exposure to the sun and fresh air, and running where the ground isn't flat. In addition, it's likely that more of us will be wearing personal tracking devices, which will offer us computer-generated personal training programmes based on our individual health metrics.

UNIT 4 MEDIATION BANK

Audio MB4.01
B = Bruna   C = Costas   J = Jim   P = Penny
B: Right, so next on the agenda is Active Week. Abe's sent through a list of ideas, but I've actually got another option I'd like to discuss. How does everyone feel about putting on some dance classes in the town square? It's active, and it doesn't need to be competitive, so everyone can join in.
C: Yeah, that's a nice idea Bruna, and I think we all agree that we need to find an activity that everyone can do. But I just don't know if dancing is popular enough. We want to get as many people involved as possible. Remember when we did the fun run a couple of years ago? People absolutely loved that.
B: Good point, so what does everyone think of that idea – about doing a fun run again?
J: Sounds good to me.
P: Yeah, the fun run was good, but I think we should try and do something different every year, which is why dance classes are such a great idea. We've never done them before.
J: That's a good point, Penny.
B: OK, thanks for the input, everyone. So, we all agree that we want something everyone can do, and I think we all want the biggest attendance possible, but Penny is worried about doing something we've done before. So, what's the solution?
C: Well, perhaps we could try and do both? Have two events instead of one this year? That way, if you're not interested in dance classes, you can do the fun run.
J: Would that work, Bruna?
B: Hmm … Abe did say we should try and choose one activity, but I can suggest two and see what he says?
P: OK, great. Thanks, Bruna!

UNIT 5

Audio 5.01
1 I'd been trying to get a job for ages.
2 We'd been waiting to meet our new boss.
3 They'd been listening to a presentation.
4 She'd been sleeping all afternoon.

Audio 5.02
SM = Sarfraz Manzoor   EW = Emily Wapnick
CH = Charles Handy   HM = Heather McGregor
SM: Emily Wapnick is an artist, entrepreneur, speaker, coach and the author of How to Be Everything: A Guide for Those Who (Still) Don't Know What They Want to Be When They Grow Up.
EW: More and more people are, erm, doing multiple things and multiple jobs, and it's not just to make ends meet, a lot of people are choosing this kind of lifestyle.
SM: She lives and works in Canada, and has coined the term 'multipotentialite' to describe folks like her.
EW: You'll have people who have five different part-time jobs, each of which they love for a different reason. They've got, you know, three different businesses that are just thriving, or they're a serial entrepreneur or they've got a career in two different areas. There's a guy that I mention who is a psychotherapist and, er, a luthier – he makes violins. Um, and he's very successful in both.
SM: And, I mean, how old are you?
EW: I'm thirty-two.
SM: And do you think that you are emblematic, or do you think you're typical of your generation in the idea of, you know, making it work by doing a variety of different, different things.
EW: Possibly. I do feel like things are moving in this direction and, you know, there's all these new, um, career models and new technology which make, er, a lot of things more possible for us.
SM: I'm just not sure whether somebody like myself would have the same capacity to learn new skills. Is there an age limit to when one can reinvent oneself or, you know, open a new door in their career or in their enthusiasms?
EW: I don't think so. I, I really believe that we can learn something new at any age.

AUDIOSCRIPTS

CH: Eighty percent of the people in corporate jobs hate them or are dissatisfied with them.
SM: This is Charles Handy, the man who popularised the idea of the portfolio career.
CH: Whereas if you're doing your own thing, eighty percent of them really like the freedom and the entrepreneurial spirit, even if they're not making an awful lot of money. It's a balancing job really.
HM: You need to know what the costs are of changing careers. So, one of the most important things is, to know what it's cost you to live.
SM: Professor Heather McGregor, 'Mrs Moneypenny' to readers of the *Financial Times*, started out in PR and communications, retrained as an investment banker, set up a highly successful business and is now an academic. If one career isn't enough, is it best to establish yourself and then switch to another in mid-life or is a portfolio of jobs a better prospect?
HM: A portfolio career is where there is almost no principal job. You know, everybody should have other things that they do in their career, apart from their main job. Otherwise, they will never advance their career. So, I have a main job and then I have other things, but I wouldn't call it a portfolio.

Audio 5.03

1 You'll have people who have five different part-time jobs, each of which they love for a different reason.
2 They've got, you know, three different businesses that are just thriving, or they're a serial entrepreneur or they've got a career in two different areas.
3 Is there an age limit to when one can reinvent oneself or, you know, open a new door in their career or in their enthusiasms?
4 Professor Heather McGregor, 'Mrs Moneypenny' to readers of the *Financial Times*, started out in PR and communications, retrained as an investment banker, set up a highly successful business and is now an academic.
5 If one career isn't enough, is it best to establish yourself and then switch to another in mid-life?
6 You know, everybody should have other things that they do in their career, apart from their main job. Otherwise, they will never advance their career.

Audio 5.05

J = Juan B = Britney L = Lisa N = Nick S = Sue A = Alison
D = David Ja = Jack

Conversation 1
J: What do you think, Lisa?
J: Lisa, you're on mute!
B: Can you unmute yourself?
L: Sorry! Yes, I think that's a very good idea.
J: There's an echo.
L: Oh, really? What about now?
J: You're still echoing.
B: Why don't you try turning down the volume on your speakers? It's worth a try because sometimes the echo's from the mic.
L: What about now?
B: That's better.
L: Well, I was just saying ... Hi, Jingles! There's a good girl!
J: Lisa?

Conversation 2
N: Hi again! Sorry, my computer crashed.
S: That's OK, Nick.
N: Um, so where were we? I think I was just ...
S: Nick? Nick?
N: There seems to be a problem with my internet connection.
S: Perhaps you could try logging off and on again? That might work because sometimes the computer just seems to fix itself.
N: OK. I'm back. Can you hear me?
S: Yes.
N: And can you see me?
S: Yes.
N: Oh good. OK, so ...
S: But now you're frozen.
N: Oh no!
S: It's OK. It's actually quite a funny picture of you, to be honest. Hold on, let me take a screen shot ...
N: What? No!

Conversation 3
A: David, can you bring up the figures on your screen for us?
D: Er, yeah. I need your permission though, as you're the host.
A: Oh. Hmm. Hang on. I can't get the screen share working.
D: Click on the icon at the bottom of the screen. It says, 'screen share'.
A: Hmmmm.
Ja: David, maybe you could post the document as a link in the chat box.
A: No, it's OK. Wait a minute. Here we go. How about that?
D: OK. Can you all see the spreadsheet?
Ja: Nope.
D: How about now?
A: Er, I think you've opened the wrong file there ...
Ja: Nice photo, David!

Audio 5.06

B = Britney N = Nick S = Sue A = Alison Ja = Jack

Conversation 1
1 B: Why don't you try turning down the volume on your speakers?
2 B: It's worth a try because sometimes the echo's from the mic.

Conversation 2
3 N: There seems to be a problem with my internet connection.
4 S: Perhaps you could try logging off and on again?
5 S: That might work because sometimes the computer just seems to fix itself.

Conversation 3
6 A: Hang on. I can't get the screen share working.
7 Ja: David, maybe you could post the document as a link in the chat box.

Audio 5.07

a Perhaps you could try switching it off.
b Perhaps you could try switching it off.

UNIT 5 REVIEW

Audio R5.01

It's never too late …
In Young Kim, 30 November
It probably feels like there's never a good time to switch careers, giving up a successful job for one that's a lot more uncertain. However, some people do manage to successfully reinvent themselves.
Michelle Obama had been working in an office doing legal work when she decided that she wanted to leave her job and do something more satisfying. For her, that meant working in public service, which was a big career change. The rest, as they say, is history!
Giorgio Armani, one of the world's top fashion designers, didn't start out in the world of fashion. He was planning to become a doctor, and had been studying medicine for three years when he decided to leave university and join the armed forces. He worked in a military hospital in Verona before moving into fashion. First, he worked in a shop in Milan and then he started designing his own clothes before setting up his own company in 1975.
Harrison Ford, who starred in *Star Wars* and *Raiders of the Lost Ark,* started acting when he was a young man. However, a few years later, he wasn't satisfied with the opportunities that he had been offered up to that point, so he decided to retrain as a carpenter. He continued in this profession for fifteen years in order to support his wife and children before he was offered the role in *Star Wars*.

AUDIOSCRIPTS

UNIT 5 VOCABULARY BANK

Audio VB5.01

1. My brother is studying agriculture at university. I think he wants to manage the family farm at some point.
2. The construction company specialises in building residential properties in the Northeast of England.
3. I have a degree in social work and have recently started a new job supporting elderly residents in the area.
4. Looking for a role in banking? Join our new personal finance team to help people with loans and savings.
5. She works in accountancy. I think her company manages the accounts of a few local businesses.
6. You have to study medicine for up to seven years before you can get a job as a doctor.
7. Journalism is a difficult industry to get into. You have to work long hours and have a real passion for news.
8. Our research team is developing new methods for scientific analysis of medical data.
9. The shift from print to digital has had a huge effect on the publishing industry.
10. We have a small consultancy business specialising in providing support for telecommunications projects.

UNIT 5 MEDIATION BANK

Audio MB5.01

F = Felix   A = Ali   E = Emily

F: Right. So, I think everyone's read the suggestion from management to move all of our meetings online. I just wanted to check in and see how you all feel about it.
A: I think it's a terrible idea! In fact, I don't think we should have any of our meetings online.
F: OK. Can you expand on that a bit?
A: Well, it's just not the same as being with people in real life.
E: I agree.
F: OK, so in what ways is it different?
E: Well, for a start, no one knows whose turn it is to speak.
F: Yeah, I agree that can sometimes be a problem. What else?
A: Loads of things really …
F: Can you give us some examples?
A: Well, sometimes people have a really bad wifi connection that can make it difficult, too.
F: Is that always an issue?
E: Well, not for us, but it is for some of people, like Nigel. His internet connection is terrible.
F: Ah, well that's definitely something to think about. So, what are the main benefits of doing things online?
E: Well, obviously it's more convenient, because we can call in from anywhere. I also find we waste less time online than we do in the office. There's less, kind of, casual chat at the start.
A: I liked the casual chat …

UNIT 6

Audio 6.02

M = Miriam   N = Nishma

M: So, I was listening to a programme this morning about the power of introverts.
N: Oh, yeah? That sounds interesting.
M: Yeah, it was really good actually. They were interviewing a woman called Susan Cain, who wrote a book called *Quiet: The Power of Introverts in a World That Can't Stop Talking*.
N: Oh, yeah. I think I heard about that book when it came out. It sounds really interesting. So, what was she saying?
M: Basically, she thinks that the world is designed for extroverts – that everything is organised around people who are bold and confident and happy to be in the spotlight. And that if you're not like that, if you're the kind of person who's quiet, or doesn't enjoy, you know, public speaking or whatever, and likes to have time to think before they speak, then you're basically at a massive disadvantage. The world just doesn't seem to listen to introverts. Take team-building exercises, for example. They're really popular with companies – loads of companies do them – but I never look forward to them, and I don't think I ever do particularly well at them.
N: Yeah, that makes sense. I mean the world's run by politicians, isn't it? And I would say you need a lot of the qualities usually associated with extroverts to be a successful politician. I mean, introverts don't make very good public speakers, do they?
M: Well, according to Susan Cain, that's not true, actually. There are loads of influential people who have been described as introverts – like Bill Gates, for example. Even Barack Obama is known to be an introvert, and for me, he's one of the best public speakers I've ever heard. Maybe it's because introverts generally like to be better prepared that they can actually be really good at giving speeches.
N: Yeah, maybe. It also, kind of depends what you mean by 'introvert', doesn't it? People always seem to think that introverts are shy and don't like being with other people. But I don't think that's true. I mean, I think I'm quite introverted, but I wouldn't say I was shy. I'm actually pretty sociable – I love being with other people. It's just that I also really enjoy spending time by myself. In fact, I'd say I actually need to spend time on my own. It's how I recharge my batteries. If I'm around lots of people for too long, I always feel like I need to go and sit quietly somewhere for a bit to get my energy back.
M: Yeah, I know what you mean. It's all about what energises you, isn't it? They actually said on the programme that rather than thinking of introverts as shy, we need to realise that they get more from being alone. They don't need other people to feel energised.
N: Exactly. And it's not just in social situations either. I had this job once in a massive open-plan office in town. I hate open-plan offices. I know they're designed to encourage social interaction, which is great if you like being loud and sociable, but personally, I find it difficult to get any work done in that kind of environment. I just couldn't concentrate! For me, being around so many people all the time was completely exhausting. In the end, I asked my manager to let me work somewhere a bit quieter.
M: Oh, yeah? So, what happened?
N: Well, there wasn't really anywhere else to go, so I used to just take my laptop and go and find an empty table in the cafeteria. It was pretty bad to be honest!
M: What? That's ridiculous!
N: Yeah, I know. Anyway, one day my manager found me working alone in the cafeteria and she told me to get back to my desk. She seemed pretty angry, actually.
M: Urgh. So, what did you do?
N: Well, I spoke to a colleague and he advised me to talk to my manager about working from home three or four days a week. I asked, but she refused to give me permission to do that. We weren't really encouraged to work from home. In the end, my manager threatened to sack me if I didn't work in the same office as everyone else. I thought her attitude was pretty unreasonable, so I ended up leaving the company and getting a better job somewhere else.
M: Well, good for you. That's kind of what the programme this morning was all about – the fact that introverts always have to adapt themselves to things that are set up for extroverts. But we'd probably all be a lot better off if we just listened to introverts more.

Audio 6.03

1. She threatened to stop speaking to me if I didn't go with her.
2. They asked us to go on holiday with them.
3. He emphasised the most important points.
4. She admitted leaving the office early.
5. They suggested practising the presentation beforehand.
6. She claimed she had a lot of management experience.

Audio 6.04

S = Samira   R = Ryan   G = Giselle   F = Fergus

Conversation 1

S: Hi, Ryan. Well done! You managed to play all the songs without making any mistakes.
R: Yeah. It was amazing! I really think the band is coming together, and I know we can make it big!

AUDIOSCRIPTS

S: Well, …
R: I mean, I was just talking to the other band members, and I was thinking maybe I'll leave university so I can practise my guitar full-time, and maybe write some new songs.
S: Ryan, I hope you don't take this the wrong way, but I'm not sure it's a good idea to stop studying.
R: Why?
S: Well, not many bands actually become successful enough to make a living from their music.
R: I know, but we're getting really good now! You have to believe in yourself!
S: Look, I'm telling you this as a friend, Ryan. I don't think you should give up your place at university. I mean, you might need your degree if you don't manage to become a rock star!
R: But how am I going to improve on the guitar if I can't practise more?
S: Well, have you thought about getting some lessons? To be honest, it might be useful to focus a bit more on your technique.
R: Yeah, but it's all about the energy in the music, not just technique! So, what would you do?
S: Well, it's up to you. But if I were you, I definitely wouldn't leave university!
R: I'll see. But it would be so amazing if we could play some of the big festivals …

Conversation 2
G: Hi, Fergus.
F: Oh, hi, Giselle. How's it going?
G: Well, I'm a bit fed up really. You know my car's in the garage again – it keeps breaking down. I really think I need a new one, but I don't know how I'm ever going to afford one!
F: Well, you earn quite a good salary …
G: Yeah, but life's expensive, isn't it?
F: That's true, but other people seem to manage. I mean, don't take this personally, but you do go out a lot, don't you?
G: Yeah, but I have to see my friends!
F: Yes, but perhaps you ought to see friends just at the weekends? Rather than every night?
G: You're probably right, but I love going out. Maybe I can save money in other ways instead. What do you think?
F: Well, it might be an idea to buy fewer clothes – I mean, you do seem to buy new clothes pretty much every week, so I'm guessing you spend quite a lot on clothes.
G: Well, not really. I usually buy things in the sale.
F: Look, I don't want you to get the wrong idea, but I just think generally you could be a bit more careful with money. My advice would be to set a budget each month, and then …
G: Yeah, thanks for the advice Fergus. Sorry, I need to take this. … Hi, Sarah! Yeah, I'm looking forward to tonight …

Audio 6.06
O = Olga   S1 = Speaker 1   S2 = Speaker 2   S3 = Speaker 3

O: One of my best friends was once mistaken for the tennis player Serena Williams and spent ten minutes taking selfies with people and signing autographs, and no one realised that she wasn't the real star.
S1: Really? But Serena Williams is really famous. Everyone knows who she is. Does your friend look like Serena Williams?
O: Yes, she does, actually. In fact, she looks exactly like her – same face, same hair, same build, even the same height.
S2: And does she often get mistaken for Serena?
O: Hmm, that's a difficult question for me to answer, because obviously, I'm not with my friend all the time, but I think probably other people have mistaken her, yes.
S3: So, where did this happen?
O: Well, we were travelling together, and were at the airport, and it started with one kid who said, like, 'Serena!' and all of a sudden, we were just surrounded by people wanting to take selfies with her, and wanting her to sign their T-shirts, their luggage, that kind of thing.
S1: And no one asked her, 'Are you Serena Williams?'
O: Er, let me think. Er, no, I don't think anyone asked that. Everyone just assumed she was Serena, especially once a crowd formed around her, you know.
S3: OK, so what did you do while your friend was being a superstar?
O: That's a good question. Er, I think I just sort of stood there. I mean, I couldn't believe what was happening, so I think I was laughing and not taking it very seriously.
S2: I'd like to ask if your friend is American – I mean, does she sound like Serena Williams when she speaks?
O: That's a good point. And that's one of the strange things, that no one really spoke to her. They just kind of smiled and handed her things to sign, so I don't think she really spoke, because she actually sounds nothing like Serena – she isn't American – she's got a British accent.
S3: Hmm, I'm finding this quite hard to believe. Are you saying she signed people's T-shirts and things with the name 'Serena'?
O: Er, I'm just trying to remember. Er, :no. In fact, she actually signed with her own name – Nana – and the weird thing is that no one seemed to notice! So, the fans were all really happy, and after about ten minutes, we just waved and walked off to catch our flight.
S1: OK, so what do we think, team? True or a lie?

Audio 6.07
S1 = Speaker 1   S3 = Speaker 3   S2 = Speaker 2   O = Olga

S1: OK, so what do we think, team? True or a lie?
S3: I actually think it might be true.
S2: Me, too. Things like this do happen.
S1: OK, we're going to say it's true.
O: Well, in fact it was … a lie!

UNIT 6 REVIEW

Audio R6.01
Burnout – and what you can do about it
We all have days when we feel we can't keep up with everything that needs doing. But what if your job starts to feel like an impossible struggle?
If you're suffering from burnout, three things might be happening. Firstly, you're probably feeling emotionally exhausted. You might find it difficult to persuade yourself to do all the jobs that need to be done. Secondly, you're starting to produce sub-standard work. Thirdly, perhaps you feel disconnected from your work. Maybe you feel resentful or angry about your co-workers and have started to take things personally.
Fortunately, there are plenty of things you can do to help yourself. Here are two things you could try.
Take care of yourself. Do more exercise and get enough sleep. Go out for lunch instead of staring at a screen. Do things to try and take your mind off work.
Look to the future. The opposite of job burnout is job engagement. Imagine what it would be like to be engaged in your work. Is there something else you would prefer to do? Could you retrain or switch companies?
If you're close to burnout, act fast and make a change.

UNIT 6 VOCABULARY BANK

Audio VB6.01
R = Rob   D = Dan   A = Ahmed   S = Samira   M = Max
R = Rose   Mthr = Mother   Dau = Daughter

1 R: Dan, I'm so sorry that I broke your phone. I didn't mean to.
   D: That's OK, Rob. I know you didn't do it deliberately.

2 A: Samira, you were the last person to use those files. You must have deleted them by mistake.
   S: No, Ahmed, I'm absolutely sure that I didn't delete them.

3 M: I'm not sure that I'll be good at that job, Rose.
   R: Of course you will, Max! You'll be brilliant at it.

4 Mthr: Remember, Julia, you have to be here on time, at ten o'clock.
   Dau: Yes, we will.
   Dau: Oh no! I knew we should have left earlier. Now, we're going to be late.

AUDIOSCRIPTS

UNIT 7

Audio 7.01
1 His medical colleagues might have wondered if he would give up his job as a surgeon.
2 It can't have been easy learning to play the piano whilst working full time.
3 He couldn't have known that he'd end up becoming a concert pianist.
4 His family must have got fed up with his piano playing sometimes.

Audio 7.02
1
My biggest regret is from when I was twelve years old. I'd started playing football when I was four and by the time I was seven, I was really good – I think partly because I had older brothers, I learnt to be tough and competitive, and I also picked up their skills. We had a goal in the back garden and we used to play out there most days. So anyway, when I turned twelve, I started attracting a bit of attention locally, you know, getting in the papers, that kind of thing. Within a few months, I was offered a trial at a professional academy, but I turned it down. At the time, there was a lot going on in my life, particularly at home, and I just wasn't mature enough to see the opportunity for what it was. I carried on playing for a few more years, then, when I was eighteen, I decided to call it a day and got a regular job, which I've been doing ever since. When I look back, I wish I'd gone to the trial. Of course, there are no guarantees in sport, but I now think I should have gone to the trial, just to see if I was good enough.

2
So, I was really into acting when I was younger. My parents took me to the theatre when I was, maybe, five or six, and I just fell in love with it and then started doing all of the school plays and everything. Then, when I was a teenager, I went to drama classes and my tutor said I could definitely make a career out of it. I thought she was pulling my leg, but she seemed convinced I had a real talent. Anyway, at the time, I was living in a small town in the north of England and there just weren't that many opportunities for actors. You kind of had to be in London to get noticed and to be invited to auditions, and at that time I didn't want to be so far away from my family. So, I stayed at home. Then, when I was eighteen, I started working in an office and basically gave up acting. Sometimes I think, 'if only I'd kept going with it'. Or maybe I should have moved to London. I suppose that's the one regret of my life.

3
When I was a teenager, I started a band with a group of friends. I was the lead singer and we played, like, heavy rock? I took it quite seriously, and I even had a singing teacher for a while. Anyway, we used to do a lot of gigs in my hometown and we were becoming quite well known. We released one song that got some radio time and got us noticed. But, it reached a point where I had to decide whether to stick with the band and try to make it, or quit and get an education. I was kind of on the fence about it until my dad suggested I try and do both. I enrolled in college three hours away and I went home to play with the band at weekends. But after a while, the travelling was too much and I felt the band wasn't really going anywhere, so I ended up leaving. Anyway, they replaced me with another singer, and less than a year later, they signed a recording contract with a big label. Now I wish I'd stayed with the band.

Audio 7.03
1 I carried on playing for a few more years, then, when I was eighteen, I decided to call it a day and got a regular job, which I've been doing ever since.
2 Then, when I was a teenager, I went to drama classes and my tutor said I could definitely make a career out of it. I thought she was pulling my leg, but she seemed convinced I had a real talent.
3 I had to decide whether to stick with the band and try to make it, or quit and get an education. I was kind of on the fence about it until my dad suggested I try and do both.

Audio 7.04
1 My exam? It was a piece of cake!
2 I applied too late to get on the course, so I missed the boat.
3 I don't like rock music. It's not my cup of tea.
4 The company failed, so it was back to the drawing board for me.
5 I don't think you'd be any happier in New York – the grass is always greener on the other side!
6 Losing my job turned out to be a blessing in disguise, because it gave me time to think about what I really wanted to do.

Audio 7.06
Hi, everyone! It's Maya here, back with another simple recipe for you to make at home. This week, I'm going to show you how to make a delicious vegetable lasagne that even your meat-eating friends won't be able to resist. Let's get started!
Now, it's quite a tricky recipe, so I'll break it down into stages and talk you through it step by step. First, let's start by going over the basics. To begin with, you'll want to get your ingredients together. You'll need about twelve sheets of lasagne – choose the kind that you don't need to cook in advance – then an aubergine, two courgettes, two red or yellow peppers, ten small tomatoes, half an onion and some garlic. For the sauce, you'll need flour, butter, milk and some grated parmesan cheese.
The next step is to make the vegetable mixture, and I'm going to roast the vegetables in the oven. So, chop the aubergine, courgettes, onion and peppers into medium-sized pieces – about two centimetres.
Then arrange them in a dish, with the tomatoes. Chop the garlic very finely and sprinkle this over the top. Pour on a little oil – I would recommend using olive oil – and add salt and pepper. You can also add some fresh herbs, but this is optional. Then put this into a hot oven for about thirty minutes.
Then for the sauce put the butter into a small pan and heat it over a low heat. Add the flour, then add the milk gradually, and keep stirring all the time. It's essential that you stir it, so the sauce stays nice and smooth. Keep stirring until the sauce thickens, then take the pan off the heat and add the grated parmesan cheese.
So, the vegetables should be ready now … Be careful not to overcook them. It's nicer if they're still a bit firm.
So it's time to make the lasagne. You'll need a baking dish, like this one. First, put a little cooking oil in the bottom. Once you've done that, add a layer of your roasted vegetables. Next, put a layer of lasagne sheets on top and then a layer of the cheese sauce. So you have three layers: vegetables, pasta, then the cheese sauce. Then add a little more grated cheese. Repeat, adding the same layers: vegetables, pasta, cheese sauce and grated cheese. If you want, you can add my secret ingredient, a little chilli, in with the vegetables or you could come up with your own secret ingredient.
The final stage involves baking the dish at 180 degrees Celsius until the top layer of cheese is golden brown. You'll want to avoid taking it out too early because it may not be cooked on the inside. After thirty-five minutes, you'll have the perfect vegetable lasagne!

Audio 7.07
1 To begin with, you'll want to get your ingredients together.
2 The next step is to make the vegetable mixture.
3 I would recommend using olive oil.
4 You can also add some fresh herbs, but this is optional.
5 It's essential that you stir it, so the sauce stays nice and smooth.
6 Be careful not to overcook them.
7 Once you've done that, add a layer of your roasted vegetables.
8 If you want, you can add my secret ingredient.
9 The final stage involves baking the dish at 180 degrees Celsius.
10 Avoid taking it out too early because it may not be cooked on the inside.

AUDIOSCRIPTS

UNIT 7 REVIEW

Audio R7.01
What's your talent?

Do you ever think to yourself, 'Perhaps I should have been an artist' or 'If only I was a dancer!'? Perhaps you say to yourself, 'I wish I hadn't given up art or 'If only I had continued to dance'. You might have given up a passion because you thought you weren't very talented at it. Someone might have made a negative comment about your work. But therein lies a problem. At that time, you were just learning, so you hadn't fully developed your talent. Imagine how things might have been different if that person had said, 'Wow, what a fantastic talent you have. You should do more of that'. To get really good at anything takes years of practice. It's not a piece of cake. But you probably stopped too soon.

Now, years later, you might feel like you've missed the boat. You're stuck in an all-consuming job you don't enjoy. Let's talk through the options, to help you figure out what you want to do. Remember, it's never too late to make a life-changing decision and go back to the drawing board and discover your true talent.

UNIT 7 VOCABULARY BANK

Audio VB7.01
1 The winner was chosen at random.
2 We met on holiday by chance.
3 My cousin arrived from the USA to visit me. It was completely unexpected.
4 Unfortunately, we arrived late and missed the show. I was so upset!
5 I feel so fortunate to have this wonderful opportunity.
6 He was struck by lightning in a freak accident.
7 She broke your phone, but it was accidental.

UNIT 7 MEDIATION BANK

Audio MB7.01
H = Henry   T = Tyra

H: Welcome back to *Explainer*, the show in which we challenge an expert to explain an interesting or challenging concept to me, in under two minutes.
Joining me this week is the psychologist and popular science communicator, Tyra Wilcox. Tyra – great to have you on the show.
T: Thanks for having me.
H: So, Tyra – what are you going to be talking about today?
T: Today I want to talk about *ad hominem* arguments.
H: OK, that sounds complicated …
T: It's actually not as complicated as you might think. Basically, it means attacking someone personally, rather than their argument.
H: Can you give an example?
T: Yeah. So, imagine you're watching a debate or a formal discussion and one of the speakers presents a really clear, well-thought-out argument. Then their opponent says something like, 'Why should we listen to someone who hasn't even finished university?'. It might be true, but it's not relevant to the argument. It's like saying that you don't like a meal because you hate the person that made it. It might be true but has nothing to do with whether or not you like the food.
H: So, it's just a bad way to argue?
T: Exactly. It's an attack on someone's character rather than their position. In other words, you criticise the person, not what they're saying.
H: OK, got it. Thanks, Tyra. Well, that's about it for this episode. Join us next week for another two-minute explanation. And in the meantime, don't forget to like, comment and subscribe. See you next week.

UNIT 8

Audio 8.01
1 Having decided to move to a city, young people face the challenging task of finding somewhere affordable to live.
2 Moving into co-living accommodation, many people find they have a ready-made community.
3 Having moved into co-living accommodation two years ago, Brad Hoffner, twenty-four, found that the people were friendly, but he was shocked at the size of the small 'box' rooms.

Audio 8.02
Thank you. Now, talking about global issues can be overwhelming. The numbers involved can be so huge that it's often difficult to fully appreciate what they mean. So, to help me explore a topic that's close to my heart, I'd like to start by putting some of the biggest issues into a simpler context.

Now, imagine that instead of over seven and a half billion people, the population of the world was represented by a village of one hundred. In this context, each villager would represent seventy-five million people. So, in terms of populations, fifty-nine of the villagers would be from Asia, sixteen from Africa, ten from Europe, nine from South and Central America and the Caribbean, five from Canada and the USA, and just one from Oceania, which is Australia, New Zealand and the Pacific islands.

Ten of our villagers would live on less than two dollars per day. Only seven would have a university education, and fourteen wouldn't be able to read. When it comes to housing, twenty-two of them wouldn't have adequate and permanent shelter, while twelve wouldn't have safe drinking water. In this village, fifteen would live without electricity and about forty without access to the internet. Sixty-two would own a mobile phone and sixteen would own a car.

Fourteen would speak Mandarin as a first language, eight would speak Hindi, seven would speak English, six would speak Arabic, five would speak Spanish, and the rest would speak over 7,000 other languages. Of these, over 3,000 are endangered and this is what I'd like to talk to you about today.

Audio 8.03
Simply put, if a language has no native speakers, it dies. Perhaps the best-known example of this is Latin. Although it's still sometimes used for formal purposes, no one learns it as their first language and it's no longer passed down from generation to generation.

So, why does this happen? Well, there are many factors that cause languages to become endangered. But arguably the most common is that the language is no longer used or taught in schools, usually because there is a more popular or 'dominant' language in the area. As a result, children are less likely to use the language at home or teach it to their children when they grow up.

So, why should we care? If we all spoke the same language, wouldn't it be easier to communicate? Well, language plays a central role in people's culture and identity. If their language dies, part of their culture will die, too. And this means their unique way of seeing the world is gone forever, because language shapes how we think.

But things **are** beginning to change for the better. People are reviving dying languages and rebuilding their cultures.

One success story is Cornish, a language spoken in the southwest corner of the UK. Cornish was barely surviving until recent decades. Then, in the twenty-first century, Cornish speakers found one another online and used social media to keep the language alive. They organised regular events to speak together in public and the result was a wonderful rebirth. Today there are street signs in Cornish and some schools teach it. This is really important. As long as young people are learning a language, it will survive.

There are many other examples of people reviving their endangered languages. One Native American tribe called the Tunica is reviving its language by teaching a curriculum based on an old Tunica dictionary and recordings of songs and stories. In Bolivia, people are working to revive endangered languages by creating blogs, virtual communities, videos and podcasts in the languages.

One tool that is helping this effort is Wikitongues. Wikitongues is a global network of people who are trying to keep endangered languages alive. They do this using different methods such as building an index of languages, providing a toolkit for identifying the needs of an endangered language, and supporting individual projects. One project is the creation and distribution of children's

AUDIOSCRIPTS

books in Nalu, a language from Guinea. Another project is building community language education programmes in Congo to keep a language called Kihunde alive. A third project involves Wikitongues recording oral histories, people talking about their lives and cultures and telling stories in their mother tongue. These outstanding projects are essential. They're a shining light in the effort to preserve languages.

All of these projects show that it's **people** that make the real difference. As long as there are people that care enough about their language to record and document it, teach it to new speakers, and use it regularly, the language will survive. Thank you.

Audio 8.05

1
I'd like to start off by saying that I completely agree with the idea that online communities are the best way to connect with like-minded people. This is true for three main reasons. Firstly, online communities allow us to connect with people all over the world, at any time of the day or night, from our sitting room. A good example of this is when I get home from work and I'm tired and I don't have very much time. I can't really go out with friends, but I can easily spend an hour or so interacting with people in my network on social media. Or when I'm away travelling for work and I can't go out with my friends, I can still keep in touch that way. As a result, I still manage to have a good social life even when I'm busy.

Secondly, online communities involve people from all types of different backgrounds and cultural experiences, which are different to my own. They allow for an amazing exchange of ideas, based on our own interests, but which incorporate different cultural values and experiences. For instance, one group I belong to has people in it from India, Argentina, Canada, the USA and Europe. In my day-to-day life, I would never have the opportunity to connect with so many different people who are all interested in the same thing that I am. The obvious impact of this is to broaden our understanding and widen our knowledge of a particular area because we can learn about it from many different viewpoints. And finally, online communities are more efficient. I don't have to waste time interacting with people I'm not interested in, but who maybe live or work near to me, or are friends of my friends. When I spend time in my online communities, I get to choose exactly who I want to socialise with in my very limited free time.

2
I'm afraid I completely disagree for the following reasons. As far as I can see, whilst online communities allow us to connect with people from around the world, face-to-face interactions are far more meaningful. Secondly, you say that online communities allow you to exchange ideas with people who are very different from you, but I don't think that's true. The evidence suggests that online communities encourage you to live in a bubble where everybody thinks in the same way as you. This would lead to the idea that …

Audio 8.07

One of the biggest problems we have in our cities is food waste. In every city around the world a huge amount of food is wasted and thrown away every day. According to our research, one-third of the world's food is wasted. Furthermore, there are large numbers of people living on the street who are hungry and cannot afford to feed themselves. On the Street Food Bank is a project which works with shops and cafés to help reduce food waste. We take food that is going to be thrown away and give it to people who need it. The project is run by volunteers. We collect food from businesses at the end of the day so it doesn't get thrown away. We collect ready-made food like sandwiches and salads, and we deliver it to people who are homeless on the streets. We started the programme because we were so shocked when we saw how much food cafés and shops in the city were throwing away every day, when there are so many homeless people on the streets who don't have anything to eat. The purpose of On the Street Food Bank is to try and solve that problem, or at least to help reduce the problem. We have an app, which businesses can use to tell us when they have food that's available to be given away. The app then notifies one of our local volunteers, who arrives to collect the food and distributes it to people who need it. We've only been doing it for about a year, but we've already had a pretty big impact on the local community. I'm really proud of what we've achieved so far.

UNIT 8 REVIEW

Audio R8.01

The artists' colony

For six artists with no regular income, housing was always a problem, as they struggled to find enough money for rent. In order to be able to live in the city, they decided to rent a spacious but not very attractive warehouse and live together that winter. Not many people wanted to live there – it wasn't a fashionable neighbourhood and most of the buildings were old and not well maintained. They learnt they were close to a railway line when the rumbling of passing trains kept them awake all night. Living in poverty had never been the plan, but at least they had something in common – they were artists and they were going to get their lives back together and change the world. As long as they had enough money to buy materials and eat, everything would be OK.

But everything went wrong immediately. While they were out shopping for mattresses, there was a flood that destroyed four paintings. In fact, if Jean-Paul hadn't come home early, all of their work would have been lost. But worse was to come. Waking up early the next morning, Jackson shivered and saw ice on the window. The heating had broken and now they were freezing.

UNIT 8 VOCABULARY BANK

Audio VB8.01

Marmalade Lane – Cambridge, UK

Cambridge is one of the most fashionable cities in the UK to live in. But price increases have meant the city has become quite exclusive and it can be difficult for young people to afford to buy or rent properties which are in good condition. Marmalade Lane is Cambridge's first co-housing community project, and its residents include families with young children, retired couples, single-person households and young professional couples. The architects have designed stylish houses of different sizes and the houses have their own character. The architecture is elegant, and even the smaller houses feel spacious. Residents live in their own houses, which are secure, but they share communal spaces and facilities, like a gym and a laundry. There is also a shared garden and a 'common house' where the community can eat together and socialise.

UNIT 8 GRAMMAR BANK

Audio GB8.01

I'd like to start off by saying that as far as I can see social media has killed the art of conversation. If you look at a group of teenagers who get together, the first thing you'll see is that they're all looking at their screens instead of having conversations with each other. I think this is really sad. Furthermore, the evidence suggests it's making people feel lonely, too.

Secondly, we can see that people often choose to text or message each other, rather than using the phone and talking to someone. Nowadays, people even finish their relationships by text. Another good example of this is in companies. Lots of office workers talk to their colleagues through messages even when they work in the same office. Some companies even use text messages to fire their staff! I think the obvious impact of this is that the more we use messaging instead of talking to people, the harder it becomes to have real conversations because we simply can't remember how to do it. We haven't had enough practice. And this leads to the younger generation never even learning the art of conversation in the first place.

VIDEOSCRIPTS

UNIT 1

Opener: BBC Vlogs

1 In my family, I probably take after my mother. She really enjoys the cinema, she enjoys reading, she enjoys travelling and that's, kind of, what I've spent a large part of my life trying to do. And I think I probably got that interest in those subjects from her.
2 Oh, I take after my father, Edward. He lives in Indiana. He has a passion for science and he's the person who gave me my love for reading and my love for books. As you can see, I've tonnes of books. And we have the very same eye colour.
3 Hmm … I believe I take after a combination of both my father and my mother. My father was a pragmatic man and the peacemaker of the family and I believe that I demonstrate those skills. My mother is very sociable and also very career focused, er, I believe that I've also got those characteristics as well. I've also been told that I look like my mother, which I consider a compliment because, er, I think my mother looks great.
4 In my family, I take after my father, more than my mother. We both have dark hair, we have dark senses of humour, er, and we both love language.
5 Who do I take after in my family? I don't think there's anyone like me to be quite honest. The rest of my family wishes they were like me, but there can only be one.

1D: BBC Street Interviews
Exs 2A and 2B

Elaine: I would describe myself as, erm, liberal, erm, I'm quite, er, happy-go-lucky, erm, I try to make the best that I can out of life, so quite positive I think?
Anna: I would say I'm bubbly, a passionate and committed person. Erm, I, I'm a people person, so I like to interact with different types of people and, like, er, get to know all different walks of life.
Valeria: So, my personality is quite curious and enthusiastic.
Elijah: Optimistic, loving and, er, creative. But sometimes I'm a bit grumpy.
Gwen: Er, I think I'm quite outgoing, erm, quite sociable, erm, I like to chat to people, meet new people, go to parties, and stuff like that – so I think I'm quite an outgoing person.
Roisin: Erm, I would say I'm friendly, welcoming … maybe a bit funny sometimes.
Collin: I'm optimistic, er, I like people, erm, I never give up.

1D: BBC Street Interviews
Exs 2A and 2C

Elaine: Generally speaking, I'm reasonably confident, erm, in social situations, erm, due to the nature of the work that I do – I recruit people worldwide. Erm, so my personality will change depending on the people that I am talking with because, erm, I will need to be a little bit more professional in how I come across, erm, in that situation.
Anna: Er, so at work, maybe I'm more serious, whereas when I go to, like, a café with my friends, er, I'm a lot more relaxed.
Valeria: I can be quite direct at work, erm, and, I think with my friends, I can be quite compassionate.
Elijah: So, if I'm hanging out with friends, I might be more talkative. If I'm with my mother, er, maybe I'll listen a little more.
Gwen: Yeah, I'm … I'd say I'm confident in most situations, but then sometimes like everybody, you know, maybe your mood's not that great and, you know, you can maybe feel, I don't know, sometimes walk into a party and just think, 'Oh, I don't want to be here!'. So, yeah, I think it varies, but not necessarily the situation, more just how I'm feeling inside myself.
Roisin: Erm, I'm probably less confident when I meet new people, whilst when I'm with my friends, I'm a bit more confident, a bit more chatty, a bit more comfortable.
Collin: Erm, doesn't change.

UNIT 2

Opener: BBC Vlogs

1 Erm, social media has a lot of impact on my life. It is a great way to keep in touch with people in different countries that I know. Erm, it's also a little bit distracting sometimes and I sometimes spend more time on it than I would like to.
2 Erm, social media has, er, quite a big impact on my professional life – I'm a furniture painter so I have a Facebook page where I have a community of followers that either buy my furniture or I create tutorials for them, so they can learn about what it is I do.
3 Social media has a big impact on my life. I don't post a lot of photos, but I spend way too much time looking at other photos.
4 I completely love social media. I don't know what I would do without it. I don't know how I did without it before it was, er, invented. Um, I just like to be able to text my friends, message my friends, erm, swap photos, arrange things, buy things. Erm, I think it's just the best thing ever.
5 Social media doesn't have a very large impact on my life. Personally, I think social media is quite harmful and I also think it's something that you grow out of as you get a little bit older. So, maybe I'm now at an age where I don't really spend much time either investing content into it or investing time into it, learning about other people. So, I would say its impact gets smaller and smaller every day that I get older.

2D: BBC Entertainment
Exs 2A and 2B

Dr Black: So, this is one of the last paintings van Gogh ever painted. Those final months of his life were probably the most astonishing artistic outpouring in history. And especially astonishing because van Gogh did it with no hope of praise or reward. Each of these pictures now is worth tens of millions of pounds, yet in his lifetime, he was a commercial disaster. Sold only one painting, and that to the sister of a friend. We have here possibly the greatest artist of all time, but when he died, you could have sold his entire body of work and got about enough money to buy a sofa and a couple of chairs. If you follow me now. …
The Doctor: Now, he'll probably be in the local café - sort of orangey light, chairs and tables outside.
Amy: Like this?
The Doctor: That's the one.
Amy: Or indeed like that.
The Doctor: Yeah, exactly like that.
The Doctor: Hello, I'm the Doctor.
Vincent: I knew it!
The Doctor: Sorry?
Vincent: My brother's always sending doctors, but you won't be able to help.
The Doctor: No, not that kind of doctor. That's incredible, don't you think, Amy?
Amy: Absolutely. One of my favourites.
Vincent: One of my favourite whats? You've never seen my work before.
Amy: Ah, yes. One of my favourite paintings that I've ever seen, genuinely!
Vincent: Then you can't have seen many paintings, then. I know it's terrible. It's the best I could do.
Vincent: It's not much. I live on my own. But you should be OK for one night. ONE night. Sorry about all the clutter.
The Doctor: Some clutter.
Vincent: I've come to accept the only person who's going to love my paintings is me.
Amy: Wow. I mean, really. Wow.
Vincent: Yeah, I know it's a mess. I'll have a proper clear-out. I must, I really must. Coffee, anyone?
The Doctor: Not for me, actually. You know, you should be careful with these. They're, they're … precious.

170

VIDEOSCRIPTS

Vincent:	Precious to me, not precious to anyone else.
Amy:	They're precious to me.
Vincent:	You're very kind. And kindness is most welcome.
The Doctor:	OK, so let's talk about you, then. What are you interested in?
Vincent:	Well, look around. Art. It seems to me there's so much more to the world than the average eye is allowed to see. I believe, if you look hard, there are more wonders in this universe than you could ever have dreamed of.
The Doctor:	You don't have to tell me.
Vincent:	I only wish I had something of real value to give you.
The Doctor:	Oh, no, no. I could never accept such an extraordinary gift.
The Doctor:	Are you thinking what I'm thinking?
Amy:	I was thinking I may need some food or something before we leave.
The Doctor:	Well, no, you're not thinking exactly what I'm thinking. Vincent! Got something I'd like to show you. Maybe just tidy yourself up a bit first.
The Doctor:	Now, you know we've had quite a few chats about the possibility there might be more to life than normal people imagine?
Vincent:	Yes.
The Doctor:	Well, brace yourself, Vinny.
Vincent:	Where are we?
The Doctor:	Paris. 2010. And this is the mighty Musée D'Orsay, home to many of the greatest paintings in history.
Vincent:	Oh, that's wonderful.
The Doctor:	Er, ignore that. I've got something more important.
The Doctor:	Dr Black – I just wondered, between you and me, in 100 words, where do you think van Gogh rates in the history of art?
Dr Black:	Well, er, big question. But, to me, van Gogh is the finest painter of them all. Certainly, the most popular, great painter of all time, the most beloved. His command of colour, the most magnificent. To my mind, that strange, wild man who roamed the fields of Provence was not only the world's greatest artist, but also one of the greatest men who ever lived.
The Doctor:	Vincent. Sorry. I'm sorry. Is it too much?
Vincent:	No. They are tears of joy. Thank you, sir. Thank you.
Dr Black:	You're welcome. You're welcome.
Vincent:	Sorry about the beard.

UNIT 3

Opener: BBC Vlogs

1 I really love, er, theatre. You can't beat the atmosphere before the curtain goes up. And every night is different … special. Theatre is special.
2 I like going to musical performances, like classical concerts, er, and jazz performances. Jazz is especially exciting. Er, it's usually at a small club. The musicians play in their own style, in their own way, and I like how they interact with each other, er, and the other musicians, to bring the music to life.
3 I love going to live comedy performances because they really improve my mood and, er, they make you see the funny side of otherwise particularly volatile situations.
4 I love going to music festivals. I love seeing my favourite artists play live, I love exploring new bands that I've never heard of before and I always find that the food at music festivals is amazing – the different food stalls with lots of different cuisines from around the world, I absolutely love. And it is fun to camp with your friends.
5 One of my favourite things to watch live is sports, especially football. And if it's my team Tottenham, even better. I find being in the stadium so exhilarating and it's so full of energy just the atmosphere that's created by the crowd. Um, whether they're singing and cheering because they're excited about what's happening on the pitch or even when they're angry at something that's going on, there's just so much energy there that you can't recreate that when you're watching football on TV in your living room, for example.

3D: BBC Street Interviews
Exs 2A and 2B

Kaelan:	I like jazz music – I'm a jazz musician myself. I like jazz because it allows me to express myself freely and improvise.
Roisin:	Erm, I listen to mostly hip hop and rap. Erm, but I also enjoy more singing songs, stuff that's a little bit more relaxed. I'd say, I'm pretty general.
Ryan:	Oh, I like all sorts of music, but I'd say probably rock music is my favourite. Er, just because I play guitar, so I … I like, yeah. I like stuff with guitars and drums, things like that.
Aslan:	Er, I like all music. I like film scores, I like hip hop, I like rock. Pretty much anything really.
Oby:	Erm, I enjoy listening to rap music because of all the different aspects of it, like the lyrics and the beat behind it.
Leanne:	Erm, I prefer, er, kind of, a soft rock. Erm, I quite like … I like singing along. Erm, so, something that's, er, yeah got a good tune to it as well.
Sophia:	I listen to a … a wide range of music, but my main would be R&B, contemporary R&B, erm, just because it's very chilled and relaxing. Erm, and I also listen to rap when I'm working out at the gym, yeah.
Lucy:	I quite enjoy hip hop music, 'cause I like the rhythms and I think it's quite good to dance to.

3D: BBC Street Interviews
Exs 2A and 2C

Kaelan:	Very important because it's my career! So, yeah. It's, yeah, very important to me.
Roisin:	Erm, I'd say very important. I don't listen to music every day, but I love going to concerts … I do listen to music on Spotify, like public platforms, but I don't play any instruments.
Ryan:	Very important, I'd say. Erm, it's the … you know … always listening to music when I walk around – it's the soundtrack to my life, I suppose.
Aslan:	Erm, I would say music is very important. Erm, there's certain bits of work where I do listen to music while I'm working and there's certain bits of work where I don't, where I can't, if it's very technical or if it's … if I'm trying to be very creative, then I can and do listen to music while I work.
Oby:	Erm, music is very important to me. I don't play the piano anymore, but I used to.
Leanne:	Erm, yeah, quite important. Erm, I … I have to say I don't like, erm, sort of, er, orchestra music so much, erm, but I do like, erm, sort of, background music, listening to, erm, relaxing things.
Sophia:	Very important, I'd say. When I wake up, the first thing I do is put on my music, when I'm brushing my teeth, listening to music, on the tube listening to music. Even at … when I'm at work I listen to music to be honest, so yeah, it's very important.
Lucy:	Music is really important to me because although I don't go to festivals, I do listen to it a lot at home and I play the piano as an instrument.

UNIT 4

Opener: BBC Vlogs

1 Um, the one thing I'd like to do to change, erm, or to improve my health, is to go out more often. Erm, to erm, do much more fitness outside – outdoors – because due to the nature of my job, I, erm, I mostly sit down. Erm, I'm in a sitting position, like, more than six or seven hours a day. So, I think I should go out more with my bike and, you know, go on a long-distance bicycle ride.
2 One thing I could do to improve my health would be to get more sleep each night. To do that, I would switch my phone off before I go to bed and stop scrolling through social media.
3 Definitely my eating. Erm, I ordered three pizzas for myself a couple of days ago. So, yeah. Changes and improvements can be made. And will be made.
4 If there's one thing I would do to change my life, it would be to take more exercise and perhaps go to the gym, because I have a sailing boat, which I sail on my own, and I would be happier if it was easier to get in and out of the boat and to be able to control the sails for the wind and not capsize.

VIDEOSCRIPTS

5 I try to be a healthy person, but one thing that I could change to improve my health is trying to do more exercise every day.

6 I try hard to be healthy – to eat the right things, to eat plenty of fruit and vegetables – and I try to exercise at least three times a week. But the one thing that I really need to do to improve my health is to drink more water.

4D: BBC Documentary
Exs 2A and 2B

Narrator: From the blackness of space our home is a blue planet. But now, satellite cameras capture a kaleidoscope of extraordinary colour.
Mr Dai and his son are nomads. They've travelled across China just in time for the bloom. These flowers will eventually produce almost 20 percent of the all the world's rapeseed oil. But they're not here for the oil. They've come to make honey.

CAPTION: Beekeeping is the most important part of our income. Our livelihood depends on it.

Narrator: But the weather is not on their side. The view from space is almost completely white. Thick cloud is blocking the sun. It's just too cold for the bees to fly.

CAPTION: It's still too cold. They don't want to come out.

CAPTION: If it stays like this for a few more days, there is no way we will make any honey.

Narrator: With a chill in the air, these bees aren't going anywhere. And time is running out.
In two weeks, the rapeseed farmers will spray pesticides over the fields, making it a dangerous place for the bees. They must move on before the spraying starts. All they can do is sit and wait for the sun. After three grey days, the clouds finally part and one and a half million bees head out to work. They must visit two million flowers to make just one jar of honey. The bees drink the sugary nectar from the flowers they visit and transfer it to the hive where it becomes honey. Food for the long winter months.
But the bees are more than just honey makers. They are one of the world's most important crop pollinators, helping plants produce fruits, seeds and vegetables. But now pesticides are contributing to a worldwide decline in the number of honeybees, and their future is under threat.
Mr Dai's window of opportunity is short, but the bees have been hard at work. He has plenty of honey. And not a moment too soon. The fields will be sprayed in two days. It's time to move on.

UNIT 5

Opener: BBC Vlogs

1 Ah. I love and admire professions that involve the use of one's hands and creativity. So, things like, being a … an artist, a patisserie chef, er, a graphic designer, er, a fashion designer – anything that involves creativity and really putting one's skills and hands to work, I just find completely inspirational.

2 There are lots of professions I admire and respect, but I think the one I admire most would have to be teachers. Erm, it's a very important job to educate young people and to keep it interesting for them.

3 Um, I would say that I especially admire professions, er, involving those who teach or who are healthcare professionals because these people make big sacrifices to better society, and to make other people happy and healthy. Um, I think any job in which you … you give something up to help another human being is a job that's worthy of admiration.

4 I would say surgeons. Um, because they're constantly under loads of pressure and I appreciate the long shifts, and the long hours they work.

5 I admire farmers because they grow our food and our food makes pizza!

6 I really admire interpreters – the ones who work at really big events and they are under a lot of pressure, they have to remember everything people have said and translate it perfectly, but nobody notices them. Erm, they are really incredible.

5D: BBC Street Interviews
Exs 2A and 2B

Kathiane: I prefer working alone because I think, er, I'm a bit of a perfectionist, and I think that when I do something alone I really perfect it in my own way, just how I want it, instead of when I work in a team and sometimes it's not easy to get everyone to be coordinated.

Aslan: I prefer working alone – I'm self-employed, so it suits me to work alone, but I do often enjoy working as a team because there's a, sort of, social aspect to it and it's enjoyable to work with people, erm, but I'd say 90 percent of my work is alone so that's obviously what suits me.

Olivia: Erm, I do enjoy working more in a team, just because I like to share … share things, share accomplishments, share, er, hard work. I think it's just so much more fun when you can bounce ideas off of people and, yeah, reflect on things more with other people around you. Erm, I think working alone is something I've done a lot of in my life, but it's not as fun to, you know, to go through things alone and to face difficult situations by yourself.

Onika: I prefer working as part of a team because when I work alone, I only have my own answer, or my own solution, but when I work as part of a team, I can, kind of, bounce ideas off of other people and it becomes more of a collective thing.

Hannah: Erm, I think I prefer working as part of a team. Erm, it's something I've always done in my job and I feel like, that you can, erm, ask other people's advice if there's something you're not confident on and you can learn from their experience, but you can also give your experience to other people, erm, and support each other, and I quite like that.

5D: BBC Street Interviews
Exs 2A and 2D

Kathiane: Erm, my old team never wanted to do the work until the last minute and would rather play around, which was incredibly frustrating because then we're always rushing. But my new team always gets straight to the point and do the work.

Aslan: Can't really think of any bad experiences, erm, most work experiences have been fairly … fairly good, fairly professional, straightforward. You know, that's … I … I can't really name anything where I thought, 'Oh, this is a terrible experience' or 'I'm having a terrible time'. It's all been pretty good.

Olivia: Er, this year I did a group project with, erm, a lot of my university course mates. And er, we had to do the whole project online, which was really difficult because some people lived in India, some people lived in the States, erm, the United States, and, erm, finding times to talk when we were all free, with the time difference, was really quite annoying.

Onika: I really enjoyed working at a team at this company called, Uptree, they're a start-up company, and we had a … every Wednesday we had, like, a group lunch, which was really fun because we all got to bring different lunches and share them together.

Hannah: A time I've worked as a team, erm, I'm a police officer, erm, and I was in a dangerous situation, er, which was very, erm, scary, and the team came to help me, erm, and we worked together to get the individual under control and make everybody safe.

UNIT 6

Opener: BBC Vlogs

1 Well, I never find any time to do any housework, er, because I'm usually doing something more interesting – er, playing some music, or a video game or … or maybe just having a nap.

2 I never find time to draw and paint which I love doing, because I always have too much studying or work to do.

3 I never find the time to read as many books as I like. Erm, I find myself distracted by easier things like watching television than reading and that's something that I'm working on to change.

4 Well, I never find the time to clean my closets and get rid of the things that I don't need. I know there are shows about this, er, and to do it properly sometimes it can take weeks. I do clean, it's just that I put everything in my closet so that it looks clean.

VIDEOSCRIPTS

5 I never find time to call people back.
6 A: Well, I … I hardly ever finish a novel …
   B: Oh, I have that problem, too.
   A: Oh, it's terrible and … because I just seem to spend all my time on either social media or watching box sets …
   B: … watching box sets because they're very, very addictive, aren't they?
   A: They definitely are.
   B: But books can be addictive, too.
   A: True.
7 I absolutely never get the time to clean my windows. I just don't like doing that. I prefer to read a book, or to play a game, or go for a walk.
8 What is something that I never seem to find the time for? A haircut!

6D: BBC Entertainment
Exs 2A and 2B

Dan:	This is my sports bag. And, er, halfway through signing it, I told Pelé to put his pen down because I thought he was ruining it.
Rob:	Lee's team.
Lee:	Well, that's very interesting. Is that a Brazil bag?
Dan:	Um, it's actually a … it's a New York Cosmos bag.
Lee:	So, when did you meet Pelé?
Dan:	Well, Pelé was the face of New York Cosmos. They paid him a lot of money to, sort of, front the rebranding of New York Cosmos. Pelé, erm, was put up for an interview.
Sarah:	What … what year was that?
Mr Motivator:	What year?
Dan:	Probably about 2011.
Lee:	So, you already had that bag?
Dan:	No, this was the bag, that, erm they gave you as a, like, a goody bag when you went to the press conference.
Sarah:	Was there stuff inside it?
Dan:	There was, um, some pencils and …
Rob:	There, there, there … 'There were'. There were some pencils.
Lee:	What did he say?
Rob:	He said, 'There was some pencils'.
Dan:	I meant to say, 'There was a pencil'.
Lee:	Look, can I be … were there any pencils or not?
Dan:	There were pencils in there, yeah.
Lee:	Oh, right. See, there was pencils.
Dan:	There were some pencils in there and, erm, a flannel.
Lee:	No, there were a flannel, there were a flannel, there were a flannel.
Lee:	May we have a look at the bag?
Rob:	I'm told it's been sanitised.
Lee:	Yeah, but he's touched it now.
Dan:	I've only touched the back handle.
Rob:	I'm going to put my arm through it like this.
Sarah:	OK, that's … that's interesting.
Dan:	Lee, if you look there, right, that says 'Pe'.
Rob:	Well, it's a sports bag.
Dan:	Which is amazing because the reason I didn't want him to sign it was because I wanted to use it in the gym, and now that's my gym bag with 'Pe' written on it, you see?
Lee:	I mean, I understand the concept of not wanting a signature if you think the bag's better, but if he's started it …
Rob:	Yeah.
Lee:	… is it not better to finish it than have just 'Pe'?
Dan:	Right, so I'd taken a Brazil shirt with me.
Lee:	For him to sign.
Dan:	For … yeah. So, I gave it to the great man and he signed the shirt, full signature on the shirt and I think it was, like, an, 'All the best, Dan, Pelé.' I turned and put it on my normal bag that I'd brought with me and, then, when I turned back, the great man had my bag that he'd picked up. And, without thinking, I said, 'Not the bag, Pelé'.
David:	And, um … What an idiot Pelé is! Put the pen down, Pelé, you maniac!
Sarah:	What must Pelé have thought of you? Because this bag was given to you for free …
Dan:	He, sort of, stared at me angrily and then he said, 'No one's ever asked me not to sign anything before'.
Rob:	I don't understand why you didn't want Pelé to sign a bag. Why?
Dan:	Because I really like the bag.
Rob:	Yeah, but have … imagine having a bag signed by Pelé, waiting until he passes on to, to a better place, and selling it on eBay.
David:	So, do you have a lot of signed memorabilia by people and you're waiting for them to die?
Rob:	Well, all that stuff I've got you to sign.
Rob:	So, what are you thinking? Sarah, do you think this could be true?
Sarah:	Erm, no, I don't think anyone would stop Pelé signing their bag. I think it's a lie.
Lee:	Mr Motivator, MBE?
Mr Motivator:	A lie.
Lee:	OK, we're saying it's a lie.
Rob:	It's unanimous. They think it's a lie. Uh, Dan?
Dan:	Yes.
Rob:	It's a great story. Was it true or was it a lie?
Dan:	I can tell you that the story is … true.
Rob:	Yes, it's true. Dan really did stop Pelé from signing his bag.

UNIT 7

Opener: BBC Vlogs

1 My hidden talent is remembering birthdays. I can remember birthdays of people I was at school with forty years ago, maybe longer. Um, it's a shame it's such a useless talent.
2 So, my hidden talent is, um, fencing. Erm, I was on my university team and took part in lots of championships. I'm not very tall, but I am quite quick and skilful.
3 Hidden talents? Ha! I really don't know if I have any. Erm, maybe not such a hidden talent, but erm, something that makes me feel good is making cakes and sweets and, I always say – baking is my anti-depressant.
4 Few people know, but I love jazz and I love to play the saxophone.
5 My hidden talent is picking things up with my foot. I can pick up a pen and even a TV remote and it always impresses my friends.
6 My hidden talent most people don't know about is that I'm actually a great basketball player. It may seem a bit surprising to everyone because I'm not that tall, but honestly, I'm really great at playing basketball.
7 My hidden talent is that I play a lot of musical instruments and my friends don't know. And also, I'm learning Persian in my spare time.
8 Yes, I do actually. Erm, not many people know that after I finished school, before I went to university, I spent a year at art college and I became a really good painter. But unfortunately, I don't have much time to do it at the moment – I have too many other things to do. So not many people have seen my paintings.

7D: BBC Street Interviews
Exs 2A and 2B

Delaney:	I'm good at making people laugh, I'm good at, erm, getting everyone else to have a good time. Erm, I'm also good at sports. Erm, and that's, that's pretty much it.
Olivia:	I … I'm quite good at cooking. Erm, I grew up in Italy, so it's, like, just, it runs in my blood. Erm, it's been all around me constantly. Er, and I'm also a really good writer and I'm training to be a journalist at the moment, so, yeah.
John:	I'm very good with words. Erm, well I suppose … I'm good at, I'm good at supporting West Ham United.
Amit:	Yeah, er, I'm good at tennis. Er, I really enjoy playing tennis. I enjoy sport in general.

173

VIDEOSCRIPTS

Kirsty:	I play football, so, erm, I'd like to think that I'm quite good at football.
Flo:	I'm good at singing as it's what I do for my career and, er, a hobby, I also horse ride and play polo. So, I'm good at that.
Constance:	I am good at science. Erm, that's my passion because I want to do medicine when I grow up, so I'm really passionate about biology and I'm, I'd say … I'd like to say I'm good at biology. Erm, because I enjoy learning about the anatomy at school.

7D: BBC Street Interviews
Exs 2A and 2C

Delaney:	Erm, I think hard work is more important. However, I do believe you still need some type of natural talent to help you in whatever skill you're … you're doing.
Olivia:	Erm, yeah, I … yeah, I personally think that hard work is a lot more important than, er, talent. Obviously, talent is great, erm, though, when it comes to anything in life, if you put enough hard work in, then you're … you're going to succeed. I believe that anyway, yeah.
John:	Well hard work is … everyone's got a certain amount of inner talent, but, erm, hard work is what develops talent, you can't get by on talent alone. Hard work – most important.
Amit:	On the one hand, er, talent is … is fundamental, because I think you do need to, erm, have some natural ability. Er, but on the other hand, talent's not enough without hard work. I think you definitely need both ingredients if you want to be, er, the best at something.
Kirsty:	Erm, I believe that hard work is more important than talent. Erm, on the other hand, I'd say that talent is definitely a necessary foundation if you want to excel at something. So, if you want to be really good at what you are doing, there does need to be a level of talent there.
Flo:	Er, definitely hard work. I believe that you've got to work hard to get anywhere in life.
Constance:	Erm, I would say that hard work is more important than having talent because having that drive and passion for something will take you a lot further than having talent. However, talent obviously plays a big part in being successful, but I think the overriding thing is being hard working.

UNIT 8

Opener: BBC Vlogs

1 Community for me means, erm, this sense of belonging, this sense of togetherness. Erm, for me to be able to know my neighbours, you know, for me to be able to go and grab a coffee with my neighbours or … you know, borrow something from them, you know? Just being able to do things together.
2 Community to me means a sense of belonging, um, a sense of being part of something bigger … bigger than yourself. Er, that's what community means to me.
3 It means helping each other, reaching out to others when they need help.
4 I live in a situation where I don't really have any family members close by, but I do still think I live in a very supportive and strong and rich community of people who are dependable, reliable and want to see you succeed, er, and flourish, in whatever way you can. So, for me, community is when you have a … a group of supportive people, who would like to see each other benefit in a way that is socially beneficial for everyone involved in that group.
5 Coming to England as an international student I was very worried about feeling lonely all the time. However, I met an awesome group of friends. So, to me, a community is a group of people who come together and make each other feel loved and cared for.
6 Community is all about finding people with the same passion. Same interests. You know, I look at the people in the building I live in and this is a very unique community because we're all artists. We all share in the love of art.

8D: BBC Documentary
Exs 2A and 2B

CAPTION:	23-year-old Julius wanted to make a difference.
Julius:	The thing about homelessness for me is the realisation that it's so easy to fall into that place and then it's so difficult to get out.
CAPTION:	So he dropped out of uni and opened a very unique café.
Julius:	So, what we wanted to do is break down the misconceptions around homelessness. When you come in you shouldn't know if the person serving you is somebody who's been in the industry for ten years or somebody who's just getting their life back together.
CAPTION:	Getting their life back together.
Julius:	So, we work with one trainee at a time and it just means that we can, kind of, focus on their individual needs. So, they start when they come on board with myself and then slowly over time as they build up their confidence, until the final endpoint of transitioning them onto whatever it is they want to do afterwards.
CAPTION:	Before training with Julius, 'Edge' had been homeless for 3 years and unemployed for 10.
Edge:	Obviously, I had nowhere to stay, had no one in my life, no structure and I was very confused, very hurt and … I had no confidence.
CAPTION:	I had no confidence.
Edge:	The training here not only showed me how to make coffee, but it also showed me how to deal with people and, how to kind of get my own confidence back. How to put myself back in life as it were.
CAPTION:	Julius also runs a scheme where customers can 'pay it forward' for food and drinks. So rough sleepers can get a meal any time they need.
Julius:	Through our 'pay it forward' wall we've given away over 7,000 coffees and 5,000 meals, …
CAPTION:	Over 7000 coffees. + 5000 meals
Julius:	… which is an impact that we're super proud of so far. I think for me the thing was that people are intrinsically good if given the opportunity and I think our job is about helping other people escape that negative cycle.
CAPTION:	Thanks to Julius, Edge is no longer on the streets. he went on to become a chef and now gives speeches on homelessness.
Edge:	I didn't think I would ever get to the other side. Even though he's only young himself, he's seen enough to understand. And he's got a big heart. Julius showed me a lot of things and helped me … get to where I am now.
Julius:	It's really nice, erm, being able to see people's journeys as they kind of exit homelessness. One day they come to us and they say, 'Oh, Julius I've got a hostel. I've got somewhere to live now.' Which is amazing and then … it sounds kind of funny but it's really nice and we never see them again because that's it.

IRREGULAR VERB TABLE

Verb	Past simple	Past participle	Verb	Past simple	Past participle
admit	admitted	admitted	know	knew	known
be	was	been	lead	led	led
become	became	become	learn	learned/learnt	learned/learnt
begin	began	begun	leave	left	left
bite	bit	bitten	let	let	let
blow	blew	blown	lie	lay	lain
break	broke	broken	lose	lost	lost
bring	brought	brought	make	made	made
build	built	built	mean	meant	meant
burn	burnt/burned	burnt/burned	meet	met	met
buy	bought	bought	pay	paid	paid
catch	caught	caught	put	put	put
choose	chose	chosen	read	read	read
come	came	come	ride	rode	ridden
cost	cost	cost	run	ran	run
cut	cut	cut	say	said	said
deny	denied	denied	see	saw	seen
do	did	done	sell	sold	sold
draw	drew	drawn	send	sent	sent
drink	drank	drunk	show	showed	shown
drive	drove	driven	shut	shut	shut
earn	earned/earnt	earned/earnt	sing	sang	sung
eat	ate	eaten	sit	sat	sat
fall	fell	fallen	sleep	slept	slept
feed	fed	fed	speak	spoke	spoken
feel	felt	felt	spend	spent	spent
find	found	found	spill	spilled/spilt	spilled/spilt
forget	forgot	forgotten	stand	stood	stood
freeze	froze	frozen	swim	swam	swum
get	got	got	take	took	taken
give	gave	given	teach	taught	taught
go	went	gone	tell	told	told
grow	grew	grown	think	thought	thought
have	had	had	throw	threw	thrown
hear	heard	heard	understand	understood	understood
hit	hit	hit	wake	woke	woken
hold	held	held	wear	wore	worn
hurt	hurt	hurt	win	won	won
keep	kept	kept	write	wrote	written

Pearson Education Limited
KAO Two
KAO Park
Hockham Way
Harlow, Essex
CM17 9SR
England
and Associated Companies throughout the world.

pearsonenglish.com/speakout3e

© Pearson Education Limited 2022

All rights reserved; no part of this publication may be reproduced, stored in a retrieval system, or transmitted in any form or by any means, electronic, mechanical, photocopying, recording, or otherwise without the prior written permission of the Publishers.

First published 2022
Sixth impression 2024

ISBN: 978-1-292-35954-0

Set in BBC Reith Sans

Printed in Slovakia by Neografia

Acknowledgements
Written by Antonia Clare and JJ Wilson
The publishers and authors would like to thank the following people for their feedback and comments during the development of the material: Charlotte Buckmaster, Charlotte Rowe, Billie Jago, Dorota Walesiak.

Text Credits:
Articles on page 26 adapted from The last of the sea nomads, Johnny Langenheim, 18 Sep 2010, Guardian News and Media Limited and The British grandmother running to Kathmandu, Financial Times, 6 April 2020 (Usborne, S), copyright The Financial Times Limited 2020; Article on page 57 adapted from First day horror stories: 'I crashed into a colleague's parked car', BBC, Alex Taylor, 10 November 2020; Article on page 69 adapted from How did our ancestors avoid distractions?, BBC, research by Miriam Quick

Image Credits:
Alamy Stock Photo: BLM Photo 33; **BBC Studios:** 7, 16, 17, 19, 28, 31, 40, 41, 43, 52, 55, 60, 65, 67, 76, 79, 88, 89, 91, 100, 101; **Brit Worgan:** 81; **Eldon Lindsay / Cornell Athletics:** 82; **Future Publishing:** Susannah Ireland 100, **Getty Images:** 27, 10'000 Hours 55, 10, 68, 74, 92, 146, Adam Hester 7, akinbostanci 6, Alejandra de la Fuente 60, AleksandarNakic 62, 63, Alexander Spatari 84, Anders Andersson 14, Anna Efetova 23, Apisak Kanjanapusit 52, 53, Carol Yepes 143, CasarsaGuru 83, Claudia Burlotti 152, CliqueImages 139, cunfek 21, d3sign 25, 95, Daniel Tsai 149, Daria Botieva / Eyeem 111, Dougal Waters 24, Drakula Images 11, electravk 68, FG Trade 152, FilippoBacci 152, Fine Art / Contributor 28, 29, Flashpop 11, fotog 125, Francesco Carta fotografo 71, Frans Lemmens 32, freedom_naruk 23, Geber86 18, Georgy Dorofeev / EyeEm 11, gremlin 59, Hinterhaus Productions 11, 45, 118, hobo_018 93, Ian Ross Pettigrew 11, Jamie Garbutt 47, Jessica Peterson 12, 13, JGalione 68, JohnnyGreig 150, Jonathan Knowles 67, Jose Luis Pelaez Inc 138, Julia Gunther 38, Jun Sato / Contributor 142, Justin Lambert 11, 84, Klaus Vedfelt 97, 148, KOLOstock 114, Kyle Monk 80, Laura Olivas 45, lechatnoir 35, Leland Bobbe 21, Lidia Utkin 84, Lilly Roadstones 152, Luis Alvarez 133, LumiNola 57, mapodile 155, Mark Metcalfe / Stringer 144, Marko Geber 11, martin-dm 22, 156, Maskot 11, Michal Kostka / EyeEm 103, Mireya Acierto 152, MoMo Productions 60, Morsa Images 84, 86, 136, MStudioImages 68, Nick David 153, OsakaWayne Studios 60, Prasit photo 98, Rafa Cortés Pascual / EyeEm 149, recep-bg 72, Reza Estakhrian 31, RichLegg 120, Rifka Hayati 46, RyanJLane 35, sarayut Thaneerat 10, skynesher 152, SolStock 34, 60, South_agency 79, SrdjanPav 135, Tara Moore 72, 152, Thomas Barwick 91, 23, 73, 84, Tim Robberts 152, Tom Werner 58, 72, 152, TommL 51, Vasily Pindyurin 21, View Pictures / Contributor 141, VioletaStoimenova 50, vorDa 56, Wachirawit Iemlerkchai 116, We Are 48, Westend61 19, 43, 8, 20, 23, 35, 45, 49, 60, 72, 84, 84, 149, 154, Yerbol Mukhanbetzhanov / EyeEm 44; **NASA:** 27; **Panos Pictures:** James Morgan 26; **Shutterstock:** ANTSTUDIO 70, Kurt Strumpf/AP 76, 77, Supamotion 35

Cover Images: *Front:* **Alamy Stock Photo:** Westend61 GmbH; **Getty Images:** adamkaz, Hinterhaus Productions, We Are

Illustrated by
Stephen Collins (Central Illustration Agency) 111, 129; Ben Hasler (NB Illustration) 96; Sam Kalda (Folio) 87; Rupert Van Wyk (Beehive Illustration) 69; Mark Willey (Designers Educational) 85